PENGUIN BOOKS

Christmas at the Ragdoll Orphanage

Suz e Lambert is the winner of Penguin and *Take a Break* ma ne's life-story competition. She lives in Newcastle, and this her first book.

Christmas at the Ragdoll Orphanage

SUZANNE LAMBERT

PENGUIN BOOKS

PENGUIN BOOKS

Published by the Penguin Group
Penguin Books Ltd, 80 Strand, London WC2R ORL, England
Penguin Group (USA) Inc., 375 Hudson Street, New York, New York 10014, USA
Penguin Group (Canada), 90 Eglinton Avenue East, Suite 700, Toronto, Ontario, Canada M4P 2Y3
(a division of Pearson Penguin Canada Inc.)
Penguin Ireland, 25 St Stephen's Green, Dublin 2, Ireland (a division of Penguin Books Ltd)
Penguin Group (Australia), 707 Collins Street, Melbourne, Victoria 3008,
Australia (a division of Pearson Australia Group Pty Ltd)
Penguin Books India Pvt Ltd, 11 Community Centre,
Panchsheel Park, New Delhi – 110 017, India
Penguin Group (NZ), 67 Apollo Drive, Rosedale, Auckland 0632, New Zealand
(a division of Pearson New Zealand Ltd)
Penguin Books (South Africa) (Pty) Ltd, Block D, Rosebank Office Park, 181 Jan Smuts Avenue,
Parktown North, Gauteng 2193, South Africa

Penguin Books Ltd, Registered Offices: 80 Strand, London WC2R ORL, England

www.penguin.com

First published 2013
001

Copyright © Suzanne Lambert, 2013
All rights reserved

The moral right of the author has been asserted

Set in 12.5/14.75pt Garamond MT Std
Typeset by Palimpsest Book Production Ltd, Falkirk, Stirlingshire
Printed in Great Britain by Clays Ltd, St Ives plc

Except in the United States of America, this book is sold subject
to the condition that it shall not, by way of trade or otherwise, be lent,
re-sold, hired out, or otherwise circulated without the publisher's
prior consent in any form of binding or cover other than that in
which it is published and without a similar condition including this
condition being imposed on the subsequent purchaser

ISBN: 978-0-718-17846-8

www.greenpenguin.co.uk

MIX
Paper from
responsible sources
FSC
www.fsc.org FSC™ C018179

Penguin Books is committed to a sustainable
future for our business, our readers and our planet.
This book is made from Forest Stewardship
Council™ certified paper.

To my precious daughter, Gemah Louise
And my grandson, Séamus Michael,

My darlings, this is for you, your heritage.

I love you both with my heart and soul.

May God bless you and angels walk with you always.

Your love for me is as essential as the air I breathe.

Mum/Grandma

Contents

Prologue   xi

Nancy's Story

Nazareth House   3

Battles   6

Chocolate Knickers   10

Holy Orders   15

The Little Ones   18

Tilly   25

The Best Knife   33

The Rag Doll   38

Time to Dance   42

The Journey Begins   45

A Grandchild   46

A Broken Promise   49

The Surprise   53

Nancy's Child

Early Years   59

No-nonsense Nancy   63

CONTENTS

Four-leaf Clovers 65

Tall Tales 67

Christopher 71

Shadows 76

Whispers 80

Shattered Dreams 86

The Very Best Clothes 91

Lucie Attwell and the Magic Whispering Conker Tree 96

Mars Bar with the Big Red Bow 103

Eileen with the Pretty Shoes 108

The Up-and-down Horses 114

Cliff Richard Christmas Wall 119

The Beach Ball 123

Mermaids 130

Parallels 136

Happy Days and Half-a-Crown 138

A Silent Kindness 141

Empty Hands 151

Pony-tails and Colouring Books 157

Her from the Home 164

Our Margy 168

Changes 173

A New Job 176

Qualifications 178

The New Wellies 183

Man in a Black Coat 185

Gratitude and Guilt 189

Guilty Secrets 195

Patent-leather Shoes with a Black Bow 203

A Real Mum 209

Susan's Story

Angel in the Upstairs Flat 215

Two Bedrooms and a Box Room 221

Fame at Last 225

Watching Handbags 230

Skinny Again 234

Love in a Hot-water Bottle 238

My Man in a Black Coat 244

Mother Earth 250

Bubble and Squeak 253

It's a Girl! 256

Celebrations 259

The New Gloves 263

Christopher and Julie 268

Family Days 271

The Lop-sided Cake 274

The Proposal 280

The Perfect Angle   285

The Last Dance   292

Titanic Trauma   294

The Letter   299

Full Circle   304

Bingo!   307

Molly   310

Hugs   316

Girls' Night In   320

The Special Clothes   326

Home   331

Reflections

Hindsight   337

Photographic Proof   341

Mum   348

Life's Lessons   353

And on a Final Note   356

To Maureen, Anne, Kathleen and Margaret   358

To Mum   360

To My Grandma   363

Acknowledgements   365

Prologue

'Mother Superior took the child and placed it in my arms. Susan, darling, that was you. You were light as a feather, and all I could think of saying was, "It's a girl." That was ten years ago.

'"Her name is Susan," the lady said. I don't think I even looked at her; I simply couldn't take my eyes off you. Oh, you were so precious and so perfect. All I cared about was holding you and, just at that moment, you opened your eyes and looked at me. Susan, I knew then and there that you and I belonged together. We still do, and always will, but, my darling, I am not your real mum.'

'I don't understand. What do you mean, "real mum"?'

I was ten years old, and Mum certainly wasn't going to talk about the birds and the bees just yet. It didn't matter anyway.

'You are my mum,' I said.

'Of course. And you are my daughter and always will be.'

That was enough for me. In that moment, I was perfectly happy to be Nancy's child.

Nancy's Story

Nazareth House

How many people have paused at those large, black, iron gates with the big pillars either side and stood at the top of the long driveway, not knowing what life holds in store for them from that moment on?

It was January 1930, and Christmas was over for another year. It had snowed almost all of December and had started again today. The snow was bright on the ground but the skies were overcast and heavy, casting a dull light on the three figures standing at the gates.

The father was smartly dressed in a suit and tie and a cloth cap covered in snow. His two young daughters, Nancy and Margaret, gripped his hands tightly. They had walked with their heads down against the snowstorm, only lifting them now, to see the stone sign carved with the words NAZARETH HOUSE. They were here.

Margaret had been full of questions; Nancy had said very little. Their mother, Anne, had lost her battle with tuberculosis and died last month, on 5 December, leaving their father, Ernest, alone with five young children. He had no choice. This was the only option for the two older girls. Luckily, his war pension would pay for it. Michael, his eldest son, was old enough to stay at home; Benny was in and out of hospital; and Mary, the youngest, he'd put in St Mary's at Spennymoor. He had to go on working. His job at the coalmine was their only source of income; and he couldn't do that and look after all the children at home.

Nancy was the one who worried him — she could be a stubborn little thing — yet she had said nothing. The children were missing their mother, and he was missing his Anne. We had no time at all together, he thought, no time at all. No matter how much I loved her, no matter how much I fought, it wasn't enough, and she was gone. A war hero, that's what they said he was. Well, the Battle of the Somme was nothing compared to this: his wife gone, and the children all split up. Nancy gripped his hand tighter. 'You all right, pet?' he asked. She nodded her head. If she spoke, her voice might have wobbled, and she didn't want to let Dad know she was afraid.

They walked in through the gates. Covered in snow, Nazareth House Convent School should have looked so picture-book pretty, but it didn't. Just like the sky, it was dark and overcast. It looked terrifying. 'Oh,' was all Nancy could think to say. Her toes felt frozen, but it was the cold inside her that was worse. That's what fear did to you sometimes, it made you feel frozen inside. As they made their way down the long driveway, watching the house emerge through the snowstorm, their footsteps made no sound in the deep, soft snow. Margaret, always with a cheeky look and a ready laugh, was silenced for once, her head up in awe of what lay ahead of her. Quiet, serious Nancy kept her head bent, saying her prayers. She was nine years old.

The driveway was bordered on one side by a wooded area with what looked like hundreds of trees and high bushes. As they walked on through the snowstorm, the house grew bigger and bigger, and they could see lights on in the windows, more windows than Nancy had ever seen before on one house. It should have looked magical, glittering like a picture on a Christmas card, but there was something eerie about it. And as they drew closer, Nancy noticed that some of the windows had bars on them. Why would anyone put bars on windows? she wondered.

4

'Bet it looks pretty in the summer,' said Dad, but Nancy and Margaret stayed silent. Summer was a lifetime away. Margaret shivered. Nancy's feet were wet and she felt as if she would never be warm again. She couldn't imagine it ever being summer or feeling the hot sun on her skin today, it was just too cold. Anyway, she wouldn't be here come summer. She closed her eyes for a moment. Please, God, let her be back home with her father come summer.

At the bottom of the drive there was a circular driveway. Now the whole building had come into view. Nancy looked up and up until her eyes were pointing straight up at the sky, blinking as the snow fell in her eyes, but she still couldn't see the top of the house. Suddenly, church bells rang out, and all three of them jumped. Margaret giggled. To the left stood a church, its lights shining through stained-glass windows. High above, they could see the church bell swaying, ringing in a new day. Margaret thought the sound of the bell was scary; Nancy thought it was absolutely beautiful. They turned from the church and made their way to a door on the right-hand side of the house. It was enormous, ornately carved in oak. Nancy had never seen a door so huge; it was almost as big as a whole house, she thought.

They rang the bell. It clanged loudly, and they stood there, waiting. What lay behind that giant door? Nancy looked over to her right, and there, through the snow, she saw a grotto with a beautiful statue of Our Lady of Lourdes. The statue seemed to be smiling at her and Nancy smiled back, feeling the beginnings of warmth, then tears stung her eyes as she heard locks being pulled back and the door was opened. I won't be here long, she thought, I simply won't. It was fortunate that there was no one there to tell Nancy that Nazareth House would be her home for the next thirty-six years.

Battles

Ernest Harmer was twenty-one years old and facing what he believed would be one of the hardest days of his life. Nothing would ever compare to this — or so he thought. It was the waiting that was hard, the not knowing what it would feel like when the time came. You were fighting for King and country, they said, and, of course, we were going to win. It would be over in no time, we were well prepared.

Ernest thought about Anne, his wife of only ten months, at home now, waiting for him to return. They planned to have children — lots of them, she had said, laughing. He would be home soon, when this was over. Anne had been so worried, those days before he left. She knew what it was like to lose someone close; two of her sisters had died of tuberculosis. She was not going to lose her young husband. And Ernest would look after Anne, when he got back. Everything would be all right. It had to be.

Ernest looked around him. Thousands of men and young boys. He smiled as he looked over at Albert, the youngest of the group, who was looking a little pale at the moment, the hands that held his rifle shaking slightly. Albert's parents were proud of their son. In years to come his mother's eyes would stray again and again to the medal next to her son's photograph on the well-polished mantelpiece and she would say to anyone who would listen that the Battle of the Somme took not only her son but her dreams of grandchildren and a house filled with laughter.

He was ready. They all were. Even the least religious were heard to whisper, 'God be with us. God bless us,' and for some, simply, in those moments before battle commenced, 'God help us.' He stood now, head held high, and as the whistle blew Ernest Benjamin Harmer took his first steps over the top on a hot summer's day on 1 July, launching himself into the Battle of the Somme.

Twenty thousand men died that day, and thousands more were injured. But the battle went on. On and on the men trudged, feet sliding in the mud, fighting on and on, the gunfire deafening and bodies all around. By November, Ernest had almost forgotten what it felt like to be home; he was tired and hungry and his heart was heavy, his spirit broken. He no longer even thought about home, and tried especially hard not to think of Anne. Each day was just another day to be survived, another day when his time in this battle might come to an end. The men were returning to the trenches when Ernest spotted him, an officer lying in the mud, his eyes open, pleading. Ernest was not about to leave this man behind. Tramping through the mud, slipping and sliding, he knelt down and lifted him up with a strength born out of sheer necessity, and he carried the officer from the battlefield on his back. He saved the officer's life. It was one act of bravery, among so many.

On his return home Ernest Harmer was awarded a medal for his bravery. He was badly injured, and the war was over for him, but there would be yet more, personal, battles to be fought in his lifetime.

Ernest worked hard in the coalmines, and he and Anne managed as best they could, along with everyone else. Their first child, Michael, was born in 1918, Nancy two years later and Margaret a year after that. A second son, Ernest Benjamin, was born in 1926, a third daughter, Mary, in 1928. Anne had suffered a stillbirth, a daughter, Violet, in 1924.

It was the beginning of December 1929, and Anne's thoughts were turning to Christmas. She wasn't feeling at all well, but she had been cleaning for days and the house was spotless. Nancy and Margaret had been a great help, as always. There was a quiet kindness to Nancy, Anne always thought. It seemed to radiate from her. She was only nine years old, but she just had a way with her, especially with the younger ones, Benny and Mary. You never really knew what she was thinking, but there was definitely a stubborn streak there somewhere. She and Margaret were as different as chalk and cheese. Margaret was always in trouble, but Anne could never be angry with her for long: she made her mother laugh and always had a story to tell. And the boys – they were growing up so quickly, poor Benny back and forth to hospital, but thankfully, the others seemed fit and well. She was grateful for that, even though the pain of losing Violet would never quite go away.

Ernest was working hard, so there should be a good dinner for them this Christmas. And there'd be little gifts – not much, but enough to make the day special for the children. She hoped Benny would be home for Christmas. He was in hospital again, but she would call them tomorrow and see what could be done. She wanted all her children together at home on Christmas Day. A proper family Christmas.

It had started snowing outside and the children were upstairs, squealing with delight. If it settled they'd be out playing in it tomorrow. Anne had taught the girls how to make paper chains and decorate stockings to hang up for Santa on Christmas Eve. It was very early: barely December, yet paper chains were already being hung all around the room, such was the excitement this year. Anne smiled as she sank into her favourite chair. She really wasn't feeling her best. The older children were happy upstairs, Mary having her nap, so she could afford to sit down, just for a little while.

The snow continued throughout December, and there was indeed enough money for a lovely Christmas dinner. Anne got her wish, and the children were all home for Christmas Day. Unfortunately, Anne was not there to celebrate with them.

Chocolate Knickers

Nazareth House Convent School had been built in 1817, and was a large, imposing structure surrounded by twenty-one acres of land in Jesmond, Newcastle-upon-Tyne. To the left of the entrance to the main house, guarded by four pillars, stood the stables, where, at one time, the horses and carriages had been kept. The house used to be called Villa Real and had been built by a man called John Dobson for a Captain Dutton and, afterwards, a string of wealthy men had lived there with their families. On the death of the last, a surgeon called Dr Gribb, in 1916, it passed into the hands of the Poor Sisters of Nazareth. It was they who had added the chapel.

The Poor Sisters of Nazareth were one of the oldest established orders in Britain. They turned the house into a live-in convent school where children over the age of five were looked after and educated. Many of the nuns of the Poor Sisters of Nazareth had dedicated their lives to looking after children in such homes. They wore long habits, some white, some black, and long strings of large rosary beads. Nancy always remembered the nuns with their arms crossed, each hand hidden in the opposite sleeve, and their heads bent in prayer. They seemed to glide along the silent corridors of Nazareth House.

What lay behind those ornately carved oak doors was a circular, three-storey parlour with a glass dome built into the ceiling. This was the nuns' parlour. Doors led off to the kitchen area, the chapel, a conservatory filled with every type of plant, and, outside, to the play areas and orchard. Nancy's dad had been right: the gardens and the driveway were beautiful in the summer, with trees and grassed areas. In spring, bluebells grew the length of the drive; the rhododendron bushes were glorious.

On the right was a clock of enormous proportions, and to the left a staircase to a mezzanine floor with a door leading to the convent area. Corridors branched in all directions on each floor, to dormitories, bathrooms and teaching quarters. Here, the children were taught basic lessons, and teachers from outside came in to teach singing, needlework and deportment. The girls wore brown pinafores with a cream shirt. In spring and summer they wore a panama hat, in winter a brown felt hat, both bearing the school badge: the intertwined letters NHC.

Time passed quickly for Nancy over the next few years. There was the daily routine of getting up early, getting dressed and getting over to the schoolrooms, topped and tailed morning and night with prayers, which were always said kneeling by the side of the bed. Nancy and the rest of the girls would all have tea together, sitting at long benches, and then, of course, there was homework and reading, or listening to the radio before bed. Weekends were divided between chores and playing, outside in the enormous grounds when it was warm and dry enough. Sundays began with Mass in the chapel and ended with benediction in the evening, with Sunday lunch and time for play in between. Before tea, everyone said the rosary together for an hour, and afterwards, the radio would be switched on.

The main event of the school year was the May procession, which all the children took part in. The girls, top to toe in white dresses and veils, the boys in shorts, white shirt and a tie. They would receive the sacrament in the Nazareth House chapel and process from there through the grounds in pairs, singing hymns — 'Bring Flowers of the

Rarest' was one of them – their hands together in the prayer position. The procession would end outside the main house, at the grotto of Our Lady of Lourdes. Nancy always remembered arriving here that first time, and the sense of comfort and warmth, in spite of everything, she had drawn from the holy statue.

Nancy missed her family, and the loss of her mother so young was never far from her thoughts, but at least she had one of her sisters, Margaret, with her, and the life of the convent seemed to suit her. And, of course, her father would visit.

Ernest would take the bus from Gateshead to visit Nancy and Margaret once a month, on a Sunday. He'd give the Mother Superior the monthly cheque for their upkeep and then spend some time with the girls. Sometimes, he'd take them out of the college and, along with Michael and Benny, they'd walk into the centre of Newcastle and take the bus from there to see Mary in Spennymoor. Even if they didn't go out anywhere, they would spend time together outside, or, if it was cold and raining, in the big playroom. Ernest always brought sweets for Nancy and Margaret when he came to visit. The rule was to hand them straight to the Mother Superior so that they could be shared out – but that didn't always happen!

On one Sunday visit, Margaret was in the sickbay with chicken-pox, and feeling very sorry for herself. It was spring, and she was lying in bed, hoping that she would be better for the May procession. They always had such a lovely tea afterwards and she had been looking forward to it. So different to Nancy, Margaret was, looking forward to the dressing up and the tea! Nancy loved all the prayers and the hymns. 'Honestly,' Margaret was heard to say, 'she'd spend all her time at the statue of Our Lady of Lourdes if she was allowed to. You'll be a nun one day yourself, our Nancy,' Margaret often told her, and Nancy would smile.

Ernest went straight to the sickbay to visit Margaret that day – the Mother Superior didn't get a look in! – and when it was time for him to leave, he handed her two bars of chocolate before saying goodbye.

Margaret wasn't so sick that the thought of a whole bar of chocolate all to herself – the second bar she would of course give to Nancy – didn't perk up her appetite. In truth, she was feeling better now; it was more because of the spots that she was being kept in the sickbay. Savouring the anticipation, she closed her eyes – only to hear Sister Augustine come into the room. What could she do with the chocolate bars? She would have to hide them, but where? There was so little time! There was only one thing for it: Margaret hastily pushed them up her knicker leg.

'Margaret Harmer, what are you doing?'

'Nothing, Sister Augustine.'

'Has your father gone? I didn't see him at all.'

'No, Sister, he has gone to see our Nancy.'

'Well, then, just look at the state of your bed, get up now and stand by the fire while I change the sheets.'

Uh-oh.

'But, Sister –'

'Margaret Harmer, do not "But, Sister" me. Get out of that bed now and stand by the fire.'

'Could I go to the toilet first, please?'

'By the fire now, and cross your arms.'

There was nothing for it but to do just that. Stand by a hot gas fire with two bars of chocolate shoved up her knicker leg. As you would expect, slowly and gently the chocolate began to melt. Just as slowly and gently it started to run down Margaret's leg. She didn't dare move. There was absolutely no way out of this. It didn't look *good — but did she dare speak and say that it was only chocolate? Sister Augustine had her back turned, changing the sheets. Ah well, sighed Margaret to herself. Then, Why not? I'm in big enough trouble anyway.* She uncrossed her arms and oh so slowly slid one down to her knicker leg, scooping up some of the delicious-smelling chocolate with her fingers. She was just about to put them in her mouth when Sister Augustine turned round.

'Holy Mother of God!' she screamed, and dropped the crumpled bed sheets on the floor.

Holy Orders

It was supper time, and they couldn't find Nancy anywhere. Usually at this time she'd be helping the little ones get ready for bed or reading them stories. The convent had started taking in children from the age of two now, and Nancy had a real way with the small ones. Sister Mary Joseph smiled as she recalled the day one of the children had broken a new toy and Nancy had insisted it was her fault. Nancy had stood in front of her with her chin up, arms folded across her chest, ready to take the blame. Sister Mary Joseph had found it almost amusing and had sent her to the church to do the rosary three times. Some punishment — Nancy had been there for over an hour, and had loved every minute. She thought nobody knew, but she loved being in the church, and even more when she had it to herself. Only thirteen years old, mused Sister Mary Joseph, but she carried with her such an air of caring. She could give you a smile and with no words your heart felt eased. No wonder the little ones loved her so much.

Sister Bernadette came back from the kitchen. She'd checked there twice now, to see if Nancy was helping to get the supper ready.

'She's such a strange little thing,' said Sister Mary Joseph, now speaking her thoughts aloud. 'She never says much, but I don't know what I'd do without her — the young ones love her, and she is such a help around the place.'

'I know,' agreed Sister Bernadette. 'She's a good, quiet, sensible girl — but she can be like a little mule too, Sister. She knows what she

wants and doesn't want, and she won't be ridden roughshod over when she's older, I'm sure of that. I wonder should we try looking in the chapel now?'

There was, as always at this time of evening, a gentle hush in the chapel; no organ was playing, no priest saying Mass. Nancy was kneeling at the altar, head bent, her hands together in prayer. The candles in the corner had flickered as the nuns opened the door, but Nancy caught nothing out of the corner of her eye. The two nuns simply stood and watched the young girl for a few moments.

'I'll go,' said Sister Mary Joseph, and she quietly walked forward to sit in the front bench, joining Nancy in prayer.

The only movement in the child was her lips, which moved in whispered prayer. Her eyes were squeezed tightly shut and she was concentrating with all her might. Nancy was fourteen now, and couldn't imagine why, all those five years ago, she had asked God to let her go home before summer came. 'I am so sorry,' she whispered now. 'Please let me stay here. Please don't make me go away. This is my home now, and the little ones need me. I will be extra good and do all my chores. Just find a way for me to stay here and be a nun like the sisters, then I can look after the children always. I love them so much, and it's wonderful when they smile, because it means they are happy, and Sister Mary Joseph says it's God-like to make others happy.'

Nancy looked up, but not with the sweet serene face of a child in prayer that you might expect to see. Oh no. This was the face of a child set in no-nonsense determination. She lifted her chin, placed her hands on her hips, and continued: 'I know you're listening, I know you can do this, and I am staying.' She paused for a moment then closed her eyes and added softly, 'Please. Please.'

Sister Mary Joseph knew without a shadow of a doubt that God would be listening. But whether he'd be laughing or crying she just wasn't sure.

It was beginning to get dark. The pretty patterns created by the sun shining through the stained-glass windows were long gone. The only light in the chapel came from the flickering candles and the altar lights. Still Nancy knelt there praying, so caught up that she was totally unaware of Sister Mary Joseph beside her.

Sister Mary Joseph also closed her eyes in prayer. She had seen so much these last years. She caught some of Nancy's words: 'Please, God, help me be a good child.'

She took a deep breath and bowed her head in prayer. If ever a child was put on this earth for a reason, it was this one. God, she said, silently. Take care of her, keep her safe and do please let her stay here with us.

Then her stomach rumbled, and Nancy looked quickly around.

Sister smiled at Nancy, and said quietly, 'Well, it is supper time.'

The Little Ones

Nancy was now in her mid-teens. As well as doing her lessons, any spare moment she had, she helped out in the nursery. She was close to Margaret, but they had such different personalities, and their own friends. Her little sister, Mary, had settled into Nazareth House well too. Their dad had moved her from Spennymoor to be with her sisters a few years back now, when she was five years old.

It was only with the children that Nancy was truly content. She couldn't imagine ever wanting to do anything other than be with them. Somehow, she could always stop their tears and find the right words to make things all better again. She had a wonderful warm feeling inside when they ran to take her hand, or cuddled in for a story, or asked her a question. It was about being needed, and Nancy wanted so badly to be needed. She'd helped her mum as much as she could when she was alive, but it hadn't been enough. Now Nancy wanted to give her love to the little ones and — was it too much to ask? — feel some of it back in return. When the other children were dreaming about toys and days out, Nancy was dreaming about having hundreds of children all around her, all tugging at her apron, sitting on her knee, listening to her stories and laughing as she tickled them or pulled funny faces. Children should always be laughing, she thought. There was nothing like it. She couldn't bear it when they cried: she'd always be the one to jump out of bed at the first sound of a sob and rush across the dormitory to comfort the crying child until they went back to sleep. She had a mother's instincts. And when she was with the young ones she didn't feel alone.

Life in the convent carried on in this way until the late 1930s. By then, though, the number of people wanting to pay to send their children to the convent had dwindled and, eventually, the money dried up. Nazareth House closed as a convent school and opened its doors to orphaned and needy children. It became Nazareth House Orphanage. Nancy, now eighteen, had been working in the nursery for years and was more than happy to stay on as a carer for the little ones. You didn't need formal qualifications in those days, just a warm heart and an easy way with the children. Some of the tears, though, were painful to witness. These children were unwanted, abandoned – not her words, other people's – but Nancy would do her best for them.

As well as her work with the small ones, Nancy was preparing to take Holy Orders. The Mother Superior had granted her permission, and Nancy was happier than she had ever been. Although it would be a few years yet before she could become a nun, she was on her way. This, she knew, was what she wanted from life.

Today was a busy day. Three new children had been brought in, one little boy who had cried from the moment he arrived, and two little girls, sisters, who simply stood there, perfectly still, looking at each other for support, frightened – and not very clean, Nancy thought. Dirty or not, though, Nancy was going to take them to see the playroom; it was always best to try to distract them by showing them something fun. She took them by the hand and led them there. Trying to placate the poor little boy – the toy soldiers and the building bricks weren't working – she picked up the kicking and screaming child. Maybe he would enjoy a bath after all. She took him into the bathroom and held him up to the window for a moment, hoping the view of the grounds would sooth him. Nancy's heart skipped a beat. Walking down the drive was a lone figure with a battered suitcase. It was her father.

That day, Ernest Harmer went straight to see the Mother Superior.

'I've come to take Nancy home,' he said. 'It's time for her to keep house for us.'

Mother Superior was at her best in these situations. 'Of course,' she said, her smile masking the shock that she was feeling. 'Come this way and take a seat. I will arrange tea, Mr Harmer.'

She had seen it all over the years: children crying when they arrived, crying again when they had to leave. She had watched so many children grow under her care to become adults, then leave, as was only right, to take their place in the world. The world these days was in a sad state. People were saying there would be another war – more death, poverty, hopelessness. Do we, she thought, prepare them for the horrors they will face outside these walls? Could anyone prepare them for it? Today, though, at the thought of saying goodbye to Nancy, there was a particular wrench in her heart. She had watched over Nancy since she was nine years old, from the moment she had arrived. If any child belonged in this Holy Order, it was Nancy. And what on earth would they do without her? She was indispensable. Well, right or wrong, Mr Harmer's tea would have to wait. Mother Superior made her way across the parlour to her room and felt the need to sit down. Oh my, she thought as she closed her eyes, her fingers now clicking the rosary beads, and she prayed, as Nancy had so many times, that God might spare Nancy this and allow her to stay where she belonged. Then she gathered herself together and headed to the kitchen to arrange the tea, and with a heavy heart proceeded slowly upstairs to the playroom.

Nancy looked up. Straight away she knew something must be wrong. Mother Superior never delivered messages personally: you were sent for, that was the way of things. Nancy gave the little boy, now calm, a reassuring hug and called for one of the other helpers to take over.

'Come to the small kitchen,' said Mother Superior. 'We might have a cup of tea.'

Nancy followed. You didn't answer Mother Superior back, but when things were frightening you simply had to stand up to them. She stopped halfway down the corridor.

'Mother Superior, please, could you just tell me? It's the Holy Orders, isn't it? Please, Mother Superior, you promised.'

This was one of the hardest things she had ever done, but it was her duty to do so, so Mother Superior took Nancy's hands in hers.

'Nancy, I don't know how to tell you this. It would seem it is your duty to go home.'

'Home?'

'Yes, Nancy.'

'Duty?'

'Your father is downstairs now, Nancy. You are to go home and keep house for him.'

Mother Superior wished that she could find some words of comfort for Nancy, but the thought of her leaving, simply not being here at the end of the day, was overwhelming. It was hard to accept, yet she knew she had to. She had no right to keep Nancy, and her father had every right to walk in and take his own child home at any point. For the first time in many a year Mother Superior felt the pain of loss so keenly she was afraid the tears would come. And that would never do.

Sister Mary Joseph knew how wrong it was to listen in to other *people's conversations, and it seemed doubly wrong somehow when you were around the corner, out of sight. But today Sister Mary Joseph listened, then proceeded to break yet another rule and ran along the corridor to tell the other nuns. They gathered, whispering to each other: 'He couldn't.' 'He wouldn't.' 'What will we do without her?'*

'The children,' said Sister Mary Joseph. 'What about the children?'

There was nothing Mother Superior could do. She squeezed Nancy's hand and said gently, 'Nancy, your father is waiting.'

Nancy slowly raised her head, looked Mother Superior in the eye and squeezed her hands back.

'Well, he's going to have a long wait then, isn't he, because I'm not going. Now, if you will excuse me, Mother Superior, I have children to look after.' And with that she turned her back on a very stunned Mother Superior and returned to the children in the playroom.

Margaret was downstairs washing her hands before tea when she was tapped on the shoulder. 'Margaret, can you come with me, please,' said Sister, who'd been given the message to pass on. 'Your father is here to take you home.'

Margaret was given the battered suitcase and told to choose some clothes from it and get changed. Margaret didn't argue and did as she was told. The clothes were too big for her. Why was she being sent home now? All those years of adapting, making new friends, going to school, the safety of living within walls where decisions were made for you, food was put on the table in front of you, clothes were provided . . . and in minutes it was over and you were back in the big, wide, scary world. And Nancy had been asked to go but had refused. Margaret felt like crying, out of anger, at the sheer injustice of it.

Nancy was shaking: for all her bravado, she was frightened. She held on to the bars of the bathroom window and watched as Margaret and her father walked away from her up the drive, carrying the suitcase between them. Not only had she answered Mother Superior back, she would have her father to face at some point. And Margaret . . . Nancy didn't have to see her face to know how angry she was, it was evident in every step she took. The children had been taken away for their tea now, but Nancy remained at the window. She felt so guilty. Margaret was gone, and it was all her fault. Mary would have no sister downstairs looking out for her now. Nancy felt frozen at the thought of having hurt another person. What should she do? Would she have to leave after all, leave the children and give up the idea of Holy Orders? Resting her forehead against the bars of the window, she closed her eyes and prayed for forgiveness.

Nancy didn't leave. She just couldn't. She spent the next year shuttling backwards and forwards between her family home at Gateshead and Nazareth House. She helped her father out as much as she could, looked after the children back at the orphanage and continued preparing for Holy Orders. Every time she thought about it, she smiled to herself.

Everything was going to be all right. Margaret, Mary and herself had survived; they would be fine. The boys had joined the army, and their father was happy at home. Everything was going to be just fine, thought Nancy again, handbag swinging in her hand as she hurried down the drive to Nazareth House after staying overnight with her father. I will be just in time, she thought, for the announcement from the Prime Minister. She would listen to it on the radio.

Say what you like, Mr Chamberlain. Nancy smiled to herself.

Nothing, but nothing, is going to stand in my way now. Life is good. Plans are settled.

That morning, at 11.15 a.m., there was an announcement to the nation. On 3 September 1939 war was declared and the Sisters of Nazareth closed any further entries into Holy Orders until further notice. Nancy hadn't reckoned on Hitler.

Tilly

What is it that draws one person to another, that instant bond? Two souls, so very different from each other, yet an instant bond on meeting. Destined to spend their whole lives together, supporting, teaching, caring for each other. Friends in every single sense of the word, each knowing what the other is thinking, when they are needed and when to step back. Ahead of them, years of laughter, challenges, and yet deep down in the soul in that moment of meeting, the knowledge that here is the person who is going to fight for you, laugh with you, cheer you on, refuse to allow you to take life too seriously and, most of all, accept you unconditionally for the person you are.

So it was with Nancy and Tilly, whose characters, views on life, beliefs and behaviour could not have been more different.

Tilly was twenty years old when she came to Nazareth House to work in the kitchens as a cook, the same age as Nancy. It was one of those instant bonds. Each one of them knew they had found a steadfast friend for life, whatever the challenges that lay ahead. And you couldn't imagine two people so different.

Tilly was such fun; she always made Nancy laugh. She loved to catch the children's eye as they walked past the kitchen and give them an illicit biscuit or piece of cake. 'Poor mites,' she would say. 'They need a treat now and again.' Tilly had been told over and over again not to do this, but she would just laugh and take no notice at all. The staff marvelled at her. She had such a devil-may-care attitude, even in her cooking. She never weighed anything and very rarely followed a recipe, just threw all the ingredients into a bowl. And still the food would turn out delicious. Nancy always boasted that her friend could make the lightest scones in the world in moments. As far as Tilly was concerned, life was to be lived and enjoyed, and she was determined to teach this lesson to Nancy.

That day, she'd literally had to drag Nancy from the nursery to come and enjoy the sunshine in the gardens. Nancy really didn't take enough time off work, give herself time to enjoy herself.

They wandered arm in arm around the garden, chatting about life, their hopes and dreams Tilly teasing Nancy about who would fall in love first, knowing Nancy would get all embarrassed. Today Nancy just smiled at Tilly, savouring her few moments of relaxation.

They both saw him at the same time.

He was raking the leaves from the grass, and pretended he hadn't noticed them, whistling as he worked. Then he slowly straightened up quickly turned round to them.

'Hello, girls,' he said, and winked. He wasn't particularly tall, but he was definitely dark and handsome.

Tilly laughed. Nancy, even more embarrassed now, turned away and pulled Tilly's arm to leave.

'Nancy Harmer, I do believe you're blushing,' said her friend.

'I certainly am not. Don't be ridiculous.'

'And you can wipe that haughty look off your face, too. You know it doesn't wash with me.'

They walked in silence for a few moments. Then:

'Did you hear that lovely Irish lilt in his voice?'

Nancy glanced back at him quickly. 'I did,' she said. 'I did.' She had to stop herself: there was no sense in being fanciful.

And in any case it was Tilly who had caught his eye, the young Irish girl he had heard about, with the ready laugh and the cheeky grin.

Nancy was looking out of the window now, at the colours of the autumn leaves. She could never find Tilly these days. Where on earth had she disappeared to now? They were supposed to be having a cuppa together. Nancy was just about to go back to the nursery when in came her friend through the kitchen door, flushed and out of breath. Nancy opened her mouth to speak but Tilly grabbed her arm, and said, 'Not now, Nancy, not now! Outside, quickly!'

Nancy was frogmarched through the door to the garden and to the statue of Our Lady of Lourdes.

'Nancy, I'm in love,' Tilly blurted out.

Whatever Nancy had been expecting, it hadn't been this.

'In love with who?' she asked.

'What do you mean, who? Are you serious? Bill, of course. Oh, Nancy, he just kissed me!'

'Where?'

'Really, Nancy! It's supposed to be me in shock! I'm going to have to shake you in a minute – now listen: on the lips in the garden under the big tree. Understand?'

'How?'

Tilly sighed and took Nancy's arm. 'We've been seeing each other for weeks now,' she said. 'He really is quite wonderful. We have so much in common, and it's serious . . . Well, say something, and please make it a sensible comment – possibly more than one word.'

Nancy was gulping and trying to steady her racing heart. Well, that's what you got for being fanciful and wondering. She looked at Tilly, who was beginning to look concerned. That brought Nancy to *her senses — honestly, what sort of friend was she being?*

They smiled at each other, then burst out laughing. Once again, arm in arm they walked around the garden and Tilly told Nancy all that had happened and how it felt to be kissed.

Nancy blushed. 'Well, I wouldn't have liked that at all,' she said.

Tilly couldn't stop giggling at that. She gave Nancy a hug and they went inside to finally have that cuppa.

Tilly and Bill were married in the small chapel in Nazareth House in July 1942, and their first daughter arrived four years later. They lived in a flat in Fenham, about five miles away, and struggled the same as everyone else during those times, but they were happy, and Nancy was simply the best friend in the world and helped out as much as she could.

Today had been particularly difficult for Tilly. How on earth were you supposed to do the housework, shop, make the tea for your husband coming home and light the fire to keep the house warm — near on impossible anyway, with only damp newspaper — with a screaming, demanding baby who had never heard of the word 'sleep'?

It's not that she wanted much out of life, she understood what was expected of her, but she slumped as she looked around the flat that day — clothes everywhere, an overflowing pile of dirty linen, nappies to be washed and, to cap it all, when she did get a moment to hang the washing up over the bath, the line snapped.

'Well,' she said, flopping down on the chair. 'If one of God's angels were sent to me now, what would I desire? Not a bag of gold, just a heavenly angel to make me a cup of tea. Is that too much to ask?'

Tilly, you're talking to yourself now, she thought. Never a good sign. The smile on her lips was replaced by a sigh as the child once again began to cry. The baby cried all day, and when Bill came home, whistling as he walked through the door, ready to tell his wife about his day and have a chat and a cuppa, as they normally did, he had his screaming daughter dumped into his arms, and Tilly sat down finally to have that cup of tea.

All night the crying went on, but even though Bill had to get up early the next morning to go to work, he lay on the bed beside his daughter, talking to her, singing in his lovely Irish voice, and, eventually, at about 3 a.m., little Maureen fell asleep. Tilly had managed to get hold of a second-hand cot, but that night there was no use for it: one small child and two totally exhausted adults had fallen finally asleep on the bed.

Tilly had paced and paced the next morning, anxious for the corner shop to open. She had been watching out of the window since early morning for Mrs Gordon to unlock the door. As soon as she had, Mrs G heard Tilly shouting and running across the road, little Maureen in her arms.

'Tilly! What on earth is wrong? Is the baby sick?'

'No,' said Tilly, 'but I need to use your telephone, please.'

Nancy was always up early with the children in the nursery but was still taken by surprise to be told just after eight o'clock, when she was clearing up after breakfast, that there was a phone call for her. Who on earth could be calling her at this ungodly hour? It had to be Tilly. Please, God, don't let there be anything wrong with the baby, she thought as she hurried to the phone.

'Nancy!'

'Tilly, what's wrong?'

'When is your next time off?'

'Why?'

'Make it today, Nancy, please.'

'I'll try,' said Nancy, and after she had put the phone down she went straight to the Mother Superior.

Nancy didn't often take time off, not even that which was due to her. There was always so much to do, and she loved looking after the children: she didn't need a day off from them. Today, though, Tilly needed her, so she made sure the other staff knew what there was to be done, put on her coat and left.

Tilly was watching out of the window. She knew her friend would come. If it had been the other way round, screaming baby or no screaming baby, she would be there for Nancy. That's just the way it was.

Nancy was on the trolley bus. It seemed to be taking ages today. As soon as it pulled up at the stop, she leapt out and ran towards Strathmore Crescent to Tilly's flat. The door was open and she could hear Maureen crying. Tilly's face had changed from thunder to relief in an instant on seeing her friend.

As soon as she'd reassured herself that there was nothing wrong with the baby, and Tilly had told her what was wrong, Nancy relaxed too, and laughed. Poor Tilly.

She'd thought that babies just slept. You fed them and they went to sleep, didn't they? Nancy gave Tilly that same knowing look Tilly had given her when she had told her about that first kiss with Bill. 'No, Tilly, that's not what babies do,' she said. 'Now make the most of it and get some sleep while I'm here.'

Walking up and down the room and rocking the little girl in her arms, Nancy was completely absorbed in the child and her thoughts began to wander. So this is how it felt to hold a really small baby. But what would it feel like to know that you were that baby's whole world, that they relied on you completely? It would be your responsibility to protect them, to love them, to ensure they grew up to be responsible adults — and then someday to let them go. The thought of it was terrifying. She looked down at the now sleeping child in her arms. Just at that moment the child reached out and grasped Nancy's finger tightly. Nancy almost held her breath and tears stung her eyes. She would be prepared to face that terror, she thought.

But would she ever be a mother herself?

Tilly had told her that you closed your eyes when you were kissed, and Nancy had been horrified at the thought of it. And as for the other stuff! It just wasn't her. Nancy did not have fanciful thoughts, or any time for them. She'd never been taught to dream, to imagine a life beyond the one she had. In her family, and at the convent, you took things a day at a time, you kept your head down and expected no promises of what the future might hold. She couldn't imagine going through all that stuff and becoming a real mum. But she had all her children at the orphanage, and they needed her love just as much as a child of her own would, if not more. And Tilly had said that she wanted lots of children, and Nancy would always be a part of their lives.

Good friend and children's nanny — that was to be Nancy's role in life. It really was best not to be fanciful. Little Maureen stirred, opened her eyes and smiled at Nancy for a moment, then went back to sleep in her arms.

The thing with tears is that sometimes there is just no way to stop them. That momentary wave of emotion takes you by surprise and, deep down inside, something hurt, but she couldn't dwell on that. Nancy put the baby in the pram — they would go for a walk — and she closed the door quietly behind her, leaving Tilly to sleep.

* * *

Three more daughters followed – Anne, Kathleen and Margaret – and, sure enough, they became as much a part of Nancy's life as of Tilly and Bill's. Nancy still worked hard at the orphanage, but she helped Tilly with the children every day off she had. She loved getting them all ready and taking them out, and it gave Tilly a much needed break to get meals prepared and the washing done. Nancy's sisters had also had children by this time, and Margaret lived nearby, so Nancy had her family to visit too. Nancy was needed, and had never been happier.

Tilly didn't know what she would do without her friend. And she couldn't tell her how much she appreciated her; she'd be embarrassed – and she knew it anyway. But Nancy deserved more. No matter how much a part of their family, and of her sisters', she was, Tilly knew that Nancy craved a child of her own – without all the nonsense, as Nancy would say. It was never going to happen, though. Tilly felt sad whenever she thought about it. 'Come on, God,' she would pray. 'Give her a break!'

God was listening, but it was to be a few years yet before Tilly's prayer was answered.

The Best Knife

It was going to be hot again today, one of those real summer-childhood days without a cloud in the sky and still hot into the evening. Nancy had been making sandwiches, oohing and aahing over her new butter knife, Tilly had been baking cakes, and the girls were all running in circles round the flat, excited about the day ahead. Margaret, Tilly's youngest, had started to cry, because she didn't understand what was going on and Kathleen was jumping up and down waving a bucket and spade about. She caught Anne on the head, and the noise level went up another notch. It was just at this point that Bill entered the room to say goodbye before leaving for work.

'You leaving me, Tilly?' he called out, seeing six bags packed to the brim with what looked like three full sliced loaves' worth of sandwiches, sweets, crisps, tea, juice, and another full of clothes.

'Unless you want to help, Bill Smalley, I suggest you leave.' Bill laughed, waved to the children and left.

'Are we going yet?' Kathleen shouted, for about the hundredth time that morning.

'We are, love. Just ten more minutes and we'll be off.'

'I'll just comb the girls' hair, Tilly, before we leave,' Nancy shouted above all the noise. Tilly laughed and told her that they would all look like they had been dragged through a hedge backwards anyway, once they had carried all the bags and battled with keeping four young children sitting still on the bus.

'Even so,' said Nancy, just as Tilly called out, 'Anne, hide that comb from your Aunty Nancy so we can get to the beach sometime today!'

It was another twenty minutes before they were out of the house, a happy family, the three younger children skipping, Maureen carrying Margaret balanced on one hip, and Tilly and Nancy carrying more bags than surely could be necessary. They'd covered themselves for every eventuality. Nancy had her special going-out bag. Plasters, bandages, antiseptic cream, scissors, sickness tablets, sun-cream, toilet roll (never any in the toilets, she said), flannels, soap and a bottle of water in case they stood in anything. What the anything was, nobody knew — and did anyone tell her about the sea? There was quite a bit of water there! Oh, and of course the new butter knife. Just a bag of chloroform and she was almost prepared for open-heart surgery!

Tilly was halfway up the street, leaving Nancy checking and re-checking that the door was locked, and eventually they were all on their way to the beach. All the way there Nancy's fingers itched to get to the comb in her pocket, but she was carrying too many bags. She would do it when they got there and, with that, she had to be satisfied.

Nancy loved these days out. She would go and get the deckchairs while Tilly spread out the towels, the girls would strip to their bathers and run off to play, and she and Tilly would settle in the deckchairs and have a cup of tea and a piece of cake.

Today, it was only just after ten in the morning when they got there, but already the beach was packed with families.

Nancy was just about to speak when Tilly jumped in.

'Nancy, we are just going to find any empty place today — not like last time, when you dragged us around the whole bay looking for the *perfect sheltered spot beside the wall, checking the angle of the sun and how high the wall was until it was nearly time for us to go home!'*

'Now, Tilly, you know how important –'

Tilly dumped the bags in an empty space then and there, and began laying out the towels.

'Run, girls, run!' she shouted, laughing at the same time.

'Tilly –'

'Oh, go and get the deckchairs! I need a cuppa.'

Once they'd had their tea, Tilly drifted off into a snooze and Nancy looked around, letting her gaze and her thoughts wander. Everywhere she looked there were families: mothers with children. Not that she was ungrateful, of course she wasn't – in fact, no one would know the four girls weren't hers. She loved them all so much, had been there to help when each new little one came along. She remembered holding each of them as a tiny baby, and had never failed to pretend – just for a moment – how it would be if she herself was a mother. I'm lucky, she chided herself, Tilly has made me part of her family and the girls love me too, I know they do. Honestly, she was being ridiculous: she had a good life, a good job, family and friends who cared about her.

She was pulled out of her thoughts by Tilly.

'Come on then, Nancy Harmer. Stop daydreaming and we'll have another cup of tea and make a start on those sandwiches.' Tilly had understood what was going on in Nancy's head. There was no sense in talking about it, and Nancy wouldn't want to anyway, so the best thing was to move on to practical things: feeding the girls.

Only, disaster struck. The flask of hot water slipped out of Nancy's hand and all the hot water drained into the sand. Nancy and Tilly looked at each other in horror.

A whole afternoon without tea. Unthinkable!

'It's the café for us then,' said Nancy. 'I tell you what — let's all go, and I'll treat the girls to chips.'

It was a noisy and busy café and the windows were so steamed up you could not see a thing through them, which was unfortunate. There were cups of tea, chips with vinegar, red sauce, bread and butter, and four very happy children enjoyed their chip butties. Nancy had such a smile on her face; she loved doing nice things for Tilly and the girls.

If only they could have seen the view!

Kathleen, having finished her butty, was drawing on the steamed-up window now and peered through the patch of window she had cleared.

'Ooh, look, Aunty Nancy, the water is nearly up to the wall.'

Lovely Kathleen.

'Mum, our sandcastles are gone,' said Anne.

'Never mind, you can make another one when we go back,' Tilly replied. Then she paused, her cup almost to her lips. She looked at Nancy, and then — pandemonium! Nancy grabbed her purse and paid as quickly as she could as Tilly grabbed the children. They ran all the way to the railings and looked down. Kathleen was right: the water was very nearly up to the wall.

Nancy opened her mouth to speak, and Tilly shouted, 'Nancy Harmer, if you say one word about this would not have happened if we had found a spot by the wall, I'll do unspeakable things to your comb!'

They stood and watched as the tide rolled in and then out, taking the last of their bags and the deckchairs with it.

'I've got my purse, anyway,' said Nancy, 'with the tickets for the return deposits on the deckchairs.'

'Oh, well, that's all right then. Wonderful. Come on then,

Nancy,' said Tilly. 'What are we waiting for? Let's just pop along to the boat station, pet, and see if we can hire a boat to retrieve the deckchairs from the middle of the ocean.'

Nancy and Tilly looked at each other and burst out laughing. They held on to each other, shaking with laughter until they could hardly breathe.

Until the final horror dawned on them — well, on Nancy anyway. The best butter knife, gone!

Tilly continued to laugh uncontrollably all the way home. Nancy was devastated.

'Don't worry,' said Kathleen, smiling at her Aunty Nancy. 'I will let you comb my hair on the bus.'

The Rag Doll

It was a bitterly cold Christmas Eve and Nancy was struggling to get thirty-six very excited children to bed. No easy task, as the snow had been falling all day and, thrilling as it was for the children, Nancy could have done without all that extra excitement. It was going to be impossible to calm the little ones down enough so that they'd go to sleep.

The war was over at last and Nancy was determined to make this a special Christmas for the children. Seventeen years I've been here now, she thought. So many Christmases. She still looked back on the day that she'd arrived, still thought about her mother, and how she'd felt first looking at those gates. And yet she'd made a life here, found a job — or more of a vocation it was really, she supposed — looking after the children in the nursery. And it was a job she loved, even on the longest, most tiring days, when the chores seemed never-ending.

Christmas Eve, and still so much to do! The orphanage was full this year — the war had added to the numbers, there was no doubt about that — but Nancy was determined that every child would have a wonderful Christmas. She was worried, though: times were hard, of course, and although they had had donations of sweets and fruit for the children, there were very few toys to give them.

There were no Santa sacks or brightly coloured stockings for these children, so Nancy had tied pretty coloured ribbons and bells, just like her own mother had shown her, to each of the socks which would dangle at the end of the thirty-six beds. Earlier today, the children had been allowed to visit the kitchen to bake biscuits with Cook. Nancy looked round the dormitory at the crumbs all over the floor and the drops of spilt milk. Who cares? she thought. The children had smiles on their faces and there had been lots of laughter as they put out the milk and biscuits for Santa and the reindeer. The story-books had been read, prayers said and, finally, the children were beginning to settle. I'll clear up when they are asleep, said Nancy to herself, and please let it be soon! She smiled.

Just as Nancy reached for the light, there was an excited whisper from one of the little girls. 'My friend at school is getting a rag doll for Christmas . . . Can you imagine how wonderful that would be, a rag doll?'

It was simply too much. Nancy felt a catch at the back of her throat and had to will the tears to stay back. One tear did manage to escape and she wiped it hurriedly away on her apron. This simply will not do, she said to herself. Pull yourself together! Lots to do, lots to do!

It was fine, really it was. A very kind benefactor to the orphanage had sent little cars for the boys, and the stockings with the sweets and oranges for each child looked so pretty. For goodness' sake, stop worrying, Nancy told herself. It had been a wonderful Christmas Eve for the children and everything had gone to plan. Her pleas to the cook to let the children bake biscuits had been granted and the children's squeals could be heard all along the corridors. The paper lanterns the children had made were draped all around the dining room and the playroom. Nancy smiled remembering the children's squeals of delight when they were hung up. Yes, it had been a wonderful day.

As night-time drew near, Nancy went to close the curtains and paused to watch the snow, still falling. 'It will be fine,' she said quietly to herself.

And yet those whispered words stayed with her:

A rag doll . . . Can you imagine?

Well, she'd have to do something; it was up to her to make it hap-pen. After all, Christmas was a time for miracles, wasn't it?

Post-war austerity for once worked in her favour. In 1946, nothing was thrown away. Old clothes were torn up into rags; buttons, rib-bons and scraps of wool were saved. Nancy got out her button box, too. Some of the rags were tied into the girls' hair to give them ring-lets on special occasions, but Nancy had another idea that night. She spread out everything she could find on the large table next to the sewing machine, then she began. Hour after hour, the snow still fall-ing, the radio in the corner of the room playing Christmas carols, Nancy rolled the rags to make dolls, sewed on buttons for eyes, wool for their hair and ribbon to tie it. She sewed until the early hours of the morning, not even stopping for a cup of tea.

It really was a miracle, thought Nancy, that she had just finished putting the last rag doll into the last stocking when the chapel bells rang six o'clock.

Today the children didn't need to be summoned twice. They jumped out of bed and rushed to the stockings hanging at the end of their beds.

'Oh my goodness, I have a rag doll!'

'Me too!'

'Me too! What colour is yours? Mine has a pink dress!'

'Oh, mine has blue eyes just like mine!'

And so it went on.

Tiredness forgotten, Nancy stood and watched them and listened to the sound of excited and happy children. Christmas is magic, she said to herself, then hurried away to begin breakfast.

If it was possible to look into someone's soul, it would have been an honour to see Nancy's at that moment. It must have been so pure and beautiful.

Somewhere in the world today those children will have celebrated many Christmas mornings with, I imagine, a little more than an orange and a rag doll. I am also sure that never will their hearts have been filled with so much joy as they were that Christmas morning in 1946 when they received the greatest gift of all: love.

Time to Dance

Newcastle-upon-Tyne, 1954

The dance hall was packed tonight. The music was so loud Molly could hardly hear herself speak, and she was chattering away non-stop because she was a little nervous. She was fidgeting with her hair, checking the pleats on her dress were not creased and re-doing her lipstick in her pretty little compact mirror. Would he be here tonight? she wondered. Ellen had said he usually came to the dance on a Monday, but he had still been messing about with his motorbike when she left home. Molly had spent hours in her bedroom that day getting ready for tonight. The full works, she thought, and out came the hair dye and rollers, new lipstick, new dress. What a fun afternoon it had been for Molly, full of anticipation, and she had laughed at her little girl, Sarah, who was dancing around her, wanting to be involved in all the excitement.

Molly and Ellen were great friends at work and it was at Ellen's house, only five nights ago, that Molly had been introduced to Ellen's brother Billy.

Billy was something else and her heart had raced from the first moment they met. They must have made up the phrase 'tall, dark and handsome' for him, Molly thought. He had jet-black hair and a way of looking at you that made your heart skip a beat. Mine, anyway, she thought. She had been warned about him, though: apparently, he could be a bit of a heartbreaker. 'Oh, really?' she had said. 'Well, maybe it's time someone took him down a peg or two!' Whether he was gorgeous or not, Molly loved a challenge, and she was a bit of a looker herself, she had been told more than once.

It was all going on around her: dancing, singing, laughing, people catching up with old friends and making new ones. Molly was usually right in the middle of everything but tonight it all faded into the background. She was thinking back to last week when she had been invited to Ellen's for tea and met Billy that first time. It wasn't that he had said much that night, just the way he kept looking over at her and smiling. Molly loved his black hair and big brown eyes. Every time she glanced over at him, he would wink at her and Molly would look away quickly, only to look up seconds later and find him winking at her again. She'd had the urge to giggle like a silly schoolgirl.

Billy had gone outside to tinker with his motorbike, and Molly and Ellen were washing up when Ellen warned her again: 'Be careful, he has got a bit of a reputation,' she said.

'So I've heard,' said Molly. 'I can cope, thank you.'

'Just telling you,' said Ellen. 'Oh, Molly, let's stay friends whatever happens.'

Molly was a good mother and loved her two-year-old daughter, Sarah, very much. Unfortunately, her marriage was over now, but she hoped one day she would marry again, maybe have more children, brothers or sisters for Sarah. She smiled, thinking of her daughter that day twirling round the room pretending to be a ballerina when she had been getting ready to go out. Even though Molly and her father were now divorced, Sarah was a happy child and loved to spend time with her father and both sets of grandparents, who all adored her.

Molly was definitely going to take Sarah to ballet classes as soon as she was three. For now, though, thought Molly, it's my time to dance.

The Journey Begins

Molly came out of the bathroom feeling very shaky indeed. This could not be happening, surely. She looked at herself in the mirror. Oh, Molly, you idiot, she mouthed to herself. It was not the first morning she had woken up feeling sick and she knew without a doubt she was pregnant. This is exactly how it had felt last time. Who on earth would she tell first, Billy or her parents? Billy would want to get married, of course. So Molly was not at all sure why this didn't feel right. I'm just confused, she thought, I need to keep this to myself until I have time to think it all through.

Unfortunately, Molly didn't have as much time as she thought. There was a knock on the bedroom door and she jumped up, pretending that she had been straightening the bed covers. 'Come in, Mum,' she shouted with forced cheerfulness.

Sarah ran to hug her grandmother. 'Go downstairs, darling, and get some breakfast,' said Molly's mother.

Then she turned her attention to her daughter.

'So who's the father then?' she asked.

Grandma was no fool.

A Grandchild

Nana Robinson had stopped banging the cupboard doors and clattering about in the kitchen and was now making up the fire. Grandad Robinson knew not to get in the way. Nana was upset. Best do nothing, he thought, and continued to sit in his favourite armchair, smoking and pretending he couldn't hear.

Nana was indeed upset and very angry. How many times had she dreamed of grandchildren, little ones running around in her kitchen helping her bake, or running around the backyard with a ball? It was the way of the world, it was what she expected. She had two daughters and a son: naturally, grandchildren would follow, quite a few in fact. This was November 1954 and Nana had already begun to prepare for Christmas. The ingredients for the cake were always prepared weeks in advance, and how, she asked herself, was she supposed to concentrate with all this hanging over them? Shame brought to her own door.

Billy had told her yesterday. Molly was expecting his child in June. Nana was shocked to her very core. This happened to other people, not them. Well, it would have to be hushed up, she supposed, and it could have been worse. It could have been one of the girls, God forbid. She felt faint. Molly wasn't even a Catholic. (Nana had to sit down and fan herself with a tea towel). A grandchild, she thought, a Robinson grandchild. Molly couldn't keep the child, Billy said, so Nana had to think of a way of doing the right thing and avoiding the shame.

Grandad Robinson was now getting very hungry, his stomach was rumbling. He put a few more logs on the fire and went back to snoozing in the chair. Nana would know what to do. A few hours later, Nana had stopped clattering about in the kitchen. Endless cups of tea had been drunk. She had a plan. They would take the child, have it baptised and put it in a Catholic home until Billy got married, which Nana was quite sure would be many years away. They could decide then what would happen. The voices of shame were screaming in Nana's head that if the child was adopted, no one would ever know, the shame would never be known and the Robinson family could continue to hold their heads up high. Nana could simply put it to the back of her mind and forget, and life would move on, as it does. There would be other grandchildren.

Grandad jumped when he heard Nana scrape back the chair and slam her cup on the draining board. No, no, no. Right or wrong, the child was a Robinson.

A grandchild, thought Nana again, sitting down once more. My grandchild. A tear had to be wiped hastily away on what was now a very dirty apron. Just look at the state of me, she thought.

She looked out of the kitchen window. It was getting dark and she needed to make up her mind. There was really only one way: Billy couldn't possibly look after the child himself and Nana would not have the shame brought to her door. The plan would be put in place. The child would be baptised, then taken to Nazareth House, a Catholic orphanage run by nuns. We can visit, she thought.

For the moment, they would tell Molly the child would be staying with them until plans had been made. It would put her mind at rest. She would get over it. The shame would never be brought to their door. They would visit. The child need never feel hurt or rejected in any way.

Nana Robinson began to concentrate on making a long overdue tea for Grandad, hoping it would get rid of the lump in her throat that was refusing to go away. A grandchild . . .

Molly never did get over it. The shame never was brought to the Robinsons' door. The secret was kept well hidden for many years, until no one cared any longer.

The feelings of rejection lay deep in the child's soul for many years to come.

A Broken Promise

The pain tore through her with a new intensity. This felt so much worse than last time — or was it just that she had forgotten how bad it could be? It was a sweltering-hot June day, too, which didn't help in the least. Molly was in between wanting it all over one minute and the next needing to hold on to this child for as long as possible. It didn't matter usually, because at the end of it there was a beautiful child to be loved and cherished, with happy times ahead. A family at home waiting to welcome you as a new mother and the new addition to the family.

Had she been able to wait another twenty years, this experience would have been so different. She'd have had kind words, mopping of her brow, choices, care, empathy regardless of the situation — but this was 1955, in a hostel for single mothers.

Eventually, it was over, but it was not the child's screams that were first heard but Molly's:

'Give me my child, she's mine, let me hold her!'

The looks of those in the room were ones of intolerance, but Molly didn't care. She had her child for now and she was going to feed her. Molly was one of the lucky single mums in this hostel. Her parents had paid extra for her to be here longer and so they left her alone.

She had pleaded and begged until her parents had paid for her to have six days with the child. Six whole days of bonding, feeding, rocking, singing lullabies and passing on every ounce of love she could give.

Molly had been promised the baby would live with its natural father and his parents, who would bring her up. Her grandmother and aunty would be collecting her tomorrow.

'Listen to me, little one,' she said now to her child. 'Never let anyone tell you I didn't love you. Your dad will explain it all to you when you are old enough to understand. This is the hardest thing I will ever do in my life and I will spend the rest of my life loving you, remembering you and missing you. You will be happy with Daddy and his family. They have promised me you will be well looked after by the family and that I should just leave it up to them. I have to believe that, one day, I will be allowed to walk back into your life. You have a sister and, one day too, I will tell her about you, I promise. You are called Susan, and I read somewhere that Susan means courage. We must both be brave now, darling.

'Tomorrow someone else will hold you, love you and take care of you, but tonight you are mine, and we have all night, just you and me.'

Molly went over and over in her head the thought that at least her daughter was to be brought up with her natural father and his parents. Billy was such fun; surely Susan would have many happy days. She would be loved, taken care of. Billy had loved Molly, hadn't he? It was just that she wasn't a Catholic and they couldn't get married. Molly no longer cared. All that mattered now was the child in her arms.

'I will not cry. I will not cry. It will be fine, I promise you, little one. I promise, I promise.'

Molly had an immense imagination, and she began to play out scenarios in her mind: Susan on Billy's shoulders, Billy throwing Susan into the air and catching her, making her squeal with laughter, father and daughter holding hands, smiling and loving each other.

Just for once, her dreams didn't help. The pain was so raw — but still she had tonight.

That night, Molly didn't sleep. She rocked and sang to her baby all night, the gnawing pain inside her growing as night turned to day. It was time.

She wasn't sure she could do it. Surely something would happen — a reprieve, a last-minute problem? — but no, they had come to take Susan.

'You need Susan's bag. Please, I have bought her things. I have to tell you how she feeds. Listen to me. Please, listen . . .'

'We have everything we need. She'll be fine.'

They took her from Molly's arms.

'She has a name, her name is Susan. She sleeps longest during the day, she is best winded lying on her tummy, she has been nursed and she won't take a bottle . . . Please, listen to me. Please, I need to tell you. You need her bag . . .'

The words fell on deaf ears. They had turned and left immediately. The people now responsible for the child were long gone. It was then that Molly began to sob, great wracking sobs louder than any sounds made during her labour. No words of empathy or understanding, no due care and attention, just a tut and 'Enough of that please', then the door was closed.

Soon, it would be time for Molly to think about going home. She had another child, a little girl, Sarah, only three years old, who needed her. The last time Molly had given birth it had been a difficult but happy experience. She had been married then. There were gifts, congratulations — all the usual happy things. Now it was different. She needed Sarah and wanted to hold her. They would be closer than ever now, no matter what happened. They would love each other, and everything would be fine. Sarah would eventually grow up and have babies of her own. Babies. She mustn't think of babies.

It was important to be strong, not today but tomorrow, before facing life never knowing what had happened to little Susan. For now, she reckoned she deserved to cry for just a little longer.

Molly's promise was not to be met.

The two women had reached the large iron gates that stood at the beginning of the long drive to Nazareth House Orphanage. Slowly they made their way down the drive carrying the tiny six-day-old child bundled up in a warm blanket. The huge wooden door had a bell pull to one side which made a loud clanging noise when they tugged on it. The child stirred. Her journey had begun.

The Surprise

It came suddenly out of nowhere, totally unexpected during this long, hot summer of 1955. The foghorn had been sending out its message since early morning, waking most of those in the surrounding coastal areas of Newcastle. By mid-morning the foghorn was nothing compared to the noise of many screaming and disappointed children standing hopefully, bucket and spade in hand, having been promised a day at the beach. There was a chilly breeze and the light mist was threatening to change to heavy rain any time soon. Typical, thought Nancy, as she wrapped yet another shawl around the sleeping child. She smiled as she looked at Susan, once more hardly able to breathe at the excitement of it all. Nancy didn't care in the least whether it was hot or cold. Nothing was going to spoil her surprise.

What on earth was all the noise about? The Lord knew Tilly's girls were never quiet, but this was something else. There was definitely something going on. Four pairs of footsteps thundered up the stairs, each of her daughters pushing and shoving to get to their mum first. It was Anne who had managed to grab the letter and had now run into the room, shouting, 'It's for you!'

Tilly wiped her hands on her apron. Who could it be from? The only letters she received were from her family in Ireland, but this had a local postmark. She opened it a little nervously.

'Who's it from? Who's it from?'

'It's from Nancy.'

53

'*Our Aunty Nancy?*' said Margaret.

Tilly was shocked — this was most unlike the Nancy she knew.

'*How strange,*' said Tilly. '*She says she has a surprise for us. She'll be here on Wednesday afternoon and she wants us all to be here. That's it. Nothing more.*'

This wasn't like Nancy at all. Never in all these years had Tilly known her to be so secretive about anything. What on earth was going on? The girls clamoured around her, but Tilly could tell them nothing. '*We'll simply have to wait,*' *she said.*

During the next two days, they talked non-stop about Aunty Nancy's surprise. Why had she warned them in a letter? It must be something huge. When Wednesday finally arrived they spent most of the afternoon taking turns to look out of the window.

'*I can see her! I can see her!*' *yelled Maureen at the top of her voice.*

Nancy could see them too, and the smile set even more firmly about her lips as she slowly made her way down the street towards them. I'm feeling fanciful, and today, I don't care, she thought.

Tilly and all the girls had their faces pressed up against the window now.

'*I can definitely see a bundle of something,*' *called Anne.*

Tilly felt the hairs stand up on the back of her neck. Nancy often bought the girls a little something when she visited, but this was no bundle of gifts. Tilly recognized this sort of bundle.

Nancy got to the door and the girls rushed down to her.

'*Wait!*' *screamed Tilly.* '*Just wait, girls!*'

It was at the top of the stairs that they met. Nancy simply handed the bundle to Tilly and said, '*Her name is Susan.*'

Tilly and the children were speechless.

After a few moments, Tilly recovered herself. '*You've been holding out on me, Nancy Harmer,*' *she said.* '*What have you been up to?*'

'Don't be ridiculous, Tilly.' Nancy blushed from ear to ear.

They all gathered round, then Susan began to cry and everyone started talking at once, Tilly shouting instructions to the girls to find a bottle and get a blanket from the bedroom. 'Must light the fire and keep the little mite warm,' she said. Even on the hottest of days these old flats could be cold.

'No explanations yet,' she went on. 'First things first,' and she busied herself with making the baby comfortable and making a pot of tea.

Her eyes were stinging as she warmed the pot, and the questions were buzzing around in her head. She had never seen Nancy looking like this — there was definitely something different about her. Being a mother made you different, of course it did, but where in Heaven's name had this child come from? Could it be Nancy's? Would she be allowed to keep it? She found herself praying again for her friend. Please, God, oh please, don't let her get hurt.

The tea tray was brought in, the biscuits handed round. It was time.

'I know what you're thinking, Tilly,' said Nancy, 'I always do, but Susan isn't to be adopted or fostered, her dad just wants her looked after until maybe he gets married, and that will be years away, and Tilly, she just feels like mine, and I'm going to speak to Billy, her dad, and tell him that I will look after her as long as he wants me to.'

Tilly had never seen such emotion in anyone, and certainly not in Nancy, her rational, sensible friend. Every word Nancy uttered tore at her heart, but they were friends and she would support her in anything.

'Well, Nancy, come on then,' she said briskly. 'We have drawers to *go through and boxes to be pulled out again. Thank God it's a girl — I have enough clothes to keep her going for years!'*

The afternoon flew by, and by the end of it there were piles of clothes, bottles, bibs, rattles and toys, all ready for Nancy to take home.

Bill's tea was not on the table ready for him that night. Instead, after a long shift at work, when he came through the door he was met by a chorus of 'Aunty Nancy has had a baby!', 'Aunty Nancy has had a baby!', and, again, boxes and bags all over the floor.

'Don't ask!' shouted Tilly. 'And don't take your coat off — you will have to go on the bus with Nancy and carry the bags.'

'Tell you on the way home,' said Nancy quietly to the poor, bemused man.

Bill went all the way back to Nazareth House with Nancy and listened to her talk about Susan. He had never seen her so animated and, like Tilly, he said nothing. Nancy's smile broke their hearts, but what could they say?

When Bill got home he looked at Tilly. Neither of them said a word. Then:

'God answered my prayers,' said Tilly.

'Well, you'd better get back on to Him then and pray she gets to keep her.'

That night Tilly put some extra coal on the fire and sat up late praying with all her heart that this baby would indeed be Nancy's child.

Nancy's Child

Early Years

So the nursery at Nazareth House had one more child now – Nancy's child – and was full to the rafters. Children who'd been orphaned in the war, their parents having fallen or died of tuberculosis or other diseases, children whose parents just couldn't cope, and, the lowest of the low in 1950s Britain, children who had been born out of wedlock. It wasn't only the mothers who were made to face the disgrace, the children too were made to feel it, and to pray for forgiveness. But not wanted? None of the children at the Nazareth House Orphanage could be that. Nancy simply would not let it happen. As long as these children were under her wing, not one of them would ever feel that.

I remember very little of the first three or four years of my life but, funnily enough, my earliest memories are of getting dressed in the morning. We had to get up especially early every day, it took so long! First came the vest, then the liberty bodice. It must have been about three inches thick. It was like putting on a mini suit of armour. The knickers came practically up to my chest, then came the petticoat, a skirt, a jumper and of course the thick woolly tights.

And still this wasn't enough protection from the elements. To go outside I would have to put on my coat, and, naturally, this had been Bought to Last. This meant that when it was new it was at least three sizes too big – to get the maximum wear out of it – so the sleeves either hung down to my knees or were turned back so many times it looked like I was wearing spare tyres around my wrists.

And who can forget the mittens on a string threaded across the shoulders and down each arm? I nearly garroted myself every time I took my coat off. Where are the Health and Safety officers when you need them?

'And make sure you take a scarf, it's cold outside. Now hurry up, you'll be late.'

Oh, come on, you have to be joking. I was wrapped up like an Egyptian mummy – there was no way I could hurry anywhere in this lot.

That feeling of being wrapped up and protected is one of my strongest memories of my childhood in the orphanage. And it was all – the layers and the feeling of security and warmth – down to Mum. I'd always called Nancy Mum. What else would I call her?

Another thing I really remember about those early years is tea time on a Sunday. That day, we'd have our tea downstairs with 'the Big Ones'. The Big Ones were aged between five and ten, so they weren't that big, looking back, but it was always a massive treat. We'd all be talking about what kind of cake Cook had baked and what would be in the sandwiches, but of course – and there was always a but – there was the rosary to be said first.

I can imagine the scene in Heaven every Sunday when God clangs the bells with shouts of warning: 'It's prayer time at the orphanage,' and a hundred thousand angels shove their fingers in their ears, throw themselves at the clouds and wait for approximately two hundred kids saying ten 'Hail Mary's, ten 'Our Father's and ten 'Jesus, Mary and Joseph's faster than the speed of light to get to the cake.

God should have been happy with us, though, because we all did as we were told. We wouldn't have dared not to. One of the things that was drummed into us was reverence. We always bowed our heads when anybody said this word – it must have been one of the rules – although none of us actually understood what it meant. All we knew was that reverence had to do with all things connected to the Church.

For example, you only got to the chapel after walking along the longest corridor you could imagine – I remember the sound of our footsteps echoing as we walked along, and the smell of wax polish on the floors – and each time we passed the chapel doors, we had to stop, genuflect and bow our heads. And as the kitchen and playroom were at one end of the building and the dormitories and dining rooms at the other, that was a lot of genuflecting. No wonder I've got bad knees and dizziness now that I'm older. I spent most of my childhood bobbing up and down like a demented yoyo and I've done more bowing and scraping than Uriah Heep.

Every Friday we'd have fish with bread and butter and, sometimes, as an extra treat, we'd have chips with lashings of red sauce. Of course, we had fish that day because it was a sin to eat meat on a Friday. Now, whose bright idea that one was, I really don't know. I can't imagine God sitting there saying, 'I know, let's punish all those who dare to dabble with a sausage roll on a Friday.' And might I ask what happened to all those poor souls who were turned away from the Pearly Gates by the meat patrol when this particular sin was abandoned? Were they all shipped in droves back to Heaven with a smack on the hand and a 'You are forgiven, my son' speech. *I*'d have been well in the huff, I'll tell you.

As I got older, I grew to enjoy spending time with the other children my age more and more. I'd spend most of my time with Mum in the nursery, as she was always working there with the small ones, but sometimes I craved companions of my own age. I was Nancy's child, but who else was I? I was stuck in the middle. The children in the nursery were too young for me now, and the big ones downstairs were told by the nuns that I didn't belong there. There was also lots of gossip. Because I was Nancy's child, they thought I was getting special treatment – and of course I had a mum, the one thing most of them didn't. But it didn't matter to me: I had imagined it all perfectly. I was going to go to school soon, I was going to have lots of friends, read lots of books and life would be wonderful – or so I thought.

No-nonsense Nancy

I was only four years old but I can still remember my first day at school. Not clearly, but the memory is definitely there. A couple of the 'Big Ones' from Nazareth House had been told to take me in, but they only took me as far as a big, derelict building just outside the school grounds and left me there to walk the rest of the way myself – if the ghosts didn't get me first. I was terrified. This went on for a whole week before I devised my clever plan. I might have only been four years old, but I was mighty creative.

Mum waved me off the next morning, and I started my long walk down the corridor and through the double doors, returning her wave. But as soon as I was through those double doors, I ran into the room above the church and hid behind the organ until I knew the Big Ones would have left.

The organ was immense; the pipes reached right up to the ceiling of the building. I crouched down on the benches and asked God to let me be safe, and not let the ghosts get me. Of course, I always promised to be good. Then I went back to Mum and said that I must have been late, as they had all gone without me. It worked: Mum had to take me to school for ever. Sorted. Day two – the very next day – blew the plan and it all went wrong.

I hadn't slept at all well the night before, as I was so

frightened about going to school. I crept into the chapel and crawled in between the pews, just as I had done the day before, but I was so tired I must have begun to doze off. This on the day there was organ practice. When the first note boomed through the chapel I got such a fright I let out a scream – and continued screaming, bringing the staff running along the corridors.

I had been caught out, but I sobbed so hard Mum just held me gently in her arms until I told her what had happened. It had to be dragged out of me, I don't know why.

Oh, my mum, the Warrior, she was ready for battle. This was No-nonsense Nancy at her best. One look at her face and even the bravest of the brave wouldn't have argued with her.

I have no idea what happened that day, but the most important thing was my plan had worked. After that, there wasn't a day that Mum didn't take me into school and stand at the school gates waving until I was inside.

Four-leaf Clovers

Once I'd settled in, I loved school. I was going to learn everything, have hundreds of friends, answer all the teacher's questions and make Mum proud. I can still to this day see the play area and the blackboard and feel the excitement of learning so many new things. I was so full of confidence: even at four years old, there was no doubt in my mind that, one day, I would be famous. And then I heard her, one of the teachers. 'Oh, her,' she said. 'She's another one that will never amount to anything. She's one of those from the home.'

So many years ago and yet this memory is one I can still recall. I am fifty-seven years old now, and those words have never left me. I wonder sometimes why I never felt like I belonged anywhere. Mum loved me, but I'd been abandoned by my birth mother. I lived with the children at the orphanage, but I wasn't one of them. I had Mum, and I also had a father. Somehow, though, there was no place for me. Somehow, I just wasn't quite good enough. The most important thing for me came to be being accepted, wanted, liked, loved. This was something that was to stay with me my whole life.

I was such a little drama queen, however, that one way of coping came naturally. It's called Let's Pretend.

To access Nazareth House you had to walk through

huge black iron gates and down a long driveway with a wooded area on one side and grass on the other. On the edge of the wood were some beautiful rhododendron bushes (Mum always had vases full of them in the nursery, she loved them so much) and I'd run past them into the trees and escape. That wood was my fantasy land, and I'd spend every moment I could in there, daydreaming about what my life was going to be like. I was going to be famous – that was for definite – and Mum and I would be rich because of it.

Over the next few years, I rehearsed all my dreams on that piece of woodland. I would dance for hours around the trees (I would be a famous ballerina). I would make up plays and act them out, trying to figure out how to make my audience laugh and cry (I would be a famous actress). I spent hours practising bows and curtseys, imagining the applause. Oh, I was such a dreamer! Then one day someone told me that over in the grassed area there were clovers, and if I found one with four leaves all my dreams would come true. Hour after hour, day after day that summer, I searched and searched, always hoping, always praying. My dreams would come true and all those people who had said I would amount to nothing would be proved wrong. And so the search for that four-leaf clover went on . . . and on.

Tall Tales

Of course, there *were* other children at the orphanage that I played with. There was Josephine, who everyone liked because of her hair. Most of us had never seen hair that long before, and it was fair and very beautiful. All the girls with long hair would have to sit on the long benches in the bathrooms before going to bed and have it wound into rags, sometimes so tight they'd actually cry out. I would have willingly put up with the pain to look as good as these girls did. And Josephine's ringlets always came out best. They would swing from side to side as she walked along, and those of us – well, most of us – who had short hair died of jealousy every time we saw her. Our hair was always parted on the right-hand side, and a clump of hair on the left tied with a ribbon. We all wanted Josephine's ringlets. We all wanted to *be* Josephine. She would say that her mother had loved her so much she would brush her hair for hours every day and tell her she would always be beautiful so long as she had those ringlets.

Meghan and Cathleen were twins, yet they couldn't have been more different from each other. Meghan was quiet and withdrawn and said very little. She'd always look to her sister to answer any question that was asked. Cathleen, on the other hand, could tell a great story. One day she told us all about their father, who was a captain on a ship – and not any old ship, but his own. He had voyaged around the world twice already, and this was why the twins were at Nazareth House, but as soon as he returned he would be coming to get them, and, if we were nice to them, they might just let us visit them on the ship. I could think of nothing more wonderful, and we spent many hours wondering what it would feel like to stand on a ship looking down at the ocean. Maybe, Cathleen said, if we were really good friends, she would ask if we could go on the next trip with them. We were all very nice to Meghan and Cathleen after that. I asked Meghan one day if it was true. 'Oh, I hope so,' she said.

There was another girl there called Lily. Her mum and dad were so rich her dad had gone off to look for a big house for them to live in and, as soon as he'd found one, they would come back for her. Make-believe was a very close cousin to Let's Pretend at Nazareth House.

The truth was Josephine's mother had never brushed her daughter's hair. She had died giving birth to Josephine. Meghan and Cathleen's father may have been far away – no one knew. He hadn't been seen since the day their mother had told him she was pregnant. Lily's father had left her mum when Lily was three days old. He had gone back home under pressure from his parents to leave the girl he loved: she'd fallen pregnant out of wedlock and they didn't want that sort in the family. 'I'll come back when things calm down,' he had said, but he never did. She kept on hoping he would come back until the day she died.

There were many other children with stories to tell, and, far worse, many children who accepted the truth of who and what they were with no sense of Let's Pretend or Make-believe, but just with a sense of hopelessness and loss. Children would cry, scream when they were taken from the arms of the people who'd brought them. The little ones just didn't understand why they were there. Some of the nuns were very kind souls, and did their best. There was one who was French, I remember, and did the most beautiful calligraphy. We would sit and watch her and she would teach us French words and tell us about life in France. And there was Sister Concepta, who kept a tin of sweets in a high corner cupboard and would beckon us into her room, place a footstool under the cupboard and let us reach in for a treat whenever we passed her door. But they could never be parents to the orphans at Nazareth House.

The bars on the window of the nursery were for safety, but I don't know how many children over the years would stand on the bench just below the window holding on to them and watching the driveway because maybe, just maybe, someday, someone would walk down that drive and come to take them home.

There was a beautiful church attached to Nazareth House, part of it built of Italian marble. One of the nun's fathers was an Italian businessman, and he had the marble shipped to Newcastle when the church was being built. The altar was gold and white and shaped like three church steeples, reaching high up into the ceiling.

Every Sunday we would put on our best clothes for Mass and walk downstairs in twos to take our place in the pews. As young as we were, we would always sit silently, head bowed, waiting for Mass to begin. The scariest part of the whole hour was when the priest, after reading the Gospel, would walk amongst us, asking questions to ensure we had been listening. Of course, I never had. Daydreaming was much more fun.

One particular Sunday, Father, who had probably noticed I wasn't paying attention, called out, 'Who can tell me what envy is?' Celia, one of the staff, who was, fortunately, sitting next to me, dug me in the ribs and whispered, 'Jealous – it means being jealous, Susan,' just before the priest wheeled round and pointed his finger at me.

'You,' he said in a booming voice. 'Tell me what envy is.'

And with my most angelic look and in the sweetest voice I could manage, I stood up and replied, 'It means being jealous, Father,' then sat down.

He eyed me suspiciously and for a moment I thought Celia might have played a trick on me. There was a pause, then 'Yes,' he said, and he turned to put the fear of God into someone else.

'Saved your skin there, kid,' said Celia, and she and I had a quiet giggle, until Mum poked her finger into our backs and told us to be quiet. Honestly, what did they want from me? I'd got the question right, hadn't I?

Christopher

The pain was much stronger today than ever before. Nancy was annoyed. Please, not today, not when there was so much to do. Dr Graham had warned her that this was not going to go away; he had given her some painkillers, but these were only a temporary measure. Last month, the pain had been so severe she had been forced to see Dr Graham during one of his visits to the sickbay.

'It's no good looking at me like that, young lady,' he had said. 'We both know you need an operation to put this right, or it will continue to get worse. How many times do I have to tell you this?'

Dr Graham had looked after Nancy since she was a young girl and knew how stubborn she could be. He also knew that behind all that bravado and no-nonsense attitude beat a heart of pure gold. She was a treasure, and he greatly admired her. He also knew the reason why she was refusing to go into hospital for the hysterectomy: there would be a six-week recuperation period afterwards. There was no mistaking the look of horror on her face at the thought of leaving Susan for that length of time.

He patted Nancy on the shoulder and smiled at her.

'Sit down, Nancy, please. Look, we have known each other many years and I really must insist you listen to me. I have a duty of care to look after you and, surely, after all these years, you know that you can trust me. Once this is all over you will never suffer these pains again. You are a good mother, Nancy, but surely there must be someone who could look after Susan for you. I promise you, if you

71

don't have this operation soon, you could end up in hospital for a lot longer than six weeks. Please, Nancy, you should think about it. Let me help you.'

'Very well,' she said.

Well, my oh my, thought Dr Graham, that must have been quite a speech I made. I've surpassed myself and actually convinced her to go ahead. Feeling extremely pleased with himself, he picked up his pen ready to begin the process to have Nancy taken into hospital.

Then Nancy looked him straight in the eye.

'I will think about it,' she said, and left.

Dr Graham snapped his bag shut and gave up.

The church bells had begun to ring. It was the start of a new day. Nancy closed her eyes and willed the pain to cease, or at least ease off a little bit. Eventually, she pulled herself out of bed to take the necessary pills to get her through it. There was a new child being brought into the nursery today, a little boy called Christopher. Nancy had read the file: his father, Danny, had been born in Ghana, and his mum was English. Danny was on his own now with his boys, and had managed to find a home with family in Manchester for Oscar, his eldest son, but Christopher was only two years old and they wouldn't be able to look after him. Poor wee mite, thought Nancy. Well, I can't let this ridiculous pain stop me getting on with my day; that little boy is going to need a lot of love and attention. Probably, though, whatever she did, there would be tears and tantrums before bedtime.

The little boy was frightened, anyone could see that. He stood in the centre of the room holding his father's hand tightly, father and son side by side, looking straight ahead in total silence. Christopher was concentrating on the ticking of the clock, counting one two, one two, in his head, like Daddy had taught him. Daddy had explained that Christopher would not be here in this place for long and that he would see him as much as possible when he wasn't working. Daddy was going to work hard and make money so they could all be a family again and return to Ghana. He had told him wonderful stories about home and all the family who were waiting to see him. Good times were coming, and soon.

Danny's face and hands were sweating, but he was trying not to let his emotions show. He was a man, a good man, and he could be strong. Men didn't cry — and certainly not in front of their children. He just kept on looking straight ahead; he'd said all there was to say, and was scared that if he even looked at his young son he might just gather him up in his arms and run. Christopher might only be two years old but he had a vice-like grip on his father's hand. So there they remained, waiting, the clock still ticking in the corner of the room.

They both looked up when they heard her footsteps in the corridor. Danny stood up tall. Oh, please, let them be good to him, he thought. Please, God, let them take good care of my son.

Nancy saw kind eyes, and recognized the pain behind them. Is this how she would feel if she had to hand her Susan over? Her heart went out to both father and son.

Danny saw a kind face, bright-blue eyes and a smile so full of empathy and compassion you could almost feel it. It was all there to see in an instant. The woman had a child with her, a little girl who looked about the same age as Christopher, maybe just a little bit older. He relaxed a little: it was going to be all right.

'Hello,' said Nancy to Christopher. 'I am Aunty Nancy.'

Christopher's head just bent to the floor.

'Sorry, he is a little bit shy and . . . well, you know . . .'

'I do know, and please don't apologize.'

Again, that kind smile, the sound of her voice that said, There, there. Everything will be all right, without her even needing to speak.

'Would you like to see the playroom, Christopher?' she went on. Still no response.

Susan could not take her eyes off Christopher, he looked so lost. But then he looked up with eyes full of tears and a bottom lip that was threatening to wobble in a big way. He just didn't understand what was going on, why this was happening. All he knew was that Daddy was going away. Maybe if he kept hold of his hand they wouldn't be able to take him. He put his head back down, gripped even harder and hoped against hope. You will need to be brave, he had been told. You must be a big boy now. He didn't understand. The fear inside was too strong to let any words get through. He didn't want to be brave, he didn't want to be a big boy, he simply wanted to stay with Daddy. Christopher wanted to stamp his foot, but he was too frightened.

Then he felt it, a small hand in his, a warm hand, and a soft voice said, 'Hello, Christopher, I'll be your friend if you like.' He liked the sound of that voice and curled his fingers around the hand. 'My name is Susan.'

Danny took a deep breath. It was time to go.

Two steps from the door, he turned back and grabbed his son.

'I will keep my promise to you,' he said. 'You know what a promise is, don't you?'

Christopher and Susan looked at each other. There was something here neither child could explain. In that instant, a bond was to be forged that even the separation of thousands of miles would never break.

Things were beginning to happen around them now: staff carrying out their daily duties, the sounds of children running up the steps from the playground into the nursery. Susan and Christopher saw only each other.

'I know,' said Susan. 'You can be my brother, and I'll be your sister. We'll do everything together. We can be like shadows that stick together for ever.'

Christopher looked up and smiled. He liked Susan.

'I'll be your big sister. I'm a whole two years older than you, which means I can look after you.'

Christopher's smile reached his eyes this time and, hand in hand, he and Susan went off to the playroom.

Shadows

The song 'Me and My Shadow' must have been written for Christopher and me. Where I went, he went, and vice versa. It didn't matter to him that I was Nancy's child and different from the other children in the orphanage. All he cared about was me, and we became closer and closer as the days went by.

One day I pleaded with Mum to let Christopher come on one of our outings to Fenwick's, a department store in the centre of Newcastle. She needed to get permission but, finally, the date was set. We were so excited! Mum didn't have a second's peace: 'Is it today?' 'Is it soon?' 'How many minutes?' Mum was demented with it. Christopher called her Mum now, too, copying me. She'd tried to explain that he should call her Aunty Nancy but stopped when he started to cry. Ooops, thought Mum. Going to be in trouble if this gets back to the nuns.

Eventually, the great day came and we were all dressed up ready for our trip to town. We sang, chatted and skipped all the way to the bus stop and had to be told more than once on the bus to sit still. I had told Christopher all about the toy department and the café, and it was the toys and the colouring books he wanted to see. We were all so happy, and Mum looked so proud and serene. Christopher was grinning from ear to ear, and I had the real fidgets. Things couldn't have been any better. This is what dreams were made of. Then we were off the bus and holding Mum's hand ready to cross the road to Fenwick's. Christopher shouted, 'Mum, are we here? Are we here?', and I called out, 'Mum, look! Look what they've got in the windows!'

I can't remember what I'd seen in the windows now. That moment is just frozen in my memory. The traffic didn't stop, but for me, it was as if everything suddenly stood still. And just because two children with different-coloured skin had called out 'Mum' to the same woman.

Some of the people around us stopped in their tracks and stared at Mum. Someone tutted, someone else looked at her with raised eyebrows, someone else muttered, 'It's disgusting, disgraceful!'

It was injustice and prejudice at its worst. Here was a woman, a wonderful, caring, compassionate soul who had dedicated her whole life to caring for other people's children, who worked more hours than was ever asked of her, never complaining, being criticized and judged by people who didn't know anything about her.

I remember both me and Christopher looked up at Mum. She was rising above it all. She held her head erect, eyes straight ahead, proud as Punch to be with us. Nothing and no one was going to spoil this day.

She gripped our hands tightly. 'God forgive them,' she said at the top of her voice, and marched us across the road to Fenwick's.

At the time I was four years old and didn't really understand the brother and sister thing. I just assumed that

Christopher was now my brother. We loved each other, after all – surely that was enough. We spent hours playing in our room. Mum and I had our own room with two single beds, and I loved it. Beside my bed was a doll's cot with my favourite doll, which played the Brahms lullaby. Mum would tuck me up in bed with a story and I would drift off to sleep listening to it.

It must have been the early hours of the morning when we were woken up by a thump on the door. Immediately, Mum jumped out of bed. There he stood in his pyjamas, head down, bottom lip stuck out in a petulant expression which meant he knew he was doing something wrong.

Christopher hung his head when Mum opened the door, and I burst out laughing. Hearing me, he ran over, climbed on to my bed and grabbed my hand. 'Oh, please, let him stay, Mum,' I said. Nancy was tired. I'll get into trouble, she thought, but tiredness got the better of her. 'Very well,' she said. 'Just this once. Now get to sleep, you two, now.'

We giggled and giggled until Mum shouted, 'All right, you two, in here now!', and we jumped into bed either side of her and snuggled in. Christopher reached over Mum for my hand and, happy and content, we slept.

This continued the next night, and the night after. Nancy gave up picking Christopher up and carrying him back to bed only to find him back at the door five minutes later. She knew when she was beaten, and gave in to him just to get some sleep. It was getting

difficult, though. After all, it was unfair to treat any child differently to another. Christopher and Susan spent every possible moment together; they loved each other so much. How on earth, thought Nancy, do I explain to Susan that this is not her brother and that, one day, he will no longer be here? It was a temporary arrangement, after all. Nancy could not even begin to think how Susan would cope when Christopher left. But children forget, she thought, once they are distracted, and Christopher would be many miles away in a new country — and Susan? Well, eventually, Susan would forget.

This time Mum was wrong. I would never forget Christopher. It would be another twenty-eight years before tiny fingers were once more wrapped around my hand, bringing me the unconditional love I craved.

Whispers

As I said, I didn't know what made a brother and sister, what tied them together, but I did know I had a mum – and I had a dad, too. While all the children at Nazareth House leaned over the railings at the playroom window, imagining their mum and dad walking up that long driveway, for me, I'd still imagine it and dream of it, but once a month, it would actually happen. Sometimes, I would close my eyes, say three 'Hail Mary's and wait, just hoping that maybe when I opened my eyes he would be there – not to take me home, because this was where I lived with Mum, and I loved her so much; but the whispered words of the past were there in my mind, and I wanted to believe that Dad missed me, loved me and wanted to be with me. He was my dad, so handsome, so much fun, always making me laugh, and I loved him too.

They were whispering in the corridor again. The nuns often whispered in quiet prayer, but this was about as far away from prayer as you could get. The whispering now came with knowing looks that Nancy could only describe as smug or sly. Still, she ignored it. She always taught the children that if something couldn't be said out loud, it shouldn't be said at all. A great example the nuns were setting the children!

Nancy could cope with words, even unkind or frightening ones — you knew what you were dealing with then, but this! They knew something, and as they were keeping it from her, it must have to do with Susan. It had been a busy day today and Nancy was hurrying to the laundry when she passed them in the corridor. She was just thinking that she was too tired to be bothered with all their nonsense today when she caught the words — still whispered, but this time loud enough to be heard: 'Won't have her much longer, that much I know'; 'No rights I'm aware of . . .'

Nancy froze, then caught her breath. Laundry, I just have to make it to the laundry, she urged herself. When she got there she dropped down on to the bench. She was fighting to keep her breath steady, and her hands were shaking. They were going to take Susan away and have her fostered or, worse, adopted. Billy had broken his promise. She just knew it. Oh, dear God, what was she going to do? I've done everything I can, she thought, kept every promise I made. Why do people have to be so cruel? 'I can't lose her, I can't,' she whispered to herself. The pain was worse than physical pain. She gripped the pile of laundry and rocked back and forth, crying with sheer frustration and anger but most of all — fear.

She stayed like that for some time, unsure whether she could stand up on her trembling legs. Susan would be drawing pictures in their room with the new crayons Nancy had bought only yesterday. Nancy focussed on that to steady her nerves: I wonder what she has drawn, I wonder what colours she has used, maybe we can put it up on the wall. Mundane thoughts but ones she needed to hold her steady.

She placed the laundry slowly in the basket to calm herself and made her way back along the corridor, thinking of Susan and her picture all the way.

What a child Susan was!

'I've drawn some ballet shoes, Mum, and I've cut them out,' she said as Nancy sat beside her.

Nancy loved her daughter with all her heart but sometimes found it extremely difficult to understand her. Susan was such a dreamer. She'd want to be a dancer, then a singer – she had the most vivid imagination Nancy had ever seen in a five-year-old. She wondered for a moment what her birth mother was like, but said:

'We could get some sticky tape and stick them to your shoes – how would that be?'

'Could we really? Ooh, Mum, I love you so much.' Susan ran to get the sticky tape, twirling excitedly around the room as she did so.

Nancy took a deep breath. She would fight this, and she could be formidable when she wanted to be. Billy. Speak to Billy: that was the answer. Never mind all this wondering what all the whispering was about; she had to know what she was facing. No rights? Well, she'd see about that one. She'd do anything she had to in order to keep her beautiful daughter. Because that is how she thought of her now and, in truth, always had: Susan was her daughter.

The telephone was in a room downstairs in the nuns' parlour, with a seat below it. She lifted the massive receiver and listened to the dialling tone, but her hand was shaking so much she replaced it. It was heavy all right, but it was her nerves that were not strong enough. She went over the conversation she would have with Billy in her mind. She needed answers, but she shouldn't push him too hard. Had he gone behind her back and had Susan fostered or adopted? No, she couldn't ask that straight out. Should she tell Billy about the plans for ballet classes, how she had saved to pay for them? No, she thought with a sigh. Any other foster parent could do that. Nancy was cold and numb, and she felt she might never be warm again. Fear clutched at every part of her. No-nonsense Nancy, who had no time for this sort of ridiculous nonsense, was frightened. 'Ridiculous!' she said out loud to herself, and grabbed the receiver and dialled.

Billy answered.

'Yoohoo, Typhoo!' That was what Dad always said on the phone – but Nancy ploughed right in.

'Have you changed your mind about Susan?' she blurted out.

'What do you mean?'

'I mean, have you changed your mind about Susan?'

'You are going to have to explain this one, Nancy.'

'Are you having her fostered or adopted?'

Nancy's heart was beating hard. She held her breath. This was it. Was she about to lose the most precious thing in the world to her? How would she bear it?

'Nancy, it has been a long week for me, and I'm sorry I haven't been to see Susan for a few weeks, but I have no idea what you are talking about. And I know that even though I haven't seen her for a while I am perfectly aware that she is always well cared for. Why in God's name would I decide to take her away from her mum at five years old and hand her over to a complete stranger –'

Her mum. *He had said* her mum.

Nancy's legs gave away, and she was never more glad of the seat beneath the telephone.

The warmth began to return to her body. It had always been in the back of her mind that Billy could one day just turn up and take Susan back. Always. He'd always said, in fact, that he'd return for her when he got married and was able to look after her.

'Billy, the nuns have been saying things, making comments.' Nancy had realized that she was still holding the receiver.

'Nothing to do with me, Nancy. Susan is happy where she is and

I can see her whenever I like. As far as I am concerned, that is the way it stays.'

That was all Nancy wanted to hear for the moment. Thanking him, she hung up.

Recovering herself, Nancy now wondered what it had been that the nuns were talking about. The fear then relief were now over-taken by anger and she marched straight to Mother Superior's office.

When Mother Superior answered the door, she immediately sighed. Nancy was never a person to be argued with. She had known her since that day she had turned up at the huge iron gates of Nazareth House, and had watched her grow up. Always sensible and in control, a serious child, and at the moment a very angry adult.

'What is it, Nancy?' The Mother Superior had never seen her so angry.

'It's the whispering,' Nancy answered. It sounded utterly ridiculous when she said it.

'Whispering?'

Mother Superior looked momentarily puzzled.

'They have been saying things, the nuns, I've heard them, saying that I won't have Susan much longer. It's cruel. What are you all planning behind my back?'

'Nancy, please sit down. No one is doing anything behind your back. We simply thought that Susan may benefit from being with children of her own age. You know the rules here: children are only in the nursery until they are five years old and then they come downstairs.'

So that's what it was all about.

'And that is better than being with her own mother?'

There was a brief silence, and then: 'Nancy, you are not —'

'*I am, I am, and even Billy said it. Of course, if you won't have it, I will leave and take Susan with me, and Billy is fine with that.*' This was extending the truth a little, but Nancy was in full flow and brimming with confidence after what Billy had said. '*Susan is my daughter and that is the end of it. Now, what do you wish me to do?*'

She held her breath. Had she gone too far? Her anger had carried her to this point, but now that it had ebbed a little she could not even begin to think where she and Susan could go from here.

'*Nancy, this has been your home for more years than I can remember. You have worked hard and asked for nothing in return except a roof over your head. Things are beginning to change, though, and some for the better. I will ensure Susan stays with you and we will discuss your work and wages in the near future. Nancy, please remember that Billy can take Susan away to live with him any time he likes. It is in his hands. Please try to remember, and not to care too much.*'

But Mother Superior knew as Nancy knew. It was too late for that.

Susan was most definitely Nancy's child.

Shattered Dreams

I stood up tall, raised my arms, pointed my toes and waited for my next instruction. I had closed my eyes to fully enjoy the moment and feel the emotion. This was it: I had arrived at my entry into the world of ballet – my very first lesson. I had the most beautiful red ballet shoes and felt like I had been dancing for ever. The teacher *was* a little scary, though: she was French and we had to call her Madame, and she had an awful habit of tapping her stick on the ground to grab our attention. Her hair was scraped back into a tight bun on the back of her head, and she looked extremely stern.

Mum had done me proud, and I was every bit as well turned out as the rest of the girls. A full ballet uniform had to be worn from day one and the fees paid a month in advance. I dread to think what Mum must have gone without to pay for this. The mothers could sit in the corner of the room to watch us but were not allowed to speak or make any noise. I think they were as scared of Madame as we were.

Her cane was tapping on the ground now, but there was no way I could hear it over the tremendous applause I could hear in my head. The audience was standing and cheering and there I was, serene and dignified, having just completed my solo performance. The stage was strewn with flowers, and the audience was shouting: 'Bravo! Bravo!' Somewhere in the distance, I heard Mum cough, and suddenly I was yanked back into the present by the vigorous tapping of Madame's cane. There were a few giggles too.

'I fail to see how you are going to learn if you spend the whole lesson with your eyes shut,' snapped Madame. 'Concentrate, please.'

I opened my eyes, and the first thing I saw was Mum. She looked mortified. After that, I concentrated for the whole hour, and afterwards I had cramp in my legs, my toes hurt and I felt as though my arms would fall off after holding them in impossible positions for what felt like hours. Surely this wasn't *ballet*? I wanted to be spinning, twirling and cavorting in leaps and bounds from one end of the room to the other, not standing still on shaking legs wondering how on earth I was going to be able to walk the short journey home. And when I did get back to Nazareth House, climbing the stairs up to the nursery felt like climbing Mount Everest. Christopher, who was sitting in the corner of the playroom waiting for me, jumped up and ran over to me. I didn't think *I*'d ever run again.

'Hello, you two. How did it go then?' asked one of the girls.

'Oh, well, it was wonderful. I loved it!'

'She's not *quite* ready for the Albert Hall yet,' said Mum, and smiled as Christopher took my hand. He couldn't quite understand the look on my face. It was pain.

'Can you stand on your toes yet, Susan?' he asked. Dear God, I could barely stand with my two feet flat on the ground!

Week after week, I went to ballet classes and, week after

week, I became more disillusioned with the whole thing. This was no fun at all – and it was about to get worse. We were to have an exam. Even the word sounded fierce, and when Madame told us, there were 'ooh's and 'aah's among the girls. We were to practise at home as much as possible.

In her broken English, Madame announced, 'My young ladies never fail. Never. I do not allow.'

I don't know why she felt she had to look at me when she said that.

That was my trips downstairs and playtimes cancelled right then and there. I spent hours in my room, using the back of a chair as a ballet bar, pointing my toes into ridiculous shapes and practising my foot and arm positions. This was seriously bordering on tedious, and I was heartily wishing I had never dreamed of being a ballet dancer. The one thing that kept me going was the thought of having to tell Mum I'd failed, so I worked hard and practised. Well, to a certain extent.

The Saturday afternoon of the exam came, and there was much excitement. There was an extremely strict-looking lady sitting at a desk in one corner of the room. If only she had smiled even a little it would have helped. But no. She just sat there, pen poised, looking like she'd been sucking lemons.

My turn came. I walked to the centre of the room, my knees knocking, trying with all my might to concentrate. I turned to the examiner, curtsied and smiled, just as we had been told to. But all I got back was a haughty lift of the eyebrow and 'Begin!'

It was the longest fifteen minutes of my life. I stretched,

pointed, went through all the feet and arm positions – doubly difficult when your knees are shaking – and, finally, thankfully!, it was over. I was thoroughly fed up by now and just wanted my mum.

'*Attention!*' Madame shouted, but I'd had enough.

I turned to the examiner, hastily curtsied, then burst into tears and ran out of the room.

When the exam results came in, all the girls and their mums gathered together. I remember Madame sweeping majestically into the room and tapping her cane for silence.

One by one, the names and results were called out. Madame smiled as she said each one, announcing 'Pass – highly commended.' This would be followed by a ripple of applause. I was beginning to look forward to my turn now. It was all about the applause, after all, and if it took passing exams to get to be a famous ballet dancer, I would just have to put up with it. Mine was the last name to be called. Madame paused. For some reason, her smile had vanished, to be replaced by a look of disgust.

'Pass,' she announced, then tapped her cane for silence. That meant no applause. A mere pass obviously wasn't good enough. Keeping my head down to avoid the smug looks of the other young girls and their mums, I made my final exit from the ballet stage.

Later that night, Nancy was sitting having a cuppa in the kitchen with Dolly, one of the upstairs helpers, and could be heard laughing and chatting.

'Oh well,' said Dolly. 'Best she finds out now – think of all the money you'll save. Do you think there is something she would like better?'

Nancy shook her head. 'God knows, Dolly. God only knows what's next.'

The Very Best Clothes

Today was a special occasion, so out came the best clothes – our Sunday best, as it used to be called. Now these clothes were so precious you were hardly allowed to move, let alone – God forbid! – eat anything or enjoy yourself while you were wearing them. No, these clothes were practically whipped from your body as you walked up the aisle out of church on a Sunday and laid away carefully until the following week.

On this occasion, however, I was to be allowed to wear my Sunday best on a day out. I had hardly slept at all the night before, because today Dad was coming to take me out. I was five years old and couldn't wait to show off my new red coat, pretty dress and shiny shoes. I was bubbling with excitement – you can just imagine! – and hardly noticed that Mum wasn't looking too happy. And the little bit I did notice, I put down to her worrying about my best clothes. It's only with hindsight that I realize how she must have felt. I was always so excited to see Dad. It must have cut her in two.

'Now behave yourself, Susan, be polite, speak properly, don't get your clothes dirty, don't eat any rubbish, no running, hold Dad's hand at all times – oh, and have a nice time.'

'Nice time' was the furthest she would go. Poor Mum

couldn't bring herself to say 'Have fun.' She must have been so worried that I'd favour him over her.

Mum worked so hard, and every penny she had ensured I was well turned out in my Sunday best for occasions such as these. I was therefore paraded through the nuns' parlour, Mum proud as could be, to meet Dad.

Dad was there waiting for me in the parlour. Of course I had a bit of an idea of how Mum would feel, so I used every ounce of composure I had not to run and throw myself in his arms. He just stood there and winked at me, and whisked me off before Mum could give him the pre-day-out talk too.

We walked sedately outside to the car, where I was met by Eileen, Dad's girlfriend. She is such a kind and gener-ous person and I love her very much to this day. She was and still is one of the most dignified and lovely people I have ever met.

So there we all were, waving and behaving most politely as Dad turned his car round and began to move up the drive. We were only halfway up when he shouted, 'OK, kid, time to have fun!' He leaned over, threw open the car door and stood me on the running board on the outside. I held on to the top of the open window and off we went, the wind in my hair, all pre-day-out warnings and rules instantly forgotten, and Dad singing at the top of his voice. Some crazy song about someone swallowing a fly, if I remember rightly.

It was an extremely hot summer's day, so Dad decided we should go to the beach. It was packed with families, and children were running in and out of the water, jumping over the waves, kids building sandcastles, egg sandwiches full more of sand than egg, and here I was with my dad, just like all the other kids. I was so happy.

There was only one major, massive problem. I was in my very best clothes! I looked down at my black shiny shoes with the buckles on, at my new coat and pretty dress. All the other kids were running wild in bathing costumes, underwear, play clothes. I looked up at Dad. 'Not a problem, kid,' he said, and laughed.

I would run around the beach in my red knickers. I was stunned. Completely and utterly mortified, and just a little scared. Dad and Eileen took my hand to reassure me that it was fine: all the other kids were doing it and having such fun. They didn't want to pressure me; they just wanted me to have a good time. Oh, I so wanted to, I really did, so, tentatively, bit by bit, I removed my coat, dress, shoes and socks and made my way to the water. After ten minutes I was squealing with delight, with Dad and Eileen helping me to jump over the waves. I was soaking wet and loving every single minute of it. I'd never had such mad fun in my life! And, today, I was just the same as everyone else. It was just perfect.

Perfect that is until I realized that, even though I'd stripped on the beach, I had a dirty mark on my dress and a scratch on my new shoes. I was utterly horrified. And of course my knickers were drenched. Naturally, Dad couldn't see the problem. He did come up with a brilliant solution, though. He tied my red knickers to his wing mirror and they flapped in the wind, drying, as we drove home. I'll be all dressed by the time I get home, I thought.

It will be fine. We sang songs all the way back to Nazareth House, but, even so, somehow I must have fallen asleep. And it was not only Mum but also the nuns standing outside the parlour door who had full view of the unholy sight of my red knickers flapping in the breeze as Dad drove down that long driveway.

They were not impressed, to say the least. Dad muttered on and on about how hot the day had been, how he'd not wanted to get the clothes dirty . . . Talk about digging yourself into a hole! Mum's face was like thunder. And there was no mistaking the looks on the nuns' faces: I had done something terribly, terribly wrong.

Honestly, it's a wonder they weren't throwing bucketfuls of holy water over me and running round in circles burning incense and chanting mantras.

I can still remember now, fifty-two years on, how I felt. Ashamed, embarrassed and very, very guilty. I looked down at my scratched shoes, full of sand, at the dirty stain on my pretty dress and the ice-cream mark on my coat. Somehow, it was all my fault, and I hung my head in shame.

I crept into bed that night with a heavy heart. I cried myself to sleep. When Mum came along later she picked me up, gave me warm milk and biscuits and a hug, and took me into her bed. 'It will all be all right,' I remember she said.

Of course I couldn't know then what I know now. Some of the nuns had never been happy about Mum being allowed to look after me, and she was constantly being told that I should be fostered out, as all the other children were. Poor Mum had always to be on her guard to show that she was bringing me up correctly. She couldn't let it seem for a moment that she wasn't, she was so fearful of losing me. I know now that that thunder in Mum's face was simply fear (well, and maybe a little bit that she'd been saving for at least six months to buy me those new clothes). And not only did she always have to impress the nuns, she could never challenge my dad, for fear of him taking me away for himself. Totally understandable – unless you're five years old.

The last thing I saw that night before falling asleep were my lovely new clothes lying across the chair.

Well, honestly! I had been sent out to play dressed as though I was attending a garden party for the Queen at Buckingham Palace. Shame I hadn't – at least I would have come home with my knickers on!

Lucie Attwell and the Magic Whispering Conker Tree

I remember that summer when I was six years old. No longer did I count the four-leaf clovers on my own, or dance around the trees in my magical forest pretending to hear the applause when I took my bow. I had Christopher now. He was there beside me every minute of every day. We'd spend hours just walking around the grounds of Nazareth House, holding hands and chattering away, but our favourite place was under the branches of the conker tree. There we would sit cross-legged while I made up stories of magical lands and adventures.

Earlier that morning Nancy had looked across the dining room and seen them sitting close together, as always, chatting excitedly about their day in the garden together. She smiled to herself and wondered why, out of all the children, suddenly, from the moment Christopher and Susan met, they had an instant bond. Nancy had tried to get them to mix with the other children but, inevitably, after a few moments, they would drift back together again. Christopher copied everything Susan did and had been caught only last week calling Nancy Mum. 'Well, honestly,' she had said to Sister, 'you try and tell him to call me Aunty Nancy. It's impossible.' Nancy sighed once more as she watched them. There was a scream from the other end of

the dining room, and she jumped. 'For goodness' sake, woman,' she said out loud to herself. 'What are you doing, daydreaming during breakfast?' She pulled herself together and went to deal with the spilt porridge and a screaming child.

A while later, Nancy paused to look out of the window as she hurried along the corridor with an armful of washing. She had a full nursery this summer and was glad of the sunny day because it meant that the children could play outside and she could get through her chores. There was a roundabout out there, swings, toys, and children were running around playing games in the sun – and there they were, Susan and Christopher, just the two of them, sitting on a raggedy blanket under the conker tree with their hands on the tree trunk. Susan must be telling him stories again. God only knew what nonsense she was filling his head with today! Christopher had bumped his head the day before because he had been walking around with one hand over his eye and couldn't see properly. 'It's all right, Mummy,' he had said. 'It's my eye patch, because I'm a pirate but a good pirate, and Susan is going to save me from the baddies.'

'If she tells you much more of this nonsense you had better tell her it's herself that will need saving . . . from me,' Nancy had said, laughing.

She'd gone out and bought Susan a Lucie Attwell book, something to read and stop her making up her own nonsense. Susan loved having it read to her over and over again, and knew the story by heart now.

Nancy was pleased when she saw Susan showing Christopher the book, pointing to the pictures and reading the stories. That's that settled, she thought. I will get her some more books.

A few nights later, after a particularly tiring day, she left them reading on Susan's bed while she sorted out the last of the daily chores then had a much needed cuppa in the little kitchen with her feet up, which was definitely called for.

The kettle whistled and Dolly called to Nancy to come and sit down. Nancy had her cuppa and began to doze off as Dolly bustled about. It was after 9 p.m. when Dolly tapped her on the shoulder, making her jump. Where on earth had the time gone? thought Nancy as she hurried along the corridor.

Darkness had begun to set in, and the little red night light was shining in the room. Christopher and Susan sat on Susan's bed cross-legged, their heads together and the Lucie Attwell book between them.

Nancy had heard Susan's voice before she reached the door. She put such expression into it, even though she was only six. Nancy smiled. How she loved her daughter . . . But wait a minute, she didn't recall Lucie Attwell telling stories about children flying around the moon on a broomstick made of chocolate. Christopher was looking at Susan, his eyes as wide as saucers, engrossed in her story. Nancy sighed. I give up, she thought. If there was one thing Susan wasn't lacking in, it was imagination.

Nancy crept into the room, sat in her comfy chair in the corner and listened to the wondrous adventures of Lucie Attwell, which certainly did not adorn the pages of any of the books Nancy had bought. Her eyes once more drooped with tiredness and the children eventually fell asleep sprawled across the bed, holding hands.

It was nearly ten when Nancy picked Christopher up and carried him down the corridor back to his own bed. 'Goodnight, darling,' she said as she kissed his forehead.

'Mummy,' he murmured sleepily. 'Mummy, tomorrow I am going to touch the magic conker tree and hear what it whispers to me.'

Nancy returned to her room to tuck Susan into bed. 'I told him the conker tree was magic, Mum,' whispered Susan. 'I told him there were such things in the world as wishing trees and if we closed our eyes really tight and believed with all our hearts our wishes would come true. Then I told him a story about horses. They were so power- ful they could run faster than the wind, and no one could catch them because they were free, but if you did catch one and rode on its back, then you were free too. We touched the magic whispering conker tree today, Mum. We listened for the whispers and wished.'

Nancy gave her daughter a hug and kissed her goodnight.

Imagination is a wonderful thing, but where does it get you? she reflected later that night. She had no time for such fancies herself.

Of course it's true that imagination is a wonderful thing – until, of course, it spills into reality. Back at school after the summer holidays, I was asked to write what I'd done during my time away from school. Some of the other chil- dren had been to holiday camps, gone on trips with their family. One young girl had even been to see family in France. That was the other side of the world to me! What could I write? I had had a wonderful summer, but I'd barely left the grounds of Nazareth House. Luckily, I had an imagination.

I wrote a wonderful story. Daddy had taken Christo- pher and me out for the day – he had a surprise for me. He had bought me a pony and I was taught to ride. The three of us rode along the beach, and I was going to be enrolled in a proper riding school and learn to ride faster than the wind. Literature was most definitely my favourite subject and my exercise book was filled with ticks. Mum would be so pleased.

Next parents' evening, Nancy got out her best clothes ready to go to discuss Susan's progress at school. She was nervous for some reason. Susan of course was always perfectly behaved and had extremely good manners – she had seen to that – and she wasn't doing badly at her lessons. It's just, Nancy felt it sometimes. All the mothers and fathers would be there. She looked down at her signet ring, the one she'd had since she was a young girl. It was her only piece of jewellery. Should she do it? Did it matter what other people thought? And would she be doing it for her sake or Susan's? Being an unmarried mother was still a stigma, and she supposed that's what people would assume. But let them think what they liked. She wavered. Still, though, it wouldn't do any harm. She looked down once more and slowly took the ring off the third finger of her right hand and placed it even more slowly on the third finger of her left, twisting it round until it looked like a plain gold wedding band. 'There now,' she said out loud, looking at herself in the mirror, and immediately felt so ridiculous she hastily put on a pair of gloves.

Nancy was well out of her comfort zone in the large school hall, which was packed with parents. Thank goodness she had worn her best coat and shoes. Her gaze fell upon a couple across the room. Money there, she thought, looking at the lady's coat, and her matching handbag and shoes. She rallied herself. Deep breath, chin up. I'm as good as they are. If I tell myself that enough times I might actually believe it! Nancy smiled to herself.

She found the table at last and was relieved to see Susan's work laid out. The marks on the maths book weren't brilliant, but then Susan hated anything to do with figures. Her English was much better. Her spelling was excellent, and English literature ten out of ten. Nancy started to feel better, a little smug even. The couple Nancy had noticed earlier were arguing now over some bad mathematics marks on their child's book. Nancy was smiling, those blue eyes twinkling as she picked up Susan's storybook and started to read. She read how happy Susan had been to be with her dad that summer, how marvellous he was, how he threw her in the air and played with her — and of course about the horse and the riding lessons. The smile drained from her face. She stood up, and No-nonsense Nancy, chin once more in the air, put the book down and walked through the school hall, seeing no one, and then to the nearest bus stop, where she sat down and began to cry heartrending sobs. She had failed. She couldn't give Susan what she wanted, she would never be loved as a real mother, loved like Susan loved her dad. Was that what Susan wished for when she touched the magic whispering conker tree? To be with her dad all the time? She tore off her gloves and almost ripped the ring from her finger to place it back on to her right hand. And she was just as bad, she thought. She'd been living in a fantasy world all these years, imagining she could be a mother to Susan.

She couldn't go back to Nazareth House and face the nuns — they'd always thought that way — and she felt that, tonight, she didn't even have the strength to put on a brave face for Susan. She crossed the road and got the bus to Tilly's. The two friends sat late into the evening drinking cup after cup of tea, Tilly's heart breaking at the unfairness of it all. They had all warned Nancy not to get too involved, but their advice had fallen on deaf ears.

It was late when Nancy finally got back to Nazareth House. She hoped Susan was in bed and asleep. She walked into the garden and stood for a moment in the shadow of the magic whispering conker tree, then slowly stepped forward and gently placed her hand on the large trunk, not knowing whether to laugh or cry. Nancy prayed, because wishing was ridiculous. Wishes didn't come true. Nancy shivered; she was cold. She looked up at the lights shining from the nursery windows and straightened herself up. She had to go in at some point; she had to face whatever challenges lay ahead of her.

The night light was on and Susan and Christopher were curled up together on Nancy's bed, fast asleep. There was a piece of paper in Susan's hand. It was a picture of Nancy, Susan and Christopher either side of her, holding her hands.

'We love you, Mummy,' it said. 'Please wake us up, we missed you.'

Immediately, the warmth returned to her body and reached inside to her heart.

'Well, now, it actually works!' she said out loud, and laughed. 'I will have to give that magic whispering conker tree another go tomorrow!'

Mars Bar with the Big Red Bow

I woke up that morning feeling that life was full of possibilities. It was Saturday, and maybe today was the day I would have the stabilizers taken off my bike.

'Will I feel different when my stabilizers are off, Mum?' I asked. 'Is that when I'll be a big girl?'

Nancy was busy in the dining room settling all the children for their breakfast.

'Hold on a moment, love, I just need to sort the breakfast –'

'Mum, if I do manage without my stabilizers, I just wondered, will I suddenly grow or something?'

Dolly was giggling and looking at Mum.

'Go on then, Dolly, you answer her. And please do not fill her head with any more nonsense.'

At that moment, one of the staff came in with two envelopes for Nancy.

Dolly looked at Nancy and opened her mouth to speak. 'That will do,' said Nancy, before she got the chance. 'Now, come on, we have children to feed. Susan, sit down and eat your breakfast, to help with all that growing up you will be doing later on.'

I ate my breakfast, but if Mum thought I hadn't seen the cards being pushed deep down into her apron pocket, she was very much mistaken. What could they be? Who would send Mum cards, and why?

However, the cards forgotten for a moment, it was time for the big event, and Dolly grabbed the bike, and we made our way to the playground.

'Well, you might have told me, Susan,' said Dolly when we were out of earshot. 'I would have got her a card too.'

'A card for what?' I asked.

'For Nancy – I mean, for your mum. It must be her birthday.'

My heart sank. Mum's birthday, today? Surely not – and I hadn't known. I felt so ashamed. We hadn't seen Aunty Tilly for a couple of weeks, and she was the only one who could have told me, the only one who would have taken me out to buy a card. Apart from her, my whole world was Mum. And of course she'd never in a million years tell me herself.

My eyes filled with tears. All thoughts of growing up were forgotten. 'I didn't know!' I sobbed.

'Oh my,' said Dolly. 'Please don't cry. Look, Susan, why don't you make her a card? That'd be a lovely surprise for your mum. But I think we should have a go taking your stabilizers off first – we don't want her to suspect anything.'

I wanted this over as quickly as possible. Part of me just wanted to dive into the drawers of my little red desk and pull out the glue and scrap paper there, but maybe Dolly was right: it would be a shame to spoil the surprise.

So off came the stabilizers, and I took a deep, deep breath. Chin up. Ready.

One foot off the ground and on to the pedal. The other halfway there.

'Ready? Steady . . . Go!' Dolly ran behind me for a few steps and then launched me across the playground.

I was doing it! Legs stretched out either side of me, wind in my hair, I was freewheeling across the tarmac. I was as free as a bird, all grown up . . . well, for about five seconds anyway. Then I lost my balance, wobbled, screamed, hit the roundabout and ended up face down in a pool of mud.

'Reckon we're done here for the day then,' said Dolly, and she picked up the bike and grabbed my hand. Inside, we ran up the stairs, bits of mud still dripping off my eyelashes, through the nursery door – and straight into Mum. Silence. She looked at me, then at Dolly, then back at me. 'I'm not even going to ask,' she said, and carried on with her daily chores.

I cleaned myself up and sat down at the red desk. Glue, crayons, coloured paper, fuzzy felt. Dolly had written out the words for me to copy. Thank goodness! I had everything I needed. I cut out some little red hearts and flowers, stuck them to the coloured paper and wrote 'Happy Birthday. Mum. I love you' in all different colours. She would love it. I'd put it on her pillow when I went to bed that night.

Then a horrible thought struck me. I had no present. Mum had given me so much and I had nothing to give her. No money to buy anything with, nothing. I got down on my knees, hands clasped together, eyes closed – I thought it was best to make a proper job of it – and I prayed. As always, I began by asking for forgiveness for all the bad things I had done. This took a while. Then:

'Please, God,' I said, 'I need a proper miracle, a real one, so that I can give Mum a birthday present, because she loves me and works really hard and I honestly didn't know it was her birthday and I promise I will make sure I never forget again.' I opened my eyes, and waited. I don't know what I was expecting, but no gift-wrapped package fell from the sky and landed on my lap. Just in case, though, I waited. And waited.

Nothing. It was with a heavy heart that I went down the stairs and along the corridor to the kitchen to fetch the milk for Mum.

At the bottom of the stairs was Sister Concepta's room. She was one of the kindest people I had ever met, always with a smile, a story and a treat for the children. 'You look sad today,' she said. And you know how it is when you're feeling really low and someone comforts you? Well, I burst into tears. Sister Concepta sat me down on the footstool and said, 'Tell me about it. Nothing can be that bad!' And between much sobbing and nose-blowing I blurted it out.

I've never forgotten how kind and sweet she was to me that day. We put the footstool under the large cupboard in the corner and reached for the sweet tin. Inside it were all sorts of different sweets, but my eyes were caught by a particular chocolate bar which I knew Mum loved.

I spent the next ten minutes decorating the Mars bar with a lovely piece of red ribbon Sister had also found in her wonderful cupboard.

'You know, Susan,' she said. 'I think your mum might just think this is the best birthday present she has ever received. You've made everything yourself.'

I ran back upstairs and hid the card and present in my red desk. I'd put them on Mum's pillow after she put me to bed that night.

It was late when Nancy finally came up to bed. Susan was fast asleep. What on earth was that on the pillow? She sat on the bed and picked up the Mars bar with the red bow on top and opened the most beautiful card she had ever seen in her life.

She looked over at her sleeping daughter, and No-nonsense Nancy cried.

Eileen with the Pretty Shoes

It was 1962. The day Nancy had dreaded for the last seven years had arrived out of the blue. She had almost managed to forget that, one day, Susan's father might get married and, if and when that happened, he had said, he would take her back. He'd always refused to have Susan fostered or adopted, knowing that she was happy with Nancy, but had said when she first came to Nazareth House that he would be able to provide a home for her if he married. Nancy had fought on Susan's behalf for the last seven years, and had gained the strength to do it because she loved the child with all her heart. She is my child, she is, Nancy would tell herself over and over again. She calls me Mum; even Billy calls me Susan's mum – surely he wouldn't take her away. But Billy had called earlier that day to say that himself and Eileen, his girlfriend of a few years now, would be along later. He had some news.

Nancy was convinced the day she dreaded had come and that he was coming to announce his marriage. When someone tells you they are getting married, it should be happy, joyful news, but Nancy was not looking forward to this news from Billy. Not one little bit.

My memories of that day were very different. I knew Dad had arrived when I heard 'Yoohoo, Typhoo!' Forgetting the rule about running in the corridor, I ran towards him at full speed and jumped into his arms, and he swung me round and round. I always loved to see Eileen, too. She was so pretty, with a peaches and cream complexion, blue eyes and fair hair. And not only was she pretty, but she had a lovely, kind manner about her too, and spirit. No wonder Dad loved her.

Dad always used to tell me a story about her, and we loved it. Billy's pride and joy had always been his motor-bike, but now there was a new lady in his life, his new, black, shiny car with running boards down the side. He had been washing and polishing it all day and was so pre-occupied he had forgotten to call Eileen.

She had been sitting quietly listening to the wireless, drumming her fingers on the table. She had spent all after-noon getting ready for her date that night, and Billy should have called hours ago. She was not used to being stood up. She knew Billy had a bit of a reputation, but she had made it quite clear from the start that she would not be putting up with any nonsense. She and Billy had fallen in love, and they both knew it was serious. They were going to see Susan the next day, so what on earth had happened today? It really was not the done thing to ring him: he should ring her. She waited another hour, then began to get annoyed, picked up the telephone and dialled the number. Billy heard the phone ringing from inside the house, put down his cleaning materials and went inside to answer the tele-phone. He had finished now anyway, he thought.

'Yoohoo!'

'Hello, Billy.'

'Eileen, how are you?'

'Fine, thanks. Just ringing to find out how your fingers are.'

'My fingers?'

'Yes. Well, I assumed they must be broken or something and you were unable to dial my number.'

Billy burst out laughing. 'On my way, Eileen,' he said, and hung up the phone. Billy laughed all the way back to his lovely new car. Eileen was fun.

And she wore the prettiest clothes. Today, I just couldn't take my eyes off her shoes. I'd never seen anything so beautiful – and they had the highest heels. Eileen saw me looking at them and whispered in my ear that she'd let me try them on later. My eyes must have been like saucers, and I gave her a big hug too. Looking back now, a mother myself, Mum must have been watching in horror, petrified that Dad and she would take me away.

Nancy's heart froze. Susan looked so happy: the three of them made the perfect family. What can I give her, just me on my own? she thought. She had no legal right to Susan, none at all, and she'd seen enough children fostered and adopted over the years to know that most children were adaptable and adjusted to living with a family. And Billy was Susan's father. All she could hope for was that perhaps she would be allowed to see her daughter, maybe take her out now and again. Nancy always kept her emotions under close control, but today she was struggling. She was sure everyone would be able to see her heart beating out of control in her breast, and hurried along

the corridor to her room for a moment to rein in her feelings. But the first thing that caught her eye was the birthday card with the hearts and flowers that Susan had made. She had stuck it on the wall above her bed with a piece of sticky tape.

It's strange the little things that can tip you over the edge. She pulled the most beautiful birthday card in the whole world off the wall, held it to her chest and cried heart-wrenching sobs like she had never cried before. Her tears dripped on to the card and she rocked backwards and forwards, feeling as though her heart had been ripped out.

No-nonsense Nancy, for the first time in her life, felt that her spirit was broken. She looked up at the dressing table and saw her holy picture of Jesus. 'Well, thank you very much,' she said. 'You were a great help. I worked hard, I gave everything I have to give to every child that comes into my care, I say my prayers daily and, dear God, I tried not to love her too much, and, guess what, I got it wrong. I love her so much I can't imagine life without her at my side every single minute of every single day . . . Dear God, I'm talking to myself.'

She had to pull herself together. There was no way she could meet Billy and Eileen looking like this. She stood up, closed her eyes and took a deep breath. Unfortunately, when she opened her eyes they rested on Susan's favourite doll, the one that played the Brahms lullaby, and once again Nancy began to cry.

It was fifteen minutes later that she rinsed her face and for the first time that year took out her powder compact and applied a little make-up. Common sense must prevail, she thought, and she began to prepare tea and cakes for when Billy, Eileen and Susan came in from the garden.

* * *

Nancy did herself an injustice that day. Susan may have loved being with her father and Eileen with the lovely shoes, but she would have to be dragged away kicking and screaming from her mum. Nancy was a wonderful mother and her daughter loved her dearly. Susan couldn't imagine spending a single day without her. She could laugh and have fun with Dad, safe in the knowledge that, at the end of the day, it would be her and Mum together, just as it should be.

What a shame that Nancy couldn't have heard the conversation that was taking place in the garden as Eileen pushed Susan on the swings. She and Billy were talking about her.

'Nancy's a bit of a tartar, you know. Even I wouldn't argue with her,' said Billy to Eileen.

'Susan seems very happy, Billy. She's delightful and so polite – Nancy has obviously done a good job,' said Eileen.

'I owe her big time – just don't tell her!' Billy laughed. 'She has looked after Susan like a daughter.'

'Well, she is her daughter, really, after all this time.'

'Yes, you're right. I would never take her off her now, you know. I said I would, when I got married, but that would be wrong.'

'Oh, Billy, it would. That would break her heart and Susan's, but let's make sure we have Susan often and take her for more days out – maybe let her stay over now and again.'

'That's a great idea.'

'Have you told Nancy that we won't be taking Susan away, Billy?' Susan had grabbed Dad's hand and was leading him to the roundabout.

'No need,' said Billy. 'She knows that.'

But Nancy knew no such thing.

* * *

It was a polite tea for everyone in Nancy's room, but there was an undercurrent that Eileen couldn't quite understand, and every time she looked at Billy he seemed not to be aware of it. Eileen kept the chatter going, but it was getting very tiring, and she began to think that Billy must be ignoring the situation on purpose. Actually, Billy found it amusing. Eileen gave him the look, the one that said, 'Enough now,' and Billy made moves to leave. Nancy took the tea things to the kitchen.

'I like Eileen, Daddy,' Susan said, jumping into Dad's arms to give him a hug.

'I like her too, Susan.' He whispered into her ear: 'Do you want to hear a secret?'

Susan forgot all about how naughty it was to whisper and keep secrets and whispered back, 'Ooh, yes, Daddy.'

'Well, I'll tell you. Eileen and I are getting married – probably in July next year.'

Nancy came back from the kitchen to say goodbye, smiling at Eileen and, preserving the niceties, told Billy how nice it was to see him. Billy gave Susan one last wink, and he and Eileen left.

Nancy turned to Susan. 'Well, what's up with you, Susan? You look like the cat that's got the cream.'

'It's a secret, and you mustn't tell anybody, but Daddy and Eileen are getting married in July! Mum, isn't that exciting!'

Susan's heart was jumping for joy.

Nancy's sank like a stone.

The Up-and-down Horses

Nancy had been saving all year so that she could take Susan and Christopher on holiday to Butlin's. They had read the brochures, and it looked like the most wonderful place on earth. It hadn't been easy for Nancy, but she had done it. Christopher's father, Danny, had given his permission, the deposit was paid and in another two months she would have the money to pay the full balance. The only problem was, it was the last week in July, and she hoped and prayed that Billy's wedding wouldn't clash with the holiday and she wouldn't lose all her money. This was Susan and Christopher's first holiday together, and they had been looking forward to it for ages, but Susan wouldn't want to miss Billy and Eileen's wedding.

Sod's law. The wedding was booked for 28 July – the Saturday Nancy, Susan and Christopher were travelling to Skegness. Billy had told Nancy he completely understood and that they should still go on their holiday.

Nancy knew in her heart that not only was this the first holiday she would have with Susan and Christopher, it could also be the last. Danny would one day take Christopher back, and that was only right and proper. She made her decision.

Saturday 28 July came. Just for once, Nancy would take a leaf out of Susan's book and enter her world of Let's Pretend. All three of them were going on holiday together, and she, Nancy, would have the two children she loved most in the whole world with her and, just like any other family, they would have fun. Yes, that was the way to go about this. It would be a perfect, normal family holiday. For the second time, Nancy slipped the signet ring on to the third finger of her left hand.

The whole week they were there, Susan ran about excitedly, joining in all the games, her eyes shining with excitement. She'd be on the stage singing songs, always first to put her hand up during the kids' shows, wanting to take part. Nancy had bought her some new clothes, and Susan loved her new pink shorts with the polka dots and the matching T-shirt. And, Christopher — well, you couldn't keep him out of the pool. At night, they cuddled up together, the three of them, in the caravan, chatting about the day's events. Christopher talked non-stop about the outdoor swimming pool, and all Susan could think about were the up-and-down horses in the fairground. She had never seen anything so wonderful. Up and down they went to the music, round and round, lights flashing everywhere, her on one and Mum behind, holding her tight. They had been on them every day, and she couldn't wait to go on again tomorrow.

Nancy enjoyed herself too, but at the back of her mind was the thought that soon it would be Billy and Eileen who would be riding on the merry-go-round with Susan. She could picture the three of them having fun together, up and down on the horses, holding Susan tight, going to the beach, opening presents on Christmas morning, Susan clomping about in Eileen's high heels. Well, I haven't got any pretty shoes like that, thought Nancy, or a car with a running board for Susan to stand on. Oh, yes, she'd seen her on it when they went up the drive.

Susan was asleep now and Nancy carried her to bed. It was their last day tomorrow, and Nancy was determined that they would have as much fun as possible. They would ride the up-and-down horses together one more time.

Susan and Christopher slept on the coach most of the way home, their heads on Nancy's lap. Nancy's eyes were closed too, but she wasn't sleeping, just trying to block out the horror of what was to come. Billy and Eileen were married, and they would be coming to take Susan away. Even through her closed eyes, the tears came, and Nancy took deep breaths to stop herself from making any noise. She held her daughter's hand tightly and somehow must have nodded off. In her dreams the music was playing and there they were, smiling and laughing as, up and down, round and round, they went.

The next time Nancy saw Billy, he turned up without warning. His wife was with him, of course. And, naturally, Susan was thrilled. Once more Nancy preserved the niceties, came forward and said hello and offered to put the kettle on, taking them all into her room to settle down for yet another uncomfortable visit. This time, though, Billy came straight to the point.

'Nancy, we have news for you and Susan.'

Nancy couldn't move, not even to sit down. If this was it, then better to face it standing. She was thankful now that Billy had not called to say they were visiting and had news. It would just have given her more time to worry. Chin up, shoulders back, No-nonsense Nancy was ready for battle.

Billy saw her expression. What on earth is the matter with the woman? he thought.

'Nancy, Eileen is pregnant. Susan, guess what? You're going to have a baby sister or brother.'

*Step*sister *or* step*brother, Nancy was about to reply, then thought better of it. She didn't want to annoy Billy.*

Eileen stepped in. 'I hope that's good news for you, Susan. Nancy, we really hope that Susan can come and visit often after I've had the baby. *It would be lovely if they could get to know each other. Even if they're not living in the same house, they should still get to know each other as much as possible. I was even hoping you might let Susan stay overnight every now and again.'*

Time stood still for Nancy. That word. Visit. Eileen had said visit, *not* live with. Visit, visit, visit. *The word went round and round in her head until she began to feel a little faint. Susan didn't notice that Mum looked a bit dazed: she was too busy jumping up and down and asking Eileen hundreds of questions, over and over, about the baby.*

Billy looked at Nancy and saw a frightened woman.

'Nancy?'

'So you're not taking her away?'

Billy was beginning to get a little angry now. 'No, Nancy, I am not taking her away. I assumed you realized that things had changed. Regardless of our earlier arrangement, I wouldn't dream of taking Susan from you.'

Susan had heard that last bit during a pause in her conversation with Eileen.

'Dad, what do you mean?'

'Nothing, pet. Just telling Nancy what a good mum she is.'

There was a pause, then Nancy pulled herself together. 'Goodness me,' she said, 'where are my manners?' *And she began bustling about, ensuring that Eileen was comfortable and letting Susan get the tea cups and saucers out of the cupboard. She could now afford to be very gracious indeed.*

They all started chatting at once now. Eileen had not been feeling too good lately, so Nancy fussed about her. They talked about all the usual worries about parenthood, not least the sleepless nights. Of course, Nancy was in her element. She reassured them that it would all be fine — it was her job, after all — and spent the next ten minutes talking about how she had coped with Susan as a baby and how she could still comfort her, as she had bonded with her when she was such a young baby. Nancy looked so happy, and Billy simply sat there and watched her with a smile on his face.

Dear God, is this what it had all been about! Had she really thought that he would walk in and take Susan away, after all these years? What must she think of him? But then, maybe he hadn't made it clear. Eileen had been right: he should have told her. Still, it had all come right now, and there was only one word to describe the look on Nancy's face now. Smug, totally and utterly smug — and Billy found it highly amusing.

That was a wonderful day for everyone: Billy and Eileen excited about the birth of their baby, due in October, Susan thrilled about having a brother or sister, and Nancy with a smile that made those beautiful bright-blue eyes sparkle with delight, delight at knowing without a doubt in the world that, next year, when Hoppings fair came to Newcastle in June, they would be together, Susan and Nancy, together once more on the up-and-down horses.

Cliff Richard Christmas Wall

Mum was up to something, we just knew it. Apparently, it was a surprise, and only if Christopher and I were very good would we find out what it was. Mum had been out for what seemed like hours now, and we had been watching the rain out of the window, watching for her return. 'Dancing soldiers' Mum called it when the rain bounced off the ground.

To pass the time we cut out pictures of Cliff Richard from the magazine Mum had bought us the week before. Christopher and I knew every single word of every single song. Our favourite was 'Bachelor Boy', and we had the radio turned up full waiting for it to be played. We carried that little radio everywhere so that we never missed it. After we'd cut out all the pictures we could find, we stuck them up on the walls. There was barely any space left! The walls were papered over with photos of Cliff and sticky tape. Then we heard, 'And now, Cliff Richard and "Bachelor Boy".' We grabbed our microphones (anything would do) jumped up on to the stage (well, the bed, for those of you with no imagination) and bounced up and down, singing along at the top of our voices.

Mum, now in the doorway, put her bags down, folded her arms and watched. Cliff burst into the chorus once more and I span around and launched myself off the stage into the audience – and saw Mum standing there.

'We were excited, Mum,' I blurted out. 'Honest, we've been waiting for hours and hours for Cliff to be on and, well, erm . . .' It was then that I noticed the bags.

'What's in the bags, Mum?' I asked, forgetting that I might be in trouble.

'Ooh, I can see lots of bright, coloured things,' said Christopher.

'You certainly can,' Mum said, laughing, as she grabbed the children and hugged them. 'Are you ready for this?'

The bags were overflowing with coloured tinsel, baubles, decorations and paper lanterns. There was even a stand-up nativity scene and silver stars.

We pulled everything out and spread it on the floor, examining it. Mum was exhausted and made her way to the kitchen for a cuppa, leaving us with the big decisions as to what would go where. Oh, the excitement!

It was still quite a few weeks before Christmas, but you could sense the excitement building in the children at Nazareth House already.

How magical Christmas was, Nancy thought, and she smiled at how much things had changed over the years. It had been hard that first Christmas without her mother, and then always struggling to ensure the children here had a wonderful time. Nancy had learned at an early age how to make lanterns and paper chains, and the ones the children made always seemed so much nicer than the ones bought in any shop. Mind you, if the squeals from Christopher and Susan were anything to go by, they seemed happy enough with the coloured lanterns Nancy had brought home that day.

Time to decorate for Christmas. Nancy smiled once more and picked up a chair to take in to begin hanging the tinsel across the ceiling.

But there was no need for the chair: there was no tinsel left to hang. Every last strand was draped around the photos on the Cliff Richard wall.

Nancy stood watching the two children, Susan now seven, Christopher five. They were covered with little bits of tinsel, the bed clothes were all crumpled, the pillows, lying on the floor, also covered in bits of tinsel. There was hardly a clear inch of floor space. Nancy felt a catch in her throat. They were so happy, and with just a few strands of tinsel and a few coloured baubles.

Everyone had warned her. And she'd tried, she really had. It had been impossible with Susan, and, she had to admit to herself now, she had failed with Christopher too. She hadn't been able to stop herself loving them as if they were her own.

'Mum, can we stay up late and wait for "Bachelor Boy" to come on the radio again so we can see all the pretty baubles and tinsel just with the night light on?'

'No,' said Nancy firmly. Two very happy faces fell.

'Oh,' said Susan. Christopher looked as if he was going to sulk.

'No need,' continued Nancy, reaching into her shopping bag. 'Now, how could I have forgotten? . . . I do have one last thing for you both.'

She produced a brown paper bag and handed it to them.

'Bachelor Boy', on record!

Nancy returned to the kitchen to start making some supper, and *for the next two hours Susan's little pink record player played 'Bachelor Boy' over and over again to two very excited and happy children.*

Nancy was busy tidying up. It was late, and there was still lots to do, but her time at the shops had been well worth it. It was nearly midnight when she finally made her way along the corridor. Reaching her room, she switched the big light off and put on the little red night light, which shone prettily on the Cliff Richard Christmas wall.

'Happy Christmas, and God Bless Cliff,' she said, smiling, as she crawled finally into bed.

The Beach Ball

It was late November 1962 now, and the excitement was building as everyone was given their jobs to make sure everything was prepared in time for Christmas. The children had been making coloured streamers for days now to decorate Nazareth House, and there was paper, glue and glitter all over the place. Mum knew the children loved this time of year and especially making their own decorations. Unfortunately, it would take the staff days to clear up after them!

Mum had no worries about the Christmas stockings this year, as there had been some extremely kind benefactors and all the children would have a lovely gift along with their tangerine and sweets. Every year some of the companies in the north-east also arranged for Christmas parties for the older children downstairs, which always caused enormous excitement. There were always lots of party games, lovely food and, most exciting of all, a visit from Santa. I was never invited to these parties, though, as Mum had been told that, as long as I was upstairs, I couldn't be included in any of the treats for the downstairs children.

This year was different. Mother Superior had discovered that I was never invited to the festivities and insisted that I was added to the list for the Christmas party.

This was a good Christmas for Mum in more ways than one, as she had been given a small wage rather than working for board, and every Saturday afternoon off. Mum and I would plan our day out well in advance but, whatever we did, it always included a trip to Fenwick's toy department, then the café. I would ask Mum over and over again to tell me the story about when she was a little girl. So there we would sit with a peach melba and a strawberry tart as she told me about walking past the shops when she was a child. How she would watch the people inside and wonder what it must be like to be able to sit in a café having a cup of tea and a cake. She'd always thought that the people inside must be very rich. Sometimes she would close her eyes and she could smell the coffee and the food people were eating inside, and she would imagine she was there too. Well, she could pick up a cup and stick her little finger up like that too! I loved this story and, of course, when I was all grown up and rich and famous, we would visit cafés every single day.

I saw the doll as soon as we walked into the toy department. It was the most incredible and beautiful doll you could ever imagine and, more importantly, it had long hair. To me, it looked almost real. It had beautiful blue eyes and its long hair was wavy and brown. I could just imagine combing it for hours. I would call her Caroline. But I knew in my heart of hearts that Mum could never afford to get me that doll. Then the lady next to us picked it up and walked to the counter. Mum and I just watched and wished.

* * *

The day of the Christmas party arrived, and Mum had such a job getting me ready. I was so excited. New dress, tights and shoes (I know now that this is where Mum's wages had gone, and why she'd never have the money to buy the doll for me before Christmas), a pretty new ribbon for my hair and a cardigan with bows on it.

All us children were paraded in twos through to the nuns' parlour to wait. The chattering stopped instantly: we knew better than to talk in here. There was a major amount of fidgeting, though. Eventually, we were taken outside to watch the cars coming down the drive to take us. There were excited yelps from the children, some of whom had never been in a car before. This was absolute luxury, and we piled into the cars with some of the nuns and members of staff, and off we went, waving all the way up the drive.

I was sitting in a red Bentley with three other children and a member of staff. We all looked at each other in total awe – in fact, we were afraid to move! Josephine looked so pretty today. Her hair had been in rags all night, and her ringlets were even more beautiful than usual. Her eyes wide and her mouth gaping open, she leaned forward and said to the driver, 'Excuse me, are you a prince?' He burst out laughing, but Josephine was tapped on the knees, told to sit still and be quiet. This was speaking out of turn; we should know better.

After a while, the party was in full swing, and it was everything we could have dreamed of. There had even been jelly and ice cream. There was so much noise, and our squeals of delight must have been heard even over the loud Christmas music that was playing. The staff stood around watching us; they must have felt a little out of control. The company had brought in their own staff to help with the children: they were doing everything they could to ensure this would be a day to remember. Naturally, we were perfectly aware of this and were taking full advantage of the situation.

I have often wondered if these people could have even guessed at the joy their kindness brought us.

And now it was time. The lights were dimmed and we all sat on the floor. Some of us held hands; others looked like they were holding their breath. Even Josephine's ringlets were still. It was time for Santa. The scream when he arrived was deafening. He was carrying an enormous red sack, and he had helpers with him who also had red sacks full of presents.

One by one the names were called out, and each child leaned eagerly forward, waiting for their name. Mary, Anthony, James, Coleen and Josephine jumped when their turn came and ran forward excitedly, smiling. On and on the names were called out – and I waited and waited, poised, ready to jump up and receive my present from Santa. It was over, and my name had not been called. There was no present for me. Santa had forgotten me. Although I had been allowed to come to the party, he hadn't put me on his Christmas list.

Some of the children looked at me as I sat there empty-handed and sniggered; others smiled kindly. Josephine offered to share her present with me. After all, we could play the game together. I had never been so ashamed and embarrassed in my life, and wished everyone would stop looking at me. Fortunately, most of the children were too busy ripping open their presents to notice, but I saw that Sister Veronica had seen, and she looked angry. Moments later, I did receive a gift from Santa. And so it was that I went home from the party with a beach ball!

A beach ball? Nancy laughed as they began looking for the balloon pump to blow it up. They were throwing it to each other and laughing, until Dolly, one of the young helpers, came into the room with Christopher, who had cried non-stop because Susan had gone to a party without him. It was Dolly who told Nancy what had happened. She caught the ball, and everything stopped. Silence. Nancy was immediately furious, but didn't say a word: she just stood perfectly still, staring straight ahead.

Susan stood waiting for Mum to throw the ball back. She began to feel frightened. What had happened? Had she done something wrong? Mum looked so angry, just staring straight over her head like that. Just when she was starting to feel better, why did everything have to go wrong again? Her bottom lip wobbled and she began to cry.

Christopher grabbed Susan's hand and decided to cry along with her. This brought Nancy to her senses. She pushed the ball into Dolly's hands, told her to look after the children and marched down the corridor, through the door and down the stairs, grabbing her coat and bag on the way.

They were left standing there, the three of them in stunned silence, then Dolly grabbed the children and they ran along the corridors to the bathroom, where Susan and Christopher jumped up on to the bench and clung on to the window bars.

There she was, marching up the drive, her handbag swinging in her hand. What on earth was she up to? Where was she going? No-nonsense Nancy was on the warpath again.

The card had been in the window of the corner shop for a few days now. Nancy had seen it earlier in the week. She greeted the shop-keeper, asked to borrow a pen, wrote the number down and left.

Back down the drive she marched, again watched by Susan, Christopher and Dolly at the bathroom window. Nancy did not, however, return upstairs but went straight to the telephone room. No permission had been granted, but Nancy was past caring.

'Hello?'

'Hello. I saw your card in the shop window, and I would like to apply, please. I am a nursery worker at Nazareth House, and I would very much like the job.'

'Oh, that's just up the road from us. My daughter, Lesley, is seven, and it's just for a few hours on a Saturday afternoon while I work from home. I'm a hairdresser.'

'I have a daughter too, of seven years old. Could I bring her along, and they could play together? She's very well-behaved.'

'Can you come on Saturday at one o'clock? We'll discuss your wages then.'

'Thank you. I'll be there on time.'

Once again, Nancy took advantage of the seat below the telephone to calm herself down. What on earth was the matter with her? From a young child she had always been sensible and totally in control. This was ridiculous. It was Susan, of course. Her stomach churned at the thought of her sitting there waiting for her name to be called. Cruel, that was the only word for it. Well, this Christmas would be perfect. She would see to it. A beach ball indeed!

Now, Nancy had to explain to Susan that they would be unable to have their weekly Fenwick's treat for a while but that she had an extra job and that Susan could come with her to it and play with Lesley, who could be a new friend for her.

The next few Saturdays, Nancy spent her afternoon off looking after Lesley and Susan, taking them for a walk or to the park if it was a nice day or watching TV if it was raining. She loved her extra job and began to help out cleaning in the little hair salon in the back room as well. After three weeks, she'd made herself invaluable, and her wage was increased just in time for Christmas.

On 25 December 1962, Susan woke up early. It was still dark, but she could just make out the shapes of presents at the bottom of her bed. Santa had been. 'Mum,' she whispered. 'Mum, can I get up?' Nancy had no trouble getting up; she had barely been asleep that night.

'Happy Christmas, darling,' she said. 'Let's see what Santa brought.'

Susan's eyes were beginning to adjust to the dark when Nancy switched the night light on. Just for once, she was lost for words. There, at the bottom of her bed, was the most beautiful doll in the world, Caroline with the long brown hair.

Mermaids

I was using my imagination and being creative – what on earth was their problem? I had seen the film on Sunday, one of those days when I was allowed downstairs to be with the big ones for tea in the afternoon. These were those special times when we had learned to say the rosary faster than the speed of light so we could have our tea then settle down to a film.

I have never forgotten that day. It was a film made in 1948 called *Miranda*, and it was about a mermaid and the effect she had on different people's lives. She was so beautiful my heart was captured. I was so totally mesmerized by the film that I couldn't even eat my sandwiches and cake. Oh, it was all I wanted out of life at that moment, to be a mermaid. How special would *that* make me! Dolly said that *sometimes*, if we wished hard enough, our dreams would come true. Mum, on the other hand, said that Dolly lived with her head in the clouds and to take no notice!

I never really enjoyed bath time as a rule, but that night I pleaded with Mum to let me have a bath. 'Now that's a new one,' said one of the staff. Our bathroom was enormous. Across one wall were tiny basins about two feet from the ground, and the other walls had benches with pegs above them. Each of us had a picture on our peg so that we could recognize it. Mine was a pink flower and

Christopher's was a blue truck. While we were put in the bath in turn and scrubbed, Mum was in the corner with the mangle, trying to squeeze the water out of the washing. It was always a noisy time and usually I was glad when it was over.

Tonight was different, though, I *wanted* to bathe and dream my imaginative dreams.

Mum was looking at me, a puzzled expression on her face. 'All right,' she said, pulling out the mangle. 'You can have a bath while I dry the clothes.'

Wonderful! I *was* a mermaid, I just knew it! Didn't I love the rain? Didn't I love the swimming pool? This explained it all. Rainwater was magic, I had been told, and as I lay there in the water I could feel myself riding the waves.

'Susan, will you stop splashing the water everywhere!'

What is it with adults? I thought. They really have no sense of adventure or imagination.

I lay in bed that night and began to dream. I was a mermaid with the most beautiful tail, and I lived in an enchanted lagoon where life was perfect and we all loved each other. We combed each other's hair and then swam the oceans with the dolphins. Life was perfect.

Nancy was tired. It had been a busy day, and she knew, as only a mother does, that Susan was up to something. I love her so much, she thought, and yet I don't understand her. Everything is a drama to her. Oh well, she sighed to herself, I'm sure I'll find out what she's up

*to in time. The last of the clothes dried, she put the mangle away and
sat down with Dolly for tea and biscuits, enjoying a relaxing five
minutes. Then Dolly said, 'Susan loved the Sunday film, Nancy.
Apparently it was about a mermaid called Miranda.'*

Light dawned. 'That explains it,' said Nancy.

It rained hard that night and all next day, until tea time
brought the sun out and we were allowed outside to play.
I remember that a few of us were sitting on the roundabout, slowly going round and round.

'I must make sure not to get my feet wet,' I said loudly.

'Why?' asked Josephine and Mary, exactly at the same
time.

'Well, surely you know I'm a mermaid?'

'Oooh, how did you find out?'

'One day when I got my feet wet in the rain. It's the
only way to truly find out.'

'Could we do that then? Find out, I mean, if we're mermaids?' said Josephine.

'Naturally, but you need to know how.'

'Please show us.'

So it was that six of us found the biggest puddle in the
playground and, after much giggling, took our shoes off
and sat in a circle, our feet meeting in the middle of the
water. I had a captive audience. All eyes were on me, and
I loved it.

'We have to close our eyes now, and imagine being a
mermaid!' I told them. I could see it all. There we were,

sitting on the waves, listening to the ocean, riding on the backs of dolphins until . . .

'*What* do you think you are doing?'

Uh-oh. It was never good to be caught out by Sister Vincent.

'Please, Sister,' said Josephine, 'we're trying to find out if we're mermaids.'

'I *beg* your pardon?'

'We're trying –'

'Yes, thank you, I heard what you said, Josephine.'

'Susan said it was the only way to truly find out.'

Such a mortified look came my way. I tell you, if I had been granted a mermaid's tail, it would have been seriously shaking, flapping about and quivering. As it was, it was my human knees that were knocking now.

In a very quiet, slow and terrifying voice, Sister Vincent said, 'Get up *now*! Go inside and remove your wet socks.'

We all got up to go. '*Not* you,' she said. 'Come over here – if you can, of course, being a mermaid and all.'

Don't get me wrong: this was not said in a joking way of any description.

I was frogmarched all the way back to the nursery in total silence. Sister Vincent made very few visits upstairs, and Mum and the staff, who were all in the dining room, looked up on hearing the footsteps in the corridor.

She marched in and pushed me forward. Mum stopped, the ladle full of mashed potato in her hand suddenly stopped in mid-air.

'What has she done?' said Dolly bravely. She was always a little afraid of Sister Vincent.

'I'll deal with this, Dolly,' said Mum. 'So, what *has* she done?'

'Got her feet wet, along with six other girls.'

'Well, it has been raining, Sister, you know.' Mum's chin was again in the air.

I closed my eyes, waiting for the rest of it.

'She cajoled six other children to sit on the wet ground and place their stocking feet in a puddle to see if they were mermaids.'

Dolly grabbed her apron and put it in front of her mouth to stifle a giggle.

'Mum, what does "cajole" mean?' I asked.

Everyone looked at me. I think this was one of those times I should have remembered to Speak When You're Spoken To.

'Be quiet and go to your room, please,' said Mum. I did as I was told and went.

Once again, I had got it so wrong. I had no understanding of why no one could understand how important it was to imagine how wonderful, exciting and amazing life could be if you just dreamed and let your imagination run wild. Why was everyone always so angry with me? The day had started out so brilliantly, full of exciting possibilities, and now, again, it had ended with my tears and me feeling that somehow I just never quite measured up to what was expected of me.

I was still sitting crying when Mum walked into the room. She looked angry. 'I'm sorry, Mum. I just wanted to be a mermaid, that's all.'

Was that a smile tickling the corner of her mouth? 'Tell

you what,' she said. 'I could find some green material and make a mermaid's tail for your doll. Come on, let's have a cup of tea and forget all about it.'

Nancy's heart felt like it would break. What on earth am I to do? she asked herself. I have never in my life thought the way Susan does. I never learned to dream; life is too hard. Nancy had always believed in being realistic and facing up to life's challenges, believing that living with your head in the clouds only led to disappointment. There were only a few instances in life when, for just a single moment, she had thought, Maybe, just maybe . . . only to be disillusioned. And yet, she'd never believed she would be a mother, and here she was, a child in her arms, crying, who needed her — and what use was she? I should know what to say, but I don't, she thought. How do I tell her that dreams are worthless, that they mean nothing? Life is hard and it hurts, and sometimes it all goes hideously wrong. But Nancy said none of these things. She just smiled, cuddled her daughter close to her and switched on the TV.

It was Billy Smart's circus, and the beautiful lady acrobats were standing on the horses' backs as they galloped around the circus ring. 'Oooh, Mum,' I said. 'I want to be an acrobat and . . .'

God, give me strength! thought Nancy.

Parallels

The examiner was smiling and nodding her head slowly. Well-pointed toes, beautiful arm positions and the perfect posture required to make an excellent ballet dancer. This child, Sarah, had promise and would go far. Molly was so very proud of her daughter.

Across town, in another hall, Nancy, too, was proud of her daughter and very pleased with herself for finding, at last, something Susan could excel in and enjoy. Tilly had told her there was a dance school not far from where they lived on the West Road. Nancy had taken Susan along and enrolled her in ballroom and Latin American dance classes, and she was loving every single moment of it. She could throw herself around the room, do a dramatic paso doble, a cheeky cha cha cha and kick her legs high with the rest of them doing the jive. This was living the dream.

The dance school had been founded by Miss Newbiggin (now Mrs Whiteside), and her daughter, Mavis, helped her run it. At the time, Nancy could never have known what a great part these kind souls would play in her and her daughter's lives.

When Nancy and Susan arrived on that first day, it was Mavis they met first, telling her all about Susan's love of dancing – except for ballet, of course. Mavis told her about all the classes they had, and it was decided that Susan would try ballroom and Latin dancing classes first. Nancy, embarrassed, explained that it might have to be one or the other and tentatively asked about costs.

Mavis is one of those people in life to whom you do not have to say anything, because their kindness and capacity to care for others is so great that words are not necessary. Mavis had seen our address, Nazareth House, on the form.

'Well, let's see now,' she said. 'Why don't you bring Susan along for, say, the next three weeks, and try out the various classes?' The fees were to be paid weekly, and any missed weeks had to be paid for, too, except in certain circumstances, such as holidays, sickness, etc. Mavis decided not to mention this at the moment, though. She would speak to Miss Newbiggin and see what could be done.

Susan worked hard and was very soon ready for her first Latin American dancing exam.

Susan and Sarah on that Saturday both received Pass: Highly Commended, and Molly and Nancy were both very proud of their talented daughters. Sarah was on her way to owning her own dance school and choreographing musical shows. And Susan was on her way to being Latin American dance champion and performing in musical shows.

Happy Days and Half-a-Crown

Mum and I were out one lovely sunny autumn day, walking, as we always did, hand in hand. 'Shanks's pony', Mum called it. I was skipping along, kicking the leaves, when my eye caught sight of something shiny. A half-crown – two whole shillings and sixpence. We couldn't have been more thrilled if we had won the pools.

'Mum, it's money! It really is . . . It's money!'

'Well, so it is. It most certainly is. Now just what are we going to do with this?'

Mum decided we should spend it on a treat for both of us, and we chatted excitedly about what we were going to do or what we could buy with it. Half-a-crown was a massive amount of money to have. After much discussion and excitement, it was finally decided that we would buy a large tin of tomato soup, some freshly baked bread and ice cream. All our favourites. Life just didn't get any better than this.

I thought all my birthdays had come at once when Mum said I could stay up late to watch TV and that we'd make a night of it and enjoy our supper together. I will never forget that day: the fun and the anticipation of just me and Mum having our special supper. I couldn't get to the shops to buy our goodies and take them home quick enough!

As soon as we entered the shop we could smell the freshly baked bread. I ran to the shelf to get the soup. Mum (as she always did, most embarrassingly) prodded the loaves to ensure they were fresh.

It wasn't until we were at the counter and Mum put her hand in her pocket that she discovered a small hole in the lining. Our lovely shiny half-a-crown was gone. Ashamed and embarrassed, we put everything back on the shelves.

'Yes, well,' was all Mum said, and one look from her told me not to say anything. There was a horrible ache in the back of my throat that was threatening to make me cry, so I swallowed and swallowed, determined not to let her see I was upset. There was no skipping on the way home, just a determined stride, one foot in front of the other, chin, as ever, in the air.

I wish I could have had some adult words to say to Mum that day. I knew how I felt, but I couldn't put it into words. I loved her with my heart and soul, and the pain I felt deep down inside now, the pain that was making me want to cry out loud, was not for me.

You know, just as a matter of interest, there is grace in receiving as well as giving. They say, as parents, when your child hurts, you hurt ten times more. Well, we feel that way too sometimes, you know. As children, we have the greatest capacity to love, so let us love you. We don't care if you are rich, pretty, fat or thin, famous or completely unknown – all we care about is that you love us and want to be with us. Time is the most precious gift you can give us and we understand if you are angry, hurt, disappointed and struggling to makes ends meet, but only if you tell us.

We have active minds and brains that understand, if you just talk to us. Involve us, ask us to help you. As children, we love nothing more than to be able to help. If you need a hug, we will hug you, it makes us feel special . . . wanted. You don't always have to be the strong one, you don't always have to stand tall, chin up in the air. Sometimes it's OK to let us be the hero. We can cope because we know you love us, as you have honoured us with your fears and worries. We can walk together hand in hand, forging a bond no one can break.

How I wish I could have said any of this to Mum back then, but I was a child who could feel all this without putting any of it into words, so I just gripped her hand tightly and walked as close to her as I could. Me and Mum against the world. Somehow it would be all right . . . and, of course, it was.

When we reached home, Mum turned to me, totally composed, as always.

'That's just the way it goes sometimes,' she said. 'But we had fun planning it, and we will still have our supper.'

So, that night, I got to stay up late, and eight o'clock found us both in the TV room, curtains drawn, snuggled up in the dark on the sofa, watching TV, drinking tea and eating sugar sandwiches. Perfect . . . absolutely perfect.

A Silent Kindness

Everyone remembers their first love. It's so very special, the emotions so new, so overpowering and all-consuming. I was no different. I will never forget him. He was my whole world, and nothing else mattered but him. Even now, on days when I catch sight of him, I remember how I felt, how much it hurt and what he meant to me. I was in love, and I spent hours writing letters to him, editing and re-editing them to make sure every word was perfect. He was, after all, the most wonderful man in the world, and I spent many hours looking longingly at the photographs of him above my bed. He even had an amazing name, Cliff Richard, and one day I would be famous and he would fall in love with me and we would live happily ever after. Well, why not? It happened sometimes surely? I was eight years old and he was the one.

I belonged to his fan club and, naturally, I was his number-one fan. Mum had no extra money for this sort of frivolity. Even now, I have no idea how she managed to pay for it or what a fan-club membership cost in 1963. Unfortunately, even fans had to pay for the club merchandise, and how could you call yourself a fan without a Cliff Richard badge? Back then, it really was all I wanted out of life. I remember sitting in my favourite place, at my little red desk, chin in hands, staring out of the window. I couldn't for the life of me imagine how I was going to get a badge, but I would figure out a way somehow.

I sat there for hours, doodling, listening to the radio, and now and again turning my head to look at the posters on my wall, just knowing that, somewhere, there was an answer. I noticed a pile of clothes in the corner of the room that Mum had asked me to sort through, and suddenly it came to me. I had heard about people selling their possessions to make money – now, what did I have that I could sell? I pulled a chair up to the wardrobe and removed all the clothes I thought wouldn't fit me any more and any old toys I no longer played with. I began to set my room up like a little shop, hanging the clothes up and sticking bits of paper to them as price tags. One of the young staff who was passing asked what I was doing, so I invited her in and she bought a couple of my cardigans and a puzzle game for her younger sister and said she would pass the word round to the rest of the staff.

I was so proud of myself. Mum would be so pleased with me. After all, even Marks & Spencer had started with a stall in a market, or so she kept telling me. It was all going wonderfully well – until, that is, word got to Mum. I heard her footsteps marching down the corridor and thought to myself, Someone's in trouble. Mum's on the warpath.

The steps came nearer and nearer. Whoops! I thought. It must be me!

She stood there in the doorway staring at me, arms folded. Never a good sign.

'May I ask what you are doing?' she said.

I was rapidly realizing that setting up shop might not have been the brightest idea.

'I was just thinking about selling my clothes so that I could buy a Cliff Richard badge,' I explained.

'Were you now? Let me have a look. The wardrobe here looks pretty empty to me – what were you planning to pin it to, your knickers?'

I intentionally let my bottom lip wobble.

'I really was trying to be helpful and make some money to buy a badge. I am so sorry, I just won't have one,' I said, and hung my head.

'Oh, please!' said Mum. 'The full drama.' And she clapped!

I looked up, and we both burst out laughing.

'You are a funny little thing, aren't you? Well, we'll have to get all your clothes back now and return the money.'

I was a little embarrassed, to be honest, but Mum was smiling as she left the room.

Later that day, Mum and I were putting all the clothes and toys back in the wardrobe and I had my most brilliant idea yet. I couldn't for a moment think why I hadn't thought of it before.

So I took pen to paper. I had Cliff Richards' fan-mail address, and I was convinced – of course – that he read every letter I wrote.

I vaguely remember writing that letter. I think it went something like this:

Dear Cliff, please could you send me a badge? My mum can't afford one yet and I'm not allowed to sell my clothes but I love you and I would like one and I have been very well-behaved.

Thank you

Susan

In all corners of the world there is great kindness, often unknown, a silent kindness that touches hearts and souls. It's rarely publicized or heard of, but it happens all the same. One such kindness responded to my heartfelt letter, possibly seeing the address of Nazareth House Orphanage.

I remember it was a school day, and it must have been late in the year, as I was wearing my winter uniform and ready for school when Mum was called and told that a parcel had arrived for me.

A parcel! Why on earth would anyone send anything to me? I never had any parcels. I remember I was so excited running downstairs with Mum to collect it. What could it be?

There it was, a big brown parcel addressed to me. Mum checked the name and address over and over, and we simply stood there and looked at it, dumbstruck. Then I just couldn't wait any longer.

'Mum, do you think we could open it now?' I said.

Still unsure, she picked it up and shook it, then immediately put it back down. Another couple of minutes of staring at the address, then slowly she began to peel off the paper bit by bit.

There was a letter attached, and Mum was reading it. I tugged at her apron: 'Please, Mum, tell me!'

'It's from Cliff.'

'Cliff?'

'Yes, Cliff.'

'Cliff Richard?'

'How many Cliffs do you know?'

Silence. We were stunned.

I couldn't speak. He was the love of my life and he had sent me a present. Oh, I felt so special. In all my life, I can never remember feeling so important. It took me a few moments to calm myself, then Mum and I looked at each other and threw ourselves at the parcel and ripped it open.

There were badges – boxes of them – posters, photographs and pens. This, then, was how it felt to matter to someone – other than Mum, of course. Someone else out there thought I was special and cared about me.

I shared everything out, of course, but Cliff had written to me personally and sent me a present and the photos, and I plastered the posters over every inch of wall I could find in my room.

I pinned the badge to my favourite jumper and danced round the room singing 'Bachelor Boy' for hours, a very happy child.

Mum had a jar where she would put spare change. It was her savings, she said, but she would never tell me what they were for. Many years later, she told me the only reason she never told me was in case she wasn't able to save enough money in time.

One afternoon, she went out, leaving me behind, something she rarely did. I played in our room, played with the children in the nursery playroom, but felt a little bit left out, to tell you the truth. I couldn't imagine for a moment why Mum wouldn't take me with her. I was soon to find out.

When she returned, she had what I can only describe as a smug, self-satisfied smile on her face, and it stayed there for the rest of the day. Finally, at bedtime, she sat on my bed and said, 'We're going to London.'

I was amazed: how on earth were we going to get to the other side of the world? And why were we going? I knew it must be for a good reason, because she still couldn't keep the smile off her face.

'It's not that far,' she said. 'And we're going on the night bus and we can sleep all the way.'

I was so excited! We were going on a bus to another world, but why? What was there to see there? Mum just carried on smiling. 'I'll tell you when we're on the bus,' she said, and I had to be content with that.

Her smile lasted all that week on the run-up to our trip to London. All she would say was 'This is your Christmas present, and it wouldn't fit in Santa's stocking,' then she would laugh. I had no idea what was going on but knew it must be very special to make Mum so happy.

We were all packed well in advance, our clothes and toothbrushes in a slightly battered overnight case – then, of course, multiple bags of things, to cover all eventualities, apparently.

It was cold that night at the bus station, but there we were with our overnight case, hot flasks, and wrapped up warm. It was freezing but we didn't care, this was an adventure, and we were chatting, laughing and holding hands as we waited for our journey to begin. Mum looked so proud. What an achievement! She had saved every penny she could, and she was about to give her daughter the thrill of a lifetime.

When the bus pulled out of the station, I looked at Mum and summoned up the courage to ask. 'So, we're going to London . . . What are we going to do when we get there?'

Mum opened her bag, pulled out a Cliff Richard badge and pinned it to my coat.

'We're going to see Cliff.'

'Cliff?'

'We're not going through this again! Cliff Richard, of course.'

Now, there have not been many times in my life when I have been speechless, but this was one of them.

She put her arm around me. 'We're going to the London Palladium to see Cliff in the pantomime *Aladdin*. Now snuggle in and go to sleep. It's going to be a long journey.'

Sleep? She had to be joking! I was going to meet the love of my life in a few hours and I was supposed to sleep? But sleep I did, eventually, and in the early hours of the morning Mum and I arrived in London. We both had our noses glued to the bus window, totally overwhelmed by this massive city. Everything seemed to be moving so fast, and it was incredibly noisy. When we got off the bus we stood there rooted to the spot, almost as if we were afraid to move as the bus moved away. What must we have looked like!

The pantomime wasn't until the afternoon, so we had a few hours to ourselves to look around. Mum was holding my hand so tight I had to keep reminding her that I had no intention of leaving her side, so could she please relax a bit. Truth be told, we both felt a little scared: this was a big, busy city.

'I have to keep tight hold of you,' said Mum. 'Bad things happen in big cities, and it is very dangerous.' Of course that just made it seem more exciting. How amazing! I was really enjoying myself now!

We chatted and walked about until at last it was time. Mum had one more surprise up her sleeve: we were to go in a taxi. We watched other people putting their hands up to flag one down and tentatively waved, loosely flapping our hands about. We must have looked totally ridiculous.

'It's just like putting your hand out for the bus, Mum,' I said, and threw my arm out – I was such a brave little girl! – and hailed a taxi. We felt like royalty! I say 'felt'; we didn't act like royalty: we were bouncing about, saying, 'Ooh, look at that! Who lives there, do you think?' 'Quick, look at this!'

When the driver asked for his fare, I really thought Mum was going to faint. 'Heavens!' she said. 'I only want to pay my fare, not buy the cab!' I'm not too sure the driver was impressed.

Our first sight of the London Palladium took our breath away. It was vast, and I remember we stood there for a moment just so we could take it all in. It wasn't until someone nudged Mum and said, 'Move along now,' that she turned, her nose in the air, and haughtily said, 'We have tickets!', and, swinging our battered case between us, we sailed forth up the steps with all the dignity we could muster.

Once inside, it was not only the Palladium that was fascinating me.

'Look at all the people, Mum! Look at their clothes!'

'Well, we are here with our tickets, just like everyone else,' she said, and, smiling and laughing, we made our way up the stairs to our seats. 'Up the stairs' is an understatement: 'up flights and flights and flights' would describe it better – we almost needed emergency oxygen by the time we reached the top. We had the cheapest seats in the back row of the gods. The stage looked absolutely tiny and we felt as though we were a million miles high, yet none of this mattered. What an adventure we were having, and I was about to see the love of my life.

Mum put some money in the slot to get the binoculars, and we sat and waited, almost holding our breath. This is it, Nancy thought. All that work had paid off, and they had actually got here. Yet another Christmas dream come true. Goodness me, I'm getting fanciful in my old age!

The lights dimmed and there was a hush throughout the auditorium. The orchestra struck up and Mum and I grabbed each other's hands.

It was a moment I will never forget. I held my breath even more, and waited, and then, to tremendous applause, there he was right there in front of me . . . Cliff Richard.

I knew Mum was watching me, smiling, so happy, and for the whole of the pantomime we laughed and clapped. We loved every single, perfect moment.

* * *

For Christmas that year Mum bought me a little gold Aladdin's lamp from the fan-club magazine. I have it still and will always treasure it.

I heard 'Bachelor Boy' on the radio the other day, and it brought it all back: my first love, Cliff Richard, and my incredible journey to the other side of the world to see him.

Empty Hands

The news fell like a bombshell. Nancy had always known this day would come – but how easy it is to put things to the back of your mind when so many years have passed. Actually, not so many years, she thought, only five. Susan was nine years old now, and Christopher seven. There was no particular day that she could recall when it had all started: she had loved Susan from the moment she held her in her arms, and with Christopher it began with compassion for a small child then grew into a mother's love. Nancy had known without a doubt that one day Christopher would be leaving the orphanage to return to Ghana, and had tried to prepare not only Susan but herself for that day. As the days and years passed, she had tried so hard to distance herself, but without success, and she had totally given up trying to make Susan understand.

Nancy was angry with herself. She should not have allowed this to happen; every child in her care was special. They all had their own little ways, their own characteristics, and although she insisted on teaching them all true values and discipline, there was always time for a kind word and a cuddle. Maybe it was seeing Christopher and Susan together. They shared such a bond. Nancy had never before seen children who spent every possible waking hour together, never arguing, never falling out and always holding hands.

She smiled, remembering the day when one of the staff had come running to her, saying she couldn't find Christopher anywhere and, no, he wasn't with Susan. The staff were beginning to get concerned.

Surely he was too small to have wandered outside into the grounds by himself? The caretaker was alerted anyway, and everyone began the search. Cupboards, dormitories, under the beds, Nancy's room, the dining room – even the other children joined in to look for him. After about fifteen minutes panic was setting in. Where on earth was he? Nancy closed her eyes and tried to think rationally. Why was Susan on her own, pushing her doll's pram along the corridors? Light dawned. No. Surely not, it couldn't be. 'Wait!' she shouted to the staff. 'Where is Susan?'

'At the far end of the corridor pushing her pram about,' said Dolly.

Nancy calmly put her hands on her hips, and smiled. 'This way,' she said to the staff, and they followed behind her as she walked purposefully along the corridor.

There he was, fast asleep, curled up in Susan's doll's pram as she pushed him along the corridors, quietly singing to him.

Susan and Nancy had been part of Christopher's journey in life for only five years, and one thing was for sure, thought Nancy: we will never see him again. There were no buses or trains that went to Ghana.

Danny had been so kind to Susan and Nancy, always turning up with birthday and Christmas presents. He always took Susan along with him on outings with Christopher, which they both loved.

Danny knew the news would be difficult to break. God had answered his prayers, and more. Nancy and Susan had not only loved his young son but made him part of their family. Nancy was making this easy for him now, saying how wonderful it was that Danny's family would be all together again and how Christopher would adjust, as he was so young. 'He'll be with his father and brother,' she said, 'surrounded by family, and that is how it should be. Now tell me the arrangements, then you can go and tell Christopher. How exciting for you all,' she finished, smiling. Danny wasn't fooled, though. The smile was nowhere near her eyes.

Danny had arranged everything. Christopher was to be transferred to the Nazareth House in Liverpool in three weeks' time, to prepare for his six-week trip to Ghana by boat. Three more weeks – that's all they had. Danny was with Christopher now, explaining it all to him, and it was time for Nancy to find Susan and somehow find the right words to say.

As it turned out, Susan already knew. She had heard the staff talking about it and was sitting in her room, looking out of the window. This is unbearable, thought Nancy, when Susan turned her tear-stained face to look at her.

'I am so sorry, darling.' There were absolutely no words that were going to help, so she said nothing more.

Nancy thought it was selfish and wrong to let her daughter see how upset she herself was. Unfortunately, the tears were falling fast and hard, and no amount of deep breaths or grin-and-bear-it attitude was making any difference at all.

They held on to each other while Nancy chattered on.

'He's being collected in a few weeks and is staying in the Nazareth House in Liverpool, where he'll be introduced to the person he's travelling with. We'll go to Liverpool and see him off. I am going to buy you that new yellow coat out of Tilly's catalogue that you like so much. On Saturday, we'll go to Fenwick's and buy some toys. I'm going to make up a suitcase full of his favourite things and we'll surprise him with it. Just think how excited he'll be. Susan, we can plan this together, you and me.'

It should have helped, but it didn't.

Together, they filled an old brown suitcase with colouring books, crayons, books to read, puzzles and toys. Susan had written a letter to Christopher, saying that when she was famous and had lots of money she would come and see him. Nancy had a couple of photographs, slightly tattered, but she wanted him to have memories of them all. It was all planned in her mind: when it was time for them to leave him, she would hand the suitcase over and he would be distracted. It would be fine. It had to be.

It was freezing cold and the Liverpool dock was breezy. Susan's new yellow coat didn't even begin to keep her warm. Danny was in Ghana with his other son, Oscar, already. When Christopher arrived, there were lots of family celebrations planned.

Susan thought her fingers would break, Christopher was holding her hand so tightly. Nancy walked behind them as the three of them boarded the ship. It was enormous, and Susan was frightened. They were shown to his cabin and met the person who would be looking after him on the journey. The adults were filling in the time with small talk; the children simply stood together, side by side, scared and shaking.

They all jumped when they heard the ship's horn.

'Time to go,' said Nancy, trying to be cheery, and she began to busy herself, showing Christopher the suitcase and telling him to open it now and see what surprises there were for him. Then she grabbed Susan's hand and they left.

They were walking too quickly when they reached the stairs and Susan fell all the way to the bottom. People were running to get to her because she had screamed as she fell. Nancy ran all the way down to the foot of the stairs, where Susan had now begun to cry.

'Mum, my coat is dirty.'

'It doesn't matter,' said Nancy, and then Susan was sick all over her lovely new yellow coat.

It was a long bus journey home and they were both exhausted and emotionally drained when they arrived home. Susan was given a bath and they both sat in silence, having a cup of tea in the small kitchen and trying to feel warm again. Nancy smiled at her daughter. She thought there must surely be something she could say to her that would help, some words of comfort, but instead she held out her hand and they walked to their room and went to bed. Susan wanted to sleep on her own that night so she could pretend that she and Christopher were curled up together like when they were little. She missed his hand being in hers. Her hand felt so empty she held hands with herself and continued to pretend.

Nancy lay there in the dark, feeling numb. What was Christopher doing now? she wondered. How long would it take for him to forget them? How long would it take for the pain in all of them to subside?

'Mum?' Susan whispered from her bed.

'Yes,' answered Nancy.

'Mum, you know God —'

'I do.'

'Mum, you know Heaven —'

'I do.'

'Mum, you know when you die —'

'Erm —'

'Will we all go to Heaven?'

'Yes, of course.'

'So, will Christopher be there?'

'I believe he will.'

'Mum, what if I go to Heaven first?'

'Then you can wait for him and be the first person he sees.'

'Like before, when we were little, when he said I made him feel better?'

'You did, my darling, you did.'
'I miss him, Mum.'
'I miss him too, darling,' said Nancy.
Finally, they slept.

Pony-tails and Colouring Books

It was the middle of the night and Nancy was lying awake yet again. The rain was pouring down outside, and the long walk to school with Susan was just not going to be possible. What should I do? she thought. The last time this had happened and Nancy had let Susan go to school with the children downstairs – after a hefty warning that they had to take care of her – she had received a telephone call from the head teacher to say Susan had been sick and wouldn't stop crying, and could Nancy come and collect her. With her imagination and funny little character, Nancy thought Susan would have loved school – making new friends, learning to read – but it simply wasn't working out that way and Nancy worried constantly that she was unhappy from the minute Nancy left her at the school gates until she collected her.

Nancy sat up now and sipped a glass of water, waiting once more for the pain in her stomach to subside, and looked over at her sleeping daughter. It was no good just sitting here thinking, it was time to make the decision about what she was going to do. She had an appointment with Dr Graham the next day to arrange the now urgent hysterectomy. Six weeks, first in the hospital, and then in a convalescence home. Six weeks at most. There were two choices: leave Susan here or ask Billy to look after her. Nancy didn't know which terror was worse, the thought of Susan being unhappy at school, enduring God only knows what on the way there and back or, and this was absolutely terrifying, the thought of Susan loving every moment of being with her father and not wanting to come back to her. It was getting light now, and Susan would be awake soon. Nancy made her decision. There was no choice, really. Susan would be safe with Billy, and happy.

Susan stirred when her mum got up to get ready. It was totally out of character for Nancy to keep her off school, but today was going to be a big day and she wanted Susan kept as close to her as possible, to ensure she was happy with everything that Nancy arranged.

'Go back to sleep, love,' she said. 'You don't have to go to school today, you can stay with me.' The sleepy but happy smile on Susan's face said it all, and Nancy made her way downstairs to the telephone to catch Billy before he left for work.

It was his mother, Nana Robinson, who answered the phone.

'Hello, Nancy, how are you and Susan?' she said. 'This is early to call, is everything all right?'

Whether it was the kind tone in Nana's voice or the fact that Nancy was worrying herself sick and had been doing so for weeks now she didn't know, but her voice was decidedly wobbly when she answered, and even Nana knew that was unusual.

No-nonsense Nancy took a deep breath and told Nana Robinson all about the operation and how frightened Susan was at school, about the bullying that had taken place on the way there and how Nancy couldn't even imagine leaving her behind at Nazareth House.

Nana had it all under control within minutes. Susan would come to live with herself and Grandad for the six weeks and be enrolled in the local primary school. Her cousins all went there, and they would take her to school and back. Nancy was not to worry for another minute and just ensure she got herself better. Billy had a car, and Nana would make sure Susan was taken to see her every week.

'*I will let you know as soon as the rest period is over and I am feeling better and well and as soon as I can come to collect her and . . .*'

Nana understood perfectly.

'*Nancy,*' *she said.* '*Let's speak plainly. Of course you are concerned about Susan, that is what makes you a good mother, and of course I will make sure you get Susan back when you are well again.*'

If I felt better I would be jumping for joy, thought Nancy, at another acknowledgement that she was Susan's mother from Billy's family. And another good thing was that Nana lived only a short walk from Tilly's and Susan could visit there if she wished. It was a perfect solution – and it meant that Susan got to change schools.

It was only three weeks later that Nancy took Susan to her new school for her first day. They sat in the big hall on a school bench waiting for the head teacher to arrive.

'*It's a school, Mum, and there's no noise,*' *said Susan. It was indeed completely quiet in this massive hall. Whispering was bad manners, Susan had been taught, but today they sat looking round them, feeling totally lost and quietly whispering to each other.*

'*Mum, there's a stage.*'

'*No doubt you will be up there at the first opportunity.*' *Nancy smiled.*

'*Mum, will the teachers be nice to me here?*'

Nancy sat up straight and looked away, anger in her eyes. So that was it. It wasn't the children Susan had been afraid of at the last school, although they had been bad enough. She'd thought at least that Susan had been safe once she was at school but, no, it had once again been adults, who should know better. Tears stung her eyes. I am her mum, and she didn't even tell me. How am I supposed to help her if I don't know?

There were footsteps in the corridor and they were coming their way. Susan grabbed her mum's hand, and they both jumped up.

'Straight as soldiers standing to attention, Mum,' said Susan.

'Ssssh!' said Nancy, but with a smile on her face. She felt a sudden surge of strength. They had got this far, hadn't they? She had fought every battle so far and won. Just let them try it again. She looked down at her daughter, took her face in her hands, and said, 'Oh yes, my darling, they will be nice to you. They had better be, that's all!'

When you know you are loved beyond reason – and I knew with total certainty that I was – the whole world is a wonderful and perfect place to live in. That day, my whole perfect life stretched out in front of me. School was going to be fun, I would have lots of new friends and, hopefully, before too long, I'd get a chance to dance on the school stage.

Nancy was not sure that Susan understood how long six weeks would be, but at least she would enjoy school and have fun with her grandparents and father, and that was enough for now.

Susan was taken to what was to be her new home for the next few weeks and settled in, with Nancy fussing around her, making sure she had everything she needed.

'Anything I need to know?' asked Nana. 'Her likes and dislikes,

*favourite toys, favourite food?' Nana looked at all the suitcases.
'What does she have?' she went on.*

'An extremely vivid imagination,' said Nancy, laughing.

*What a perfect adventure this was, thought Susan. She would
start her new school the next day and travel there and back with her
cousin Graham, who she had played with earlier today. Tomorrow
she would have an exciting day at school and then play with Eileen
and Dad, who were coming to see her after work. It wasn't until
bedtime that, even with all the excitement, Susan was beginning to
feel a little strange without Mum.*

'Nana?'

'Yes, love.'

'How long is six weeks?'

'It's no time at all.'

'Nana, will Mum be all right without me?'

*'She will, love, and Daddy is taking you to see her at the end of
the week. Now, before you go to sleep . . . I know this is all very new
to you. Is there anything you would like while you are here?'*

'A pony-tail.'

'Pardon?'

'A pony-tail. Mum won't let me have one.'

*Nana Robinson burst out laughing, tucked Susan up into bed
and went to tell Billy that Nancy had been right, Susan was a funny
little thing, then she went to find an elastic band.*

*The next morning Susan could have cried with joy. Not only did
she have a new school, lovely cousins, and fun with Nana, Grandad
and Daddy but, most importantly of all, she had an elastic band in
the back of her hair holding a pony-tail. No well-groomed hair with
a perfect bow on the side today! Susan bounced all the way to school,
holding her cousin Graham's hand and swinging her pony-tail. Well,*

actually, it was a little stump of hair about an inch long, but im-agination is a great thing!

Nancy, had she known, would have been utterly mortified.

She'd had the operation at last, and the moment Nancy opened her eyes she asked for Susan.

'Your husband has been on the phone,' the nurse said, 'and we told him he could bring your daughter in later on today.'

If Nancy had been well enough, she would have laughed. Instead, she just mumbled, 'I haven't got one.'

The nurse patted her hand and said, 'There, there. They'll all be here later,' and Nancy fell asleep again. When she woke up, still in pain but feeling lots better, she spent the rest of the afternoon until visiting time dozing and checking the time on the clock.

When the time came at last, Nancy watched Susan and Billy playing at the end of her bed, Susan laughing and giggling at her dad as he threw grapes in the air and caught them in his mouth. If she hadn't been so pleased to see Susan, she would have said something: if these were the sort of things they were teaching her, she was not impressed. Billy caught the look on Nancy's face and said he would take a walk while she and Susan had some time together. Nancy heard all about the pony-tail Susan had every day for going to school and was, as previously predicted, absolutely mortified. She closed her eyes and imagined the unimaginable thought of uncombed hair and elastic bands. I have to get better soon, she thought, get out of here and get everything back to some sort of normality – like Susan using a comb, for starters.

Nancy had a smile pasted on her face, one of those where it just doesn't quite reach the eyes, when she watched her lovely daughter walk away from her, waving all the time, holding her daddy's hand

and looking extremely happy. Fortunately, Susan didn't see or hear the tears her mum cried into her pillow that night.

It was the middle of the night, and completely quiet. There was only one light on in the ward, on Sister's desk, where she sat filling out paperwork. Nurse Wilson was just returning from checking on her patients.

'Everything all right, Nurse?' asked Sister.

'Yes, Sister. Just the lady in the end bed muttering in her sleep. Something about a comb . . .'

Her from the Home

I was back home at Nazareth House now, and so happy to be in my own room with Mum once more. It was sad about the loss of the pony-tail but, all the same, I had begun to fret for Mum after about week three and kept asking for her all the time. Although Mum was sad that I had been sad, I bet she was also secretly very pleased that I had missed her.

It had all gone so well. Mum seemed thrilled at how quickly I had settled into my new school, and the teachers said I was a clever little girl and doing very well. There was to be a birthday party tomorrow, for a little girl called Julia, and I had been invited. All the children had to take their party clothes to school that day, and Mum had bought a lovely little blue vanity case and written the address of Nazareth House on an envelope and stuck it over the mirror so that Julia's mum and dad knew where to bring me after the party.

The party the next day could not have been better. Games, threepenny bits in the scones and flags in the sandwiches – these people must be so rich, I thought. There were songs and dancing too, and Julia had loved the book and colouring pens I had given her, all wrapped up in pretty paper, with a bow on top. It had definitely been the most brilliant day – until, that is, it was time to go home, and I opened my new pretty blue vanity case with the address inside.

'What's this?' asked Julia's dad.

'It's my address, where I live.'

That instant of stony silence said it all.

'I wasn't aware this girl was from the orphanage in Jesmond,' he said to his wife.

I had no idea why it would even be a problem, but all the other children were looking at me in embarrassment. It had been assumed that I still lived in Fenham with my grandparents – which apparently was acceptable – but from the moment they realized that I lived in Nazareth House, I was an undesirable party guest. I was given a lift home in total silence and, as I got out of the car, I heard Julia's father say, 'Well, at least, I suppose, she was well-behaved.' Prejudice and ignorance alive and well.

There was definitely a change from that day on at school. I was no longer Susan with the little pony-tail, I was her from the home, who didn't tell the truth about where she lived in order to get an invite to a party. And it was to get worse before it got better.

That day in class we knew something was going on, because our teacher was huddled in a corner with the head. We were all sitting quietly, waiting to find out what it was all about. I had no idea why, but one of the girls, Victoria, kept looking at me with what I can only describe as a smug look on her face. It was beginning to frighten me just a little. Still, all this had nothing to do with me, so I ignored her. The head teacher left the room, and I was called out by the teacher in front of the whole class and shown a book, Victoria's book, which had been scribbled all over with bright-coloured crayons.

'Is there something you want to tell me, young lady?' asked the teacher.

'No.'

'No what?'

'No, there's nothing I want to tell you.'

'I meant, you should say, "No, Miss Hunter."'

'No, Miss Hunter.'

The children behind me were beginning to giggle, and the teacher was not stopping them.

'Why did you destroy this book?'

'I didn't, I didn't –'

'You were seen. Own up now.'

That was the moment in life, as young as I was, that I understood the pain of being accused of something I had not done. I simply could not understand why the teacher did not immediately say, 'Very well, that's fine,' and understand that I would never have done such a thing.

I was humiliated in front of a classroom of children, all for something I did not do and never would have done, and this by an adult, a teacher who was constantly talking about the value of being polite and respectful. That obviously didn't include the teachers to the children – or at least not if you were *her from the home*.

The tears were running down my face and I was sobbing, but the teacher just stood there with the book in her hand, saying she would wait as long as it took for me to own up to this atrocity. No way, not a chance I was going to do that, so I was sent to the head teacher's office to explain myself. She smiled at me, which made me feel a little better, and asked me to sit down. She began to explain very sweetly that we all made mistakes from time to time, and for many different reasons, but once you had owned up to them you could move on and be forgiven, and it was time to put all nonsense aside and do just that. So I said I was sorry, was duly forgiven and promised that my mother would not be told about the incident – as long as it was not repeated, of course. I was to pray for forgiveness for five minutes then return to my class. Victoria and her friends continued to laugh and point at me for the rest of the day. If the teacher had taken even a moment to think, she would have realized that I had been set up. Instead she simply shook her head and said, 'Stupid child. Still, it's no more than I would have expected.'

In all these years, I don't think I have ever quite recovered from this incident, which is still perfectly clear in my mind, and I am to this day outraged by anyone who does not and will not believe me when I tell them the truth.

It was a few years after this that one of the girls in my class, who I was then friendly with, told me that it had indeed been a set-up and that Victoria herself had done it. I made a pact with myself that day. I would always try to be strong enough to take the rap for any indiscretions or mistakes I had made, but I would fight tooth and nail before apologizing ever again for something I had not done.

Our Margy

Our Margy was so cool. The height of fashion, long brown hair, slim, and a whole four years older than me. I just wanted to be her. There were always friends, girls *and* boys, knocking on the door for her, and they would all sit on the wall outside the house with her, chatting and laughing.

I would keep disappearing to go to the bedroom window and watch, fascinated, and sometimes she would let me go down and join them.

I would quiz her for hours about who the boys were, what their names were, and she would tell me all about them and which ones she liked the best.

Our Margy was amazing: she knew everything. One Thursday, I remember, we were both very excited because the corner shop was selling new crisps – and hey! not any old crisps, hold on to your hats . . . these were cheese-and-onion-flavoured crisps. The whole country was going crazy about them. It was so old hat to eat the plain bags of crisps that had a little blue packet of salt inside to sprinkle all over them (Oh, how health conscious we were in the sixties!). Now, you had to be seen with a bag of cheese and onion in your school satchel.

Every Thursday after school I would go to Aunty Tilly's for tea, and Mum would come along later when she had finished work. Every second Thursday we would stay over, as Mum now had a morning off on a Friday. I would always look forward to these sleepovers.

I would spend these evenings following our Margy about and asking hundreds of questions. Naturally, she always wore the latest fashions, and I would plead with her to keep her clothes and let me have them when she outgrew them. I was always one season out of fashion of course, but who cared? I thought I was the bees' knees in our Margy's clothes.

One particular fashion was the most incredible, wonderful invention I had ever seen. It was called a bloomer suit. This was a silky dress with splits up the side and a pair of matching silk shorts underneath. Every magazine was displaying models wearing these, and I just couldn't wait to own one. I turned to Mum, who said no before I had even had the chance to finish my sentence.

'Well, Twiggy is only sixteen, and she wears the latest trends,' I remember saying.

'And you,' said Mum, 'are not Twiggy. Now I don't want to hear another word.' Mum may have been angry, but she wasn't as angry as I was

I wanted to be a fashion icon. How was I supposed to get famous if I didn't have the latest in high-street fashion? I stomped off in what I can only describe as a teenage huff to see our Margy, who would understand exactly how I felt. I sighed, watching her. There she was in her bedroom, measuring all her skirts to ensure they were six inches above the knee.

'Mini-skirts,' she told me. 'It's the latest trend.' And we

sat there on her bed while she told me all about designers like Mary Quant.

It was all very well, but I wanted a bloomer suit. However, Margy may have been cool and fun, but she was also fair. 'You know, I think it might just be that Aunty Nancy can't afford one. Mum got mine out of the catalogue for my birthday, otherwise I don't think I would have one either.'

I felt ashamed. No one knew more than me how Mum struggled to make sure I had everything I needed. I would make it up to her later and never mention it again. We lay on the bed, our Margy taking her skirts up and me absorbing everything I could in her magazines.

There it was on page six, the answer to all my problems. Be your own designer, make it yourself. In my mind I went through every single dress I owned, and I knew at last I had the right one – and just the occasion for it. Mum would be so thrilled I had been so inventive! Friday night, out came the dress from the wardrobe, and I spent the whole evening cutting and sewing. It was wonderful. Mary Quant, eat your heart out, love!

Every summer, the whole of Aunty Tilly's street went on a trip to Seaham, where there was a fun fair. It was always the most wonderful day. We all had our tickets in advance for the rides and were travelling to the Haymarket bus station in Newcastle, where there was a special bus to the fair.

No one was going to believe how trendy I was this year, I thought. I had borrowed a pair of cool sunglasses and a beaded bag from one of the staff to go with my designer outfit, and I could hardly breathe with the anticipation. I hurried off to get ready. Mum and I were going to meet Aunty Tilly and the girls in Newcastle. I lifted my outfit carefully out of the wardrobe. My own creation. Just think where this could lead! Other people might like me to make one for them. Maybe I could be a famous fashion designer.

I was ready. The side seams weren't quite perfect, but they would have to do. I put the glasses on, slung the bag on my shoulder and strutted to the TV room, where Mum was chatting with some of the staff and Sister Evangeline was reading to the children.

Head held high, I made my entrance. Unfortunately, I couldn't see anyone properly because the glasses were so dark. However, I did notice the deafening silence when I entered. I waited, not too sure whether this was the response I had expected.

'*What in God's name?*' shouted my stunned mother.

There were a few stifled giggles in the background.

I was beginning to wonder what their problem was. Maybe, I thought, I should remove the glasses, but I was a little afraid of what I might see. I needn't have worried. The glasses were removed for me, then the handbag.

'Do we have a mirror in our bedroom, Susan?' Mum asked.

I nodded.

'And did you actually manage to look in it?'

'I made it myself —'

One of the staff burst out laughing, unable to control herself any longer. Even Sister Evangeline had her hand over her mouth to stop herself from laughing.

Apparently, a pink, straight, flowered dress split up the sides to the armpits with bottle-green knickers underneath was not acceptable attire. To be fair, though, I *had* sewn a couple of pink flowers on to my knickers.

I turned on my heel to leave with as much dignity as I could muster. Honestly, some people have no imagination.

Changes

It was now 1965 and major changes were taking place. This was the swinging sixties and although, in general, single parenthood was still very much considered a disgrace, there were also the beginnings of a new world, where girls were fighting back against prejudice and ignorance and keeping their children. Welfare benefits for single mothers had recently been introduced and there was a change of mood in the country. The sixties was a time of standing up for what you believed in, flower power and free love. I was ten years old and didn't really understand it all, but there was always our Margy to keep me up to date.

Nazareth House was also changing, and what used to be the old laundry building was converted into a mother and baby home. Not all of these mothers were being forced to give up their babies. Instead they were given somewhere to live with their little ones while housing and benefits advice were organized for them. Others stayed with their babies until they were adopted.

Nazareth House was not always as full of children as it used to be. There were now 'family group homes' where children of all ages were placed temporarily while waiting to be found foster homes or adoptive parents, or until their parents were ready to take care of them. These were ordinary houses in ordinary streets, and the idea was to bring these children up in a family atmosphere.

My thoughts during this time were focussed on the bullying I was receiving at school. It was never-ending, and something I still kept to myself, every day, safe in the knowledge that I would be sent to a different comprehensive school to the rest of my class. I was determined to fail my 11+ exam to make sure of this.

It would, of course, have been simpler to tell Mum, Aunty Tilly or our Margy what was going on, but the fear that had been instilled into me that I wouldn't be believed was enough to keep me quiet. I hadn't forgotten the episode with the colouring book.

Today, Mum was waiting for me at the top of the drive, which was very unusual. She said she wanted to talk to me about a big change in our lives. That day, Mum had been for an interview at a family group home for the role of house mother to twelve children. They were aged between two and fifteen, and it was a wonderful opportunity for her, she said, and more money. There was only one problem.

'I am so sorry,' she said, 'but it means changing schools. Fenham is simply too far away. The other children in the home go to a very good school in Walker, and you could go with them.'

I could have burst with joy. I flung my arms round Mum and told her that I would very much love that and that, as long as we were together, everything would be fine. I never really gave Mum's job or the new home we would be moving to before my eleventh birthday a second thought – all I cared about was leaving school and being with other children my own age who were all going to the same school. I wouldn't have to fail my 11+, and deal with Mum being annoyed about it; I could work and take a glowing report to my new school in Walker. Unfortunately, in the event, I still failed my 11+ and my report wasn't exactly glowing, but who cared? I was all set and ready for my new adventure.

A New Job

Both Mum and I loved our new home at once. Mum, I suppose, had been worried that it would be a wrench for me. After all, Nazareth House had been the only home I had ever known and, on top of settling into a new school and making new friends, she must have wondered if I'd be able to adapt. Of course she never really knew how I'd react to anything. She always thought I lived with my head in the clouds. She needn't have worried, though. I was perfectly happy and loved my new school, and I couldn't stop talking about Elaine, my new best friend. I thought she was perfect in every way. I also got on well with the children in the house. Life was good for both of us and Mum was very happy.

She was greatly valued in her new role as house mother, and took to it quickly. The home was two houses with interconnecting doors, and one side of the house was for the girls and the other for the boys, with a common lounge and dining room. Mum made it quite clear – of course! – to all the children when she first started that she would accept no nonsense from them, but at the same time she listed all the good things they could do together. 'Just wait and see,' she said.

'What happens if we're naughty?' asked Gary, one of the younger children. 'What happens if we're bad?'

'Listen,' said Mum – or Aunty Nancy, as she'd soon become known to them. 'Listen, all of you. Firstly, I will not have the word "bad" used. You are not bad, it is simply the behaviour that is unacceptable. You are still good. And I do not expect anything special, just polite behaviour and for you to do what I ask you. Is that understood?'

'So I'm not bad, Aunty Nancy?'

'No, Gary, you are not bad.'

'Well, can we watch *Match of the Day*, then, because we're not allowed to now?'

We all waited while Aunty Nancy thought about it.

'Very well,' she said. 'I am going to have to trust you in advance, as I believe it is on tonight.'

'It is,' everybody said, and held their breath, waiting.

'You understand I am trusting you in advance, therefore you must not let me down?'

Lots of little heads nodded.

The tradition started there and then: Saturday night was *Match of the Day*, and the boys were allowed to stay up. They were extra thrilled that very first night when Mum came in with a trolleyful of sandwiches, biscuits and juice. She had gained their respect and, from then on, they all loved their Aunty Nancy.

Qualifications

I was doing very well in my dancing competitions and had won lots of medals, but I still talked about being an actress. Other people did it. Other people had dreams and got famous. You didn't have to have lots of money, just lots of talent, and you had to work very hard. Mum hadn't been surprised when at the last open evening at school they had said that drama was my favourite subject and that I was very good at it. The class teacher apparently said that if I worked as much as I talked and dreamed I would be a very good student. Mum wasn't very pleased by that!

Mum wanted to tell me I would succeed, of course she did. Any parent who loves their child as much as Mum did me wants their child to know from day one that wishes really do come true if you believe hard enough and that it is those who persevere day after day that eventually achieve their goals.

Mum wanted to do this, but she couldn't. This was long before any self-help books were published, long before motivational speakers talked about fighting for what you wanted and told inspirational stories of those who had achieved greatness just by believing it would happen.

Mum couldn't tell me these things because, quite simply, she didn't know how. Never in her whole life had

anyone told her that things would be all right, that she was
something special and was going to achieve great things.
Life was hard, and that's just the way it was. If you dreamed
a dream you were heading for a fall, and nothing had ever
proved otherwise. No one person was ever going to hold
Mum's hand and take all her worries away, telling her that,
no matter what happened, they would stand by her side.
You just had to get on with it. Mum had given her heart to
children that no one wanted, loved or felt able to handle.
She knew that children needed not only a cuddle (that was
never enough), they needed to understand the bound-
aries, to have good manners, to know how to show and
earn respect – and yes, even as children, they deserved to
be treated fairly. Even the youngest of children received
this talk from Mum, and in a way they could understand.
She would cry silent tears for the children who kicked and
screamed when they were brought to her. She never quite
understood why, after they had been hurt and neglected,
they would still prefer to stay with 'our mam' or 'wor
Billy', who had never and never would give them any love
at all. Mum would try with all her heart to help them feel
safe, wanted, special, when she tucked them up in bed and
they were crying for those left behind.

Some parents, however, were simply unable to cope,
very often through no fault of their own. Mum was determined not only to help the children but the parents, and
this new job at the family group home was a chance to do
just that. She was already doing her best in the case of one
child in her care and fighting the mother's side.

Laura had been unable to cope after being left a single

parent and trying to hold down a job to make enough money to make ends meet. There were no extras or pretty clothes for her little girl, but Laura refused to believe that anyone could love her more than she did, so she fought and battled on until, eventually, with all the extra hours at work and not enough to eat for herself, she collapsed at work. Her daughter, Sally, was taken into care. Unfit mother, they said; no food in the cupboards, out at work all the time and the child left with a neighbour. No one listened, they just judged and condemned. Until Mum, that is, who held Laura's hand when she came to visit and gave her cups of tea, and listened and heard when Laura told her about having been forced to give up her daughter, about people telling her she was selfish to keep her, and how much better off the child would be with someone else.

'How,' said Laura, 'does money make you a better parent? I work hard, and I may not have much money, but what I have will always be used to feed my daughter. And no, I can't buy the latest books, but just a few weeks ago I took some paper from work that nobody wanted and Sally and I made our own book with our own story and spent hours colouring it all in. Oh, Nancy, please don't let them take that away from me. I'll try so hard. Please help me.'

There was to be a case conference the next day, and Nancy was ready for them. One of the social workers was newly qualified and ready to make her mark on the world.

Full of herself, thought Nancy, on meeting her for the first time.

The social worker was rustling importantly through her papers, then she looked at Nancy with a haughty expression on her face.

'And your qualifications are –?'

Nancy looked up and raised her eyebrows, but she didn't speak. Oops, thought Michael, one of the social workers who worked with the people housed in family group homes, she really shouldn't have done that. This was going to be an interesting meeting. He had the greatest respect for Nancy and even as head of department he would never have spoken to her that way. He smiled to himself. 'I don't think I would have dared,' he said to one of the nuns later. 'She had the most incredible way of putting you in your place without even speaking.'

Nancy still didn't speak and the social worker was beginning to look a little uneasy. Nancy looked over at Michael, who smiled at her, still amused as to what she would do.

Nancy placed her hands on her hips, chin in the air and looked the social worker straight in the eye. 'My qualifications, young lady?

'Fifty years of loving, giving, teaching and caring for children of every age and race, whatever the circumstances. A knowledge that can only be gained from experience, not learned. The capacity to understand the situation from every single angle, not only the one that we think we can see. I have looked into the eyes of hundreds of parents and children and I know the truth when I see it and, young lady, no qualification in any college in any country will teach you that one. I value justice being done, and today Sally needs to be returned to her mother. What Laura needs is constructive help and, in my world, any parent who fights to keep her child out of love and works every hour God sends to ensure they stay together is to be congratu-lated, not condemned.'

Nancy stood up then and looked at Michael. 'You gave me this job because of my experience, not because of any qualifications on paper. You believed in me, so trust me. I know what I am doing and I suggest you finish this meeting soon so we can all get on. I know I am extremely busy today.' And with that, No-nonsense Nancy stood up, nodded and left the room and the meeting.

Laura got her child back and, ten years later, a wedding invitation was posted to 'Aunty Nancy' from Sally, hoping she would attend as a guest of honour in thanks for not only her kindness to Sally in the short time she had been in her care but also for her belief in her mother, who had been her rock and was very proud to be the person walking her daughter down the aisle. 'Thank you, Aunty Nancy,' she wrote. 'You saw in my mum something no one else did, and we will never forget that.'

Mum and I both went to Sally's wedding, and we had a great day. On the way home that evening Mum told me the whole story. Sometimes, she said, you have to trust your instincts, because, when you see and hear the truth, it is very beautiful indeed.

The New Wellies

So, I had a best friend at last. Elaine, she was called, and she had the most amazing auburn hair. I was totally in awe of her; she always had trendy clothes and the most amazing yellow jumper. Most importantly, Elaine couldn't have cared less where I came from or who I was. All that mattered was that we made each other laugh. She was such a clever girl too but also very shy, and she hated being the centre of attention in any way. In class, when Elaine was asked a question, if I thought she was struggling I would immediately answer to save her embarrassment, and on one particular parents' evening Mum was told that if I worked as hard as I talked I would be an A-class student and would she please remind me that I was not a mouthpiece for Elaine? Oops! In trouble again.

This was a wonderful time for me, thanks to Elaine. At last, I had a friend whom I could trust with all my dreams and, in forty-six years, she has never let me down. Sometimes I think I must have done something really good to deserve her in my life. Oh, she was funny, though, and her shyness was something I struggled to understand. Bless her, she was once told off in class and made to stand in the corner. She blushed so much even her legs went red, and I laughed so much I was sent outside to calm down. She was, and still is, one of the sweetest and kindest people I have ever known. Forty-six years after we first met, we are still the greatest of friends. She has been my support through so much, and we still spend many hours looking back and laughing.

Oh, my heart was singing tonight, though! Finally, it was my turn to be the trendsetter. Tomorrow was going to be an incredible day, a red-letter day, one I would remember for ever. You see, tomorrow, at school, I was going to be the belle of the ball. Yes, me! I had new wellies – but, wait for it, this is cutting-edge stuff – they had zips! This was fashion at its highest. I didn't walk to school that day, I strutted like I was a supermodel gliding down the catwalk, placing one foot delicately in front of the other. Well – almost! I tripped up and ended face first in Mrs Higgins's hedge, but hey ho! I had new wellies and I was the Queen of Fashion!

Man in a Black Coat

Why does Christmas pull on the heartstrings so much? Is it because for some it's a time of suffering and loneliness but for others a time of joy and happy endings?

I don't know why, but this particular Christmas sits in my mind. I think I must have been about twelve years old. I remember, I was sitting with Mum and some of the children from the family group home at the Midnight Mass carol service on Christmas Eve. Their families weren't there. The parents or family members of some were in prison; some were sick; others were not allowed to look after their children for one reason or another; others were simply unable to cope.

My Christopher would be with his family tonight and I wondered for a moment how Christmas would be celebrated in Ghana. As I did every Christmas since he had left, I wondered if he would remember me. Mum got letters from Danny, keeping us up to date, yet, years later, the loss of Christopher still hurt. He was older now, but he would have understood. I could have told him, without any guilt, how I missed his unconditional love. Often, still, I would hold my own hands and pretend he was still there with me.

I remember the choir was singing 'Silent Night', and, as I looked around, I could see that these children were happy, even though they had every reason to be sad. They had seen all the presents around the tree, Mum had let them all help with the preparations for Christmas dinner the next day, ensuring they were involved, and they were all looking forward to a fantastic day. So what was my problem? I watched all the couples in the church, who seemed to be either holding hands or smiling at each other, and all the parents with children on their knees. Midnight Mass always made me cry, and Mum never understood why. 'You are such a little drama queen,' she would laugh, and I would laugh too, but it hurt. I wanted what those other families had.

Across from me there was a father with two young children on his knee, and each time Mum was busy looking after the other children I took the chance to look over and watch him. He had a black woollen coat on and his wife a red one with gold buttons. That is how much notice I was taking, and how strongly implanted that Christmas Eve is in my memory. I wondered for a moment if Dad, Eileen and their daughter, Jane, were at Midnight Mass and looking like that. Does Dad wish I was there too? I wondered, and at that moment Mum took my hand. 'You all right?' she asked.

Can you even begin to understand how selfish I felt at that moment? Next to me sat my mum, who had loved me from the moment I was placed in her arms and would give anything to make me happy. How unbelievably hard it is to know that you have everything in the world in front of you and yet somewhere inside a pain so bad it threatens to ruin everything in your world. I smiled at Mum, and said, '"Silent Night" always makes me want to cry.'

'Me too, darling,' she said.

I made a promise to myself that night. Sometime in the future I was going to be that lady over there with the husband in the black coat. He would look at me like that and I would bounce my children on my knee. During the second verse of 'Silent Night' he would put his arm around me, just like this man did to his wife. He would love me, protect me, be kind to me even when I got things wrong and burnt the tea, like I did last week when I was helping. He would laugh with me but, most of all, he would love me unconditionally. It would be all right if I made a mess of things because he would accept me for who I was. Mum said miracles happened when you least expected them, so one day he would just be there, and it wouldn't matter if I was Nancy's child – if I was unwanted, wanted, clever, stupid, beautiful, average – he would ask me to marry him because he loved me, and I would finally be accepted, and he would never criticize me because he would know that was what hurt me the most. He would know there is no greater pain than trying your best and having only your failures pointed out. He would know that all I had ever wanted out of life was to belong. To truly belong to a family where I was valued, needed and respected, even if I wasn't perfect.

I closed my eyes that night and prayed so hard that I would get it right and be a good enough person, always remembering and fighting against the voices in my head that said I was worth nothing, that I would never amount to anything and, most of all, that I was unwanted. I may have been only twelve years old but, of course, in my heart of hearts, I already knew better than that. Still, though, even now, the smallest criticism reminds me of those hateful words and the pain they caused me.

The choir was still singing 'Silent Night'. He would make everything all right, he would make life safe, he would love me unconditionally. I closed my eyes and prayed to God to bring me my very own man in a black coat.

Gratitude and Guilt

When I woke up that day there was nothing to show that this would be different from any other Saturday when, hail, rain or shine, we would have our weekly trip to Newcastle, regardless of whether we needed anything or not. 'Window-shopping', Mum called it. 'Completely pointless', I called it. Secretly, though, even as a teenager I still loved our cuppa and cake in Fenwick's, and today Mum said she was feeling particularly flush and we could have lunch there too. So there we were, enjoying a cheese omelette and planning which shop would be graced by our presence next.

Fate deals us a strange hand sometimes, and this was particularly true today. Billy and Eileen didn't often shop in Newcastle, but it was such a lovely sunny Saturday, and a day out seemed like a good idea. They both worked hard and it was rare that they got a day off together, so lunch in town and a browse around the shops sounded like fun.

Molly was also in Newcastle that day, not for a fun day out or lunch but for a double shift at work. It had been a long day already and she had been on her feet for what seemed like hours.

All she could think of was getting home, putting her feet up and having a cuppa.

She saw him as soon as he walked through the shop door. She would have recognized him anywhere. My goodness, he hadn't changed much at all, just looked a little older — but then didn't they all? Her heart was racing. She should look away, really she should, but still she looked. Susan, where was Susan? Was she with him? The woman with him was obviously his wife. Molly knew Susan would be fourteen years old now. And, probably, like her own children, a day out shopping with their parents would be the last thing they would choose to do. Maybe Susan was at home, but the two of them were looking around, as though for someone else. Molly's hands were shaking. Was she about to see the daughter she had given away all those years ago? What had they told her? What would she say? What did Susan look like now?

She had imagined the reunion with her daughter over and over again, but not like this. It should be in a beautiful place with them throwing their arms around each other, crying tears of happiness. Oh, it was so much nicer that way. Not like this. Molly had to get away quickly. She turned to her colleague and said she was feeling sick, and moved to leave the counter.

Too late. Billy turned and looked straight into her eyes.

'Molly!'

'Billy.'

'How are you?' they both said together.

Pleasantries were exchanged to cover the awkwardness. Eileen was introduced and it was explained that they were having a day out with their daughter, Jane. So that's who they were looking round for earlier, thought Molly. A million thoughts were rushing around her head. Where was Susan? Should she ask? Would she be able to forgive herself if she didn't? It was amazing, she thought, that she could smile and chat easily with all these thoughts running through her mind. Jane joined them then and was introduced.

They chatted for a few moments longer then said their goodbyes, wished each other well and turned to go their separate ways.

'How is Susan?' Molly blurted out.

Billy turned back. 'She's fine, Molly. Fourteen years old now, you know.'

'Yes, I know. I haven't forgotten.'

'No, well, take care, Molly.'

There were hundreds more questions begging for an answer, but Billy was gone. A nudge in the ribs brought Molly back to the job in hand. They were busy and her colleagues were asking if she was OK. She forced a smile and went back to work.

Fate, however, had not yet finished with these families that day.

Billy walked out of the store, and straight into Mum and me.

I was always thrilled to see my sister, Jane, who I liked very much, and after saying hello to Dad and Eileen, she and I stood to one side to have a chat. We were deep in conversation when for a moment I looked up and saw Mum's face. Now there's an expression I recognize, I thought. Lips pursed, chin in the air and the no-nonsense attitude well in attendance. What on earth was Dad telling her?

Goodbyes were said and promises made to meet up soon, in the summer holidays, and we all went on our way.

This is when the dithering began. Now this was a very unusual situation: dithering was most definitely my department, not Mum's. Eventually, I said, 'Are we or are we not going into this shop?'

'Well. Yes . . . no . . . erm, maybe.'

I was shocked: Mum was being indecisive. It was really rather funny. Funny, that is, until two hours later we were still window-shopping and the novelty of our Saturday outing was wearing extremely thin.

I never gave cheek but, on this occasion, having had quite enough, I said, 'For goodness' sake, can we just go home? I'm absolutely exhausted.'

'Well, all right,' said Mum, still dithering. Honestly, what was the matter with her? 'Just one more shop,' she said.

'Just one more shop' indeed!

Mum told me later that her heart was pounding. What was she playing at? What she was doing was utterly ridiculous and not in the least rational . . . however, one step in front of the other, she was walking towards the shop.

Then she paused. 'Just being nosy . . . this is ridiculous.'

'Mum?'

'Sorry, love.' Oh no, she thought, did I really say that out loud? They had reached the department where Molly worked now. Oh well. Here goes.

There was no mistaking her. Susan was her absolute double. Nancy was horrified at what she was doing. This is wrong, so wrong, she thought, and this was confirmed when Susan left her

*side and walked straight towards the counter where Molly stood.
Nancy was rooted to the spot. It took all her resolve not to scream
out 'NO!'*

*And so, after fourteen years, mother and daughter faced each
other, neither one knowing who the other was. Susan thought the lady
was pretty, Molly thought the girl was polite, and how lovely that she
was out shopping with her mum, who was now calling for her.*

'Susan! Susan!'

'Coming, Mum.'

*Molly's eyes welled up. This was just too much, on top of every-
thing else.*

'Nice name,' she said.

*Susan smiled at Molly. 'Thank you,' she said, then walked over
to her mum, linked arms with her and left the shop.*

*Nancy was immediately filled with guilt. I can't think why I did
that, she thought. What on earth was there to achieve by looking at
Molly? It was unforgivable. What if she had recognized Susan?
No, that was ridiculous. Still, she felt so guilty. Life was so strange.
Who would believe that all three families would meet in the same
place at almost the same time? Well, thought Nancy, that's what you
get when you let your emotions run away with you. And I'm so lucky,
Susan and I are so close, even though she's a teenager now and is
growing up so quickly. Nancy was just glad and grateful that Susan
had noticed nothing. Lesson learned, she thought to herself. Be
thankful everything is still all right, and think no more of it.*

I knew of course only too well that something had happened that day and that it had to do with what Dad had

said to Mum. Of course, if Mum didn't want to tell me about it, that was the end of it.

As for Mum putting that day behind her, well, that was easier said than done. Molly's image haunted her after that day: she hadn't missed the look on her face when she had called out my name. Susan.

As for Molly, she was rushed off her feet for the rest of the day and it wasn't until she finally sat down on the bus for her journey home that she allowed herself to think about how she felt. It had been a shock, that was certainly true – for a moment today she had thought she might see her daughter. She thought about Susan often, of course, and especially on her birthday. Oh well, nearly home now, so she turned her thoughts forward to her husband, who would have the kettle on, and her four other children, whom she loved dearly.

It was beginning to get dark and looked like rain. Molly smiled, thinking how strange things can be. Fancy that young girl being called Susan.

Guilty Secrets

It was completely silent. Tears make no sound when they fall. I was crying, the tears falling silently on to my cheeks and then dripping on to the sheets. There was no sobbing or screaming, no shouting or laboured breathing as the tears continued to fall. The screaming was inside, where the pain was fighting to be heard.

I thought about her that morning as soon as I woke up. I was fifteen years old today, and Mum had arranged a fabulous day for me, as she always did on my birthday. I wish I could have been more excited about the party and the presents. Instead, all I wanted was to be left alone to dream about her. Molly. Where was she? What was she doing? Did she remember me, or had she conveniently forgotten all about me? More and more these days, I found myself thinking about her, especially on my birthday, but there was no one I could tell. In fifteen years, no one had ever told me anything about her. Who was she? What were the circumstances when she had me? Why did she give me away? . . . Surely I deserved to know – but who was I supposed to ask? Not Mum, that was for sure. She'd be hurt after all she had done for me.

It had been the programme on TV the night before that had started me thinking. For some parents and children, the reunion was heart-warming and wonderful, yet, sadly, for others, the parents or children had their own lives to lead and did not want to be put into contact with each other. Maybe then it was better not to know? The idea of being rejected twice was unthinkable. Yet hadn't those children on the programme thought they were unwanted? And how amazing it was for me to realize that they had the same questions I did.

Last night, just before I went to bed, I looked in the mirror and wondered if I looked like her. Did she love music and dancing? What colour were her eyes? . . . I could have gone on for ever with my questions. I closed my eyes and pretended she was like those other mothers who had found their children and had cried tears of happiness at the reunion. I wanted to be one of those children. I wanted her arms around me. Suddenly, there were tears in my eyes. Not because Molly may have forgotten about me but because there was my mum downstairs, doing everything she could to make this a happy birthday for me. How ungrateful was I? As a young child, I was told I should pray for forgiveness and be grateful – after all, I had been born out of wedlock, which made me a bad child. Fortunately, it was 1970 now, and I knew this to be untrue, yet somewhere deep down in my subconscious, a part of this feeling still sits, waiting to be resurrected when I'm feeling vulnerable.

Who knew better than me, after being brought up in an orphanage, about all the children who never found the love I had been given? The guilt I felt was worse than any emotion I had ever experienced. The nuns must have been right: there must be badness deep inside me for me to think these thoughts. I couldn't cry today, I couldn't be that selfish; Mum had arranged a lovely birthday party for me and friends were coming for tea. Maybe, though, there was one person I could talk to. Elaine. She would know what to do. I put on a brave face and went ahead and enjoyed my day.

Honestly, I deserved an Oscar for my performance that day. Not one single person knew that, secretly, I felt sad. Except, of course, Elaine, who at the end of the day, after saying goodbye, said to me, 'Great party! You can tell me what the matter is tomorrow.'

The next day Elaine's answer was quite simple: ask your dad — surely he knows. She was right, of course, and I immediately realized that this was a great idea, especially as, during the summer holidays, I was going to spend a long weekend with him, Eileen and Jane.

The days passed so slowly until then, and all I could think of was Molly. Could it possibly be that Dad could give me answers? I assumed that he had never told me anything because he had no knowledge, but there had to be things he did know, like the colour of her hair, her eyes, her likes and dislikes. I prayed every day: Please let me know a little about her, and please forgive me for even wanting to know. This was a very difficult time for me, and I had never felt so confused, excited or guilty in my entire life.

After what seemed like months, it was finally time to go to Dad's. Mum saw me off at the railway station with, as usual, a hundred do's and don't's. I always had to reassure her how much I loved her on these occasions when I was to spend time with Dad and curb the excitement I felt at spending time with him. Poor Mum! I looked out of the window as the train pulled away and saw her beautiful face smiling up at me as she hurried along with the train, waving to me as if she wasn't going to see me for months. I would be home again in three days, but still my heart swelled with love for her. I sat back and wondered what on earth I had been thinking, I had so much already – but I was determined to learn more this weekend.

Dad had a great weekend planned, which started with a family meal out. There was lots of lovely food, laughing and catching up. This still didn't stop me from wondering when I would get my chance to talk to him, though. I finally got up the courage to ask much later that night, when we were sitting chatting in the cottage in front of a roaring coal fire.

'Dad, I was just wondering if you could tell me anything about Molly – but please don't tell anyone I asked.'

'I will tell you anything you want to know, Susan,' he said. 'In fact, just wait there a moment . . .'

He was gone ages, and I was worried. My hands were shaking and my heart was beating so fast. I sat there in the semi-darkness in front of the coal fire trying not to think about Molly but praying that, at long last, I might learn something.

Then Dad tapped me on the shoulder. 'There you go,' he said, and he handed me a photo of Molly, my birth mother. At last, after all this time, there she was. I couldn't speak. I just stared at the photo. She looked so much like me. She was sitting on a rock on a hillside, with her head thrown back, laughing. I loved her. I loved her with all my heart and soul. She was me, my mother: same eyes, same face, same expression. Dad and I sat there in the firelight in total silence.

'When I look at you, I see her,' he said. 'The likeness is uncanny.'

Still, I could not speak.

'She wanted you, but she already had a child, called Sarah. You must understand, Susan, in those days she would have been thought an unfit mother to be pregnant again, outside marriage, and she was so afraid of losing Sarah, who was three years old then. It's so different now. Back then she had no choice, but I know she loved you. She begged her parents to let her spend time with you, and she had you for six days.'

At last I found my voice. 'What was she like?'

Dad laughed. 'She was fun. Had a lovely singing voice, was a bit of a drama queen, and she loved to dance.'

I felt that I couldn't take my eyes off the photograph, but eventually I looked up and said, 'I wonder where she is now.'

'I don't know where she lives,' said Dad, 'but she was working in Marks and Spencer's last year – but then you know that.'

'Sorry? What do you mean?'

'You know – that day we met in town. I assume Nancy told you that Molly was working in Marks and Spencer's there?'

I felt as though I was holding my breath. I was shocked, numb. After a while I broke the silence.

'No, actually, I didn't know, Dad.'

'Oh well,' he said matter-of-factly. 'She looked well, and she has four other children now and seems very happy. I told her about you, that you were fourteen now and were doing really well.'

'Great,' I said. 'And thanks for the photo. I'm glad you told me.' Just say anything, I was thinking to myself. I needed to get away and be on my own.

Shortly afterwards I said goodnight and went to bed.

I have never since then or before felt so furious. Anger, frustration, a sense of injustice – it was all there. Did people not think I deserved to know? After all, she was my mother – my birth mother. Mum had given me every-thing, yet she and I would have never been together if Molly hadn't given birth to me in the first place. How many people had told me I wasn't wanted – or that I was a bad child, God forgive them. I could barely contain my fury but still I cried silently; I had to, I was sharing a room with my sister. I curled up in all the blankets and sheets, pushing them against my mouth and face so I would not be heard, and cried on and on.

When finally I began to calm down I at last understood what all the dithering that Saturday in town had been about, and what Dad had told Mum. I lay for hours trying to remember going into the shop but the only thing I could even vaguely recollect was being called away from the counter. I had no idea whether the woman there had been Molly or not. I seemed to remember a lady I thought was pretty. Still I cried, whether in anger, at the injustice or in sadness I can't remember – but I do recall the pain.

As morning drew near I knew I had to pull myself together. I thought about all the children who would never know one mum, never mind two, and began to feel horrendously ungrateful yet again. In any case, I had a plan, a really good plan.

I was fifteen years old now, and Mum often had to work at weekends at the family group home, so on the first Saturday I had free, myself and Elaine went into Newcastle. 'Well, here goes,' she said as we made our way into Marks and Spencer's. Poor Elaine. I dragged her round for at least two hours, to no avail. Over the next few months I tried going into the shop at different times on different days, hoping for a glimpse of her. I just knew I would recognize her if I saw her. What the plan was if I did see her was another matter altogether. I promised myself I just wanted to look and wouldn't say anything to her, in case I upset her.

I gave up after about six months. Obviously, she was no longer there and I was destined never to meet her. Over the next few years I never purposely went to Marks and Spencer's to find her. However, on the days I did shop there, I always looked out for her, just in case.

There were other ways, of course, I know that now, but then I was fifteen years old and had no one to talk to who could help me. I knew I had the most wonderful mum, Nancy, and she was everything a child could hope for, yet still, deep down inside somewhere, there was a longing, an emptiness, something missing. I did have the photograph, though, and every night I secretly said goodnight to my birth mother and kissed it. God bless Nancy and Molly, I would pray, one for being the kindest, most incredible mum any child could ever wish for, and the other for just being my mum. I hoped and prayed that she remembered me, and that God would forgive me for loving them both. Before I got up from my knees I would always slide my hand under the bed and hide my photograph once more under the carpet.

Patent-leather Shoes with a Black Bow

It wasn't the greatest of starts. It could have been worse, but then it could have been better. Who, I wonder, decides which one of us will be born to a life of privilege, and who will not? By privilege I don't mean wealth and all it brings – a big house, nannies, tables full of food, the best schools, the latest in clothes – but the certain knowledge from the day you are born that you are wanted, needed and loved unconditionally, that there is someone who from that moment on will always feel you are wonderful, regardless of whether you become a success or a failure.

'Unconditionally' is the important word here. It means that no matter what happens – if we get it wrong, don't turn out the way you want us to, try our hardest but still don't succeed – there you are, still loving us and telling us that it's all right, there's always a next time. And even if there isn't a next time, who cares, because whatever happens, there you will be, standing by our sides, believing in us.

Of all my dreams in life, this was the one that mattered most, the one I would never give up on. I wanted someone to love me for who I was, not who I could possibly be. I decided early on in life that I would wait for the man in the long black coat who would pick me up and say,

'Hello there, it's me!' and take my hand, and I would live happily ever after. Must stop reading fairy tales!

It was to take many years before I realized that I was already surrounded by the kind of love that lasts for ever, blessed as I was with friends who would stand by my side through thick and thin. Some would let me cry on their shoulder and tell me I was a good person; others would laugh with me and tell me to get a grip – which, to be honest, did me the power of good.

I never felt pretty; my friends were always prettier than me. The first disco I went to, when I was fifteen years old, taught me that. The evening felt full of promise, and I had a new hairdo, a new dress and new shoes. I remember the shoes more than anything. They had high heels with little bows on the back, and were black patent leather so shiny you could see your face in them. I was so proud and felt very grown up in them. It followed of course that I would be the belle of the ball just by wearing them. All the boys would notice me. That night Elaine, as usual, looked absolutely amazing with her beautiful long auburn hair, now no longer wavy but straightened (with an iron and brown paper), and with legs up to her neck, shown off by her little mini-skirt.

We were grown up now and could be trusted to go to the disco and come back on our own with no nonsense. Fifteen years old, and I had been let out to a party on my own for the very first time! And don't forget I was wearing black patent-leather shoes with a bow.

We met at the bus stop in Walker outside the Turbinia pub, two very excited girls. I admired Elaine's straight hair and she admired my shoes. Neither one of us had ever even smelt, let alone drunk, alcohol before but maybe today was the day? After all, we were grown up now. It was decided we would go to the pub and have half a cider each before the party.

'Let's not link arms,' said Elaine. 'It makes us look young.'

'OK. Anything else?'

'Well, we should chatter as we're walking in . . . ooh, and I'll jiggle keys in my hand – our Janet does that – it'll look like we have car keys.'

'OK. We ready then?'

'Yes, let's go.'

We hovered a bit in front of the door and then – deep breaths – in we went, women of the world.

Side by side, each placing one foot delicately in front of the other, swinging our handbags, jiggling keys, chattering about something or other, we opened the door. I got as far as putting one foot with its new black patent-leather shoe through. The jukebox had just finished blasting out a song. The landlady turned her head to look at us. Momentary pause. We looked at each other then turned on our heels and ran as fast as our feet would carry us. We screamed with laughter all the way to the school disco.

This school disco was really my first chance ever to meet boys. The school I attended was a comprehensive for boys and girls, but it had separate buildings for the two. The boys had the gym, we had the swimming pool, and we got together only when necessary. This year, however, the powers that be had decided that the girls and boys should celebrate together, and the school Christmas party was arranged, creating much excitement among both boys and girls.

Tonight, with my new shoes, there came the possibility of meeting the man of my dreams. Elaine and I had visited the boys' building over the last few months with our class. We'd been taken to their newly equipped gym, where, I have to say, I think I got a bit carried away on the trampoline. I must have thought that I was ready for the Olympics and, causing much hilarity, got my nose stuck in the springs when my somersault went hopelessly wrong. Elaine laughed so much she was banished to the changing room. Tonight, though, was different: we were young ladies – groomed, sophisticated and totally hot stuff with our straightened hair and new shoes.

The boys we had watched through the windows of the swimming pool on the diving board were already at the disco, trying to look cool and failing miserably. We walked past, our noses in the air. Honestly, who did they think they were to us? We were so above them. We really felt like we were the queen bees.

After a few minutes, our favourite song, 'Spirit in the Sky', came on, and we were ready to take to the dance floor.

'Hey, you!' one of the boys shouted.

'Don't turn around,' said Elaine.

Too late. I turned, to see a group of boys on the edge of the dance floor, and smiled.

'You must have the worst pair of legs I have seen in my entire life,' said one, and the whole group burst out laughing. My heart sank. I knew of course that I was considered skinny, and I knew, looking around, that I was definitely not as pretty as some of the other girls, but still, there was always hope. Or there was until that moment.

The evening was ruined for me, but I pretended to enjoy myself, when all I really wanted to do was go home and hide my legs away for ever.

It meant that there was absolutely no nonsense that night, and I could eventually leave, to catch the bus home, back to Mum. I would be safe and sound with her. Mum was waiting for me and wanted to hear all about it. I remember I said I was very tired, refused any offers of supper or tea and made my way to the bedroom. Mum, as mothers do, knew there was something wrong straight away.

'Nothing bad happened, did it?' she said. 'Because if it did, you need to tell me.'

I wanted to tell someone, I really did. It had hurt so much; I didn't like being laughed at and humiliated. Today had held so much promise, and now I felt ridiculous. Tears pricked my eyelids. Mum would understand, I thought.

Looking back as a mother myself, Mum must have been so worried. God alone knew what had happened; she had gone through every possible horrendous scenario in her mind all night. She'd wanted to go with me to meet Elaine at the bus stop, but they'd all told her not to. 'How much do you want to embarrass her?' they'd said. 'She is a good girl, Nancy. Trust her and let her go'– and so she had.

So Mum must have been sweating, because she knew me well, as mothers do. Something had happened, and she wanted to know what it was.

'Mum, a boy said I had the most horrible legs he had ever seen in his life,' I said miserably.

There was a pause, then I heard her breathe a sigh of relief.

'Susan,' she said, 'just be grateful you have two of them,' and smiled to herself.

She didn't understand, after all.

I smiled at her, said goodnight and pretended everything was all right. It was only when she turned out the light that I let myself cry. I had been totally humiliated in front of everyone. Even with beautiful black patent-leather shoes with a bow on the back I still wasn't good enough. How was I ever going to find my man in the black coat with horrible legs that any decent man would laugh at? I vowed that night never to wear a dress again unless it was with boots so that my legs would be hidden. And I never have.

A Real Mum

I can honestly say that I do not know how it feels to want a child so much and to be told you are unable to have one naturally, or to go through treatments and spend every month waiting to see if you are finally on the way to being parents, only to be disappointed again and again. I know this can be the case for a lot of adoptive parents, and I can't find enough praise for you, or for anyone who takes on a child that is not their own, whatever their circumstances. I have heard these people say to their child time and time again, 'We were so lucky to get you.' Take it from me: it is us who are lucky to have *you*.

How hard that speech must be! That day you tell your child that they were adopted, wanting so much to make it easy for them, letting them know they were chosen and how special they are. I wonder how many say that they are not our real parents. But of course you are our real parents. You fought to have us, loved us, picked us up when we fell, comforted us when we cried at the school gates on our first day at school, coped with the teenage huffs, held our hands when our hearts were broken for the first time, cried at our weddings because you didn't know where the time had gone, scared that this might mean you lose a little piece of us that has always been yours. What's not real about that? You may not be our birth parents, but you are and always will be our parents: the mother and father who bonded with their child and made their lives and their family complete.

All we ask is that you don't make us feel guilty. That day when we find out you are not our birth parents doesn't make us stop loving you and wanting to spend the rest of our lives with you. You are and always will be our parents, yet somewhere inside us there are questions. Who do I look like? Does Mum/Dad think about me? Do I have brothers and sisters? Will I ever meet them? For me, over-coming this guilt was the hardest thing I ever had to face, this guilt I felt knowing that my mum had faced challenge after challenge, always keeping strong and making me feel truly wanted and loved, but still wanting to know about Molly, my birth mother. It was horrendous.

And of course there is another part to it – those mothers who have to give up their babies. I applaud their courage. I cannot for one single moment understand how you must have felt. For many of you, the choice was taken away from you, but your sacrifice has granted a kind, lov-ing soul somewhere the chance to have a child. What greater gift is there than that?

This was the day Mum would give that speech.

I was only small but I don't remember exactly how old I was when Mum tucked me up in bed one night, saying she had something to tell me. Never being one for great exhibitions of emotion, she simply took my hand and said, 'I have a story to tell you . . .

'When I was a little girl I used to see all the babies in their prams outside in the back lane and I could hear them cry and I would run up and rock the pram, always wondering why the baby was crying, and wanting to help. I asked God to send me lots of children, and so he did. I looked after all the children in the nursery and helped them to be happy until they went home or were adopted. Then one day a little baby only six days old was brought to the front door in the nuns' parlour. This was long before the baby home was built, and there was no room for the child. I was walking through the parlour and I heard a lady say that she couldn't keep the child and there was nowhere for the baby to go. Oh, Susan, my heart froze. Mother Superior did not look too impressed. There was a pause, and then Mother saw me, as I'd dared to come and have a look, but I couldn't see the baby, as it was bundled up in a blanket. I knew, though, that it must be really tiny. Mother looked at me and said, "Nancy, would you be prepared to take care of this child for the moment? I appreciate you already have a full nursery, and this child would have to be kept in your room so as not to disturb the others." I had said yes before she even finished the sentence, and I was holding my arms out, and Mother took the child and placed it in my arms. Susan, darling that was you. You were light as a feather, and all I could think of saying was, "It's a girl."

'"Her name is Susan," the lady said. I don't think I even looked at her; I simply couldn't take my eyes off you. Oh, you were so precious and so perfect. All I cared about was holding you and, just at that moment, you opened your eyes and looked at me. Susan, I knew then and there that you and I belonged together. We still do, and always will, but, my darling, I am not your real mum.'

'I don't understand. What do you mean, "real mum"?'

I don't remember how old I was, and Mum certainly wasn't going to talk about the birds and the bees just yet. It didn't matter anyway.

'You *are* my mum,' I said.

'Of course. And you are my daughter and always will be.'

That was enough for me. In that moment, I was perfectly happy to be Nancy's child.

Susan's Story

Angel in the Upstairs Flat

In June 1971 I turned sweet sixteen. I had a lovely birthday party, but the celebrations were also for Mum. We had been through so much, and we had survived. We both knew that the days were over when anyone could complain that she was being selfish and that I should be adopted or fostered. My father was never going to turn up and take me away. The truth is, he would never have done that, to either of us, but for Mum the threat had always been there. It was now my choice . . . but was she happy? Not really. Now no one could take me away from her for legal reasons, she worried that I would leave her of my own accord. 'Oh,' she said. 'You're all grown up now. Mrs Brown's daughter left home last week, and she was only seventeen.' Poor Mum. I only wish she could have seen into the future and known that from the very first day she had held me in her arms I was totally and utterly Nancy's child and she would always be a massive part of my life.

No one was going to take me away, but we did have a different problem now.

'Not again.' Mum sighed. 'Here we are, back at square one.' During our time together in the Nazareth House nursery, Mum was always being told that I shouldn't be there as I was too old, regardless of whether I was her daughter or not. It was only Mum's determination and threats to leave that kept me with her. Now, as my six-teenth birthday was approaching, Mum was being told that when I turned sixteen I would have to leave the family group home where Mum was a house mother, as all the other children did, and move into the girls' hostel and live there. The nuns who ran the home had tried to find a way round this but there simply wasn't one. My bed would have to be made available as soon as possible. Another child needed it.

I had just started my first job, as a receptionist, and was receiving a weekly wage of £25. I was actually rather enjoy-ing it, despite the fact that my first choice of career was to be an actress. The Careers Advice Bureau had almost laughed me out of the office when I told them that.

Mum was always telling me I needed to start being sen-sible and that the only way to get on in life was to keep my feet firmly planted on the ground. Well, that day when I left the careers office with an appointment for an inter-view as a receptionist I felt as though my feet were firmly planted in concrete boots. I didn't realize then how won-derful it would feel to be surrounded by positive and kind people who did everything they could to help me begin my career. It was fun too, they were a jolly bunch, and they took me to lunch at the nearby pub a couple of times a week, which I thought was such an adventure and a mas-sive treat. So it was just when things were going well that I came home to the news that I was surplus to require-ments yet again.

However, this time, I had the answer. 'Mum, why don't we get our own home? I'm working now and we could manage together,' I suggested. We talked for hours. We had never had to pay our own bills and manage our own home before, but as we talked, we began to get excited. We sat on in Mum's room late into the night, deciding on our plan of action. This would be a real adventure, the two of us together.

It was only three weeks later that Mum came hurrying to tell me we had been offered a flat in Beresford Road in Byker and that she had the keys. With the slip of paper grasped in her hand, we grabbed our coats and went in search of our very own first home.

We stood and looked up the steepest street I have ever seen. 'I reckon there's snow at the top,' I said, but Mum didn't laugh.

'Let's just pray number twenty-four is near the bottom, or we'll need mountain boots,' she replied.

Her prayers were answered – thank you! – number one was where we were standing, so number twenty-four wasn't far up. It had a green door, and we just stood there for a moment. Mum's hand was shaking as she tried to place the key in the door. The first thing I noticed was the cold – it was freezing! – and the wallpaper could not have been more hideous.

'Come on,' said Mum, with a smile pasted on her face that didn't fool me one bit. 'Let's have a look around.'

There was a long corridor, and to the left was a large bedroom with a gas fire. Straight ahead of us was the living room, which had a door into the second bedroom. We were both totally silent, neither of us able to think of anything to say.

I looked at Mum, and my heart went out to her. 'Look, Mum, this second bedroom is a lovely size,' I said, and put my hand out to lean on the wall. As I did so, all the plaster crumbled and dropped out from the bottom of the wall-paper, where it had come away from the wall with damp. Thank God for a sense of humour! We both started to laugh.

'Well, it's not exactly a palace, Susan. Never mind. Just you wait and see – I will have it homely in no time. It could be worse.'

How, exactly, I failed to see. It was worse already: it had an outside toilet and the kitchen consisted of a sink and benches. I was totally mortified. 'You mean I actually have to get up and go outside to go to the toilet?' I said.

'Well, I did when I was a child,' said Mum, starting to look nervous and upset.

'But it's so dirty and cold.'

We stood there in total silence, both desperately trying to think of something positive to say.

Then she was there, our saviour, the angel in the upstairs flat.

There are many heroes in this world, and many of them never receive any recognition or any reward, yet there they are, giving, caring, sharing, loving and helping us keep our sanity and our grip on life.

Our angel upstairs was also called Nancy. Her smile always flooded her eyes and she was one of those people who were always there when you needed them, happy to help, never complaining. Nothing was ever too much for her. She breezed into the room where we were standing, introduced herself and said, 'Come on upstairs. I have the kettle on and some sandwiches ready.'

We just stood there smiling, looking totally dumb-struck. 'Come on,' she said. 'Follow me,' and follow her we did.

Nancy had two small children, Dawn and Lisa, who were sitting in front of a roaring coal fire happily playing with their father, Alan. Nancy and Mum chatted without stopping and after about two hours we all felt like we had known each other for ever.

'Now don't you worry,' Nancy said. 'You two get your-selves away. Just leave the door open and I will do what I can.' She then listed the names of the neighbours, who had all asked who was moving in and did they need any-thing. I had never before and have never since met this kind of community spirit. The people living in this street had very little but what they had they were always willing to share. Everyone knew everyone else and if you sneezed in the front room at lunchtime, by tea time people were knocking on your door asking if you had a cold and offer-ing remedies. 'Curtain-twitchers', Mum used to call them, always lifting the corner of their net curtains to see what was going on, but inside every one of those houses lived people with hearts of pure gold.

We returned, as arranged, that evening after Mum had finished work. I have never in my life before or since been so totally and utterly taken aback. The first thing I noticed was the doorstep – it was gleaming. Who cleans door-steps, for goodness' sake! The door was open and there was a delicious smell coming from inside. Somehow,

Nancy upstairs had managed to beg, steal or borrow beds, bedding, an oven and a kitchen table. There was a wonderful warmth and glow from the fire, and there were piles of curtains in the corner and a couple of upright chairs. This is what I saw. Mum smelled the wonderful clean smell of bleach in what was now a spotless flat.

'Well, come on in then,' said Nancy from upstairs.

Now, it was no longer just a flat, a place to live in, it was a home, and Nancy had done this in one single day, and not for someone she knew, someone she cared about, not for relatives or friends, but for complete and total strangers. She gave me a massive hug, and I hugged her back. Now Mum, as I have previously said, is not one for public displays of emotion – in fact, she finds them hugely embarrassing. This didn't bother Nancy, though. She grabbed Mum, gave her a hug and said, 'Come on then, stick the kettle on. I'm gagging for a cuppa.'

We lived in that damp and falling-to-bits flat for two years, and loved it. I would come home from work and, before I had my key in the door, Nancy would be calling down, 'Come on up. I've kept you some tea. You must be starving.' Nancy, Alan, Dawn and Lisa would invite us along on their Sunday outings, and we would have a fantastic time. Mum often babysat for Nancy and we got to know the children really well. They had invited us not only into their family but into their hearts.

I look back now so thankful for Nancy's kindness and generosity. I loved her very much and count her as one of life's true heroes.

Two Bedrooms and a Box Room

No amount of love and caring, however, was going to keep those flats standing for much longer. After a while I shared a bed with Mum, as the walls in the other bedroom were crumbling and we were unable to light the gas fire in there. And the bathroom was a bit primitive: we really did have one of those massive tin baths you put in front of the fire and fill with buckets of water. Me having a bath in it was probably not a pretty sight, and most embarrassing, as I was a teenager now, but in some ways, climbing into a steaming tub of bubbly, hot water in front of a massive roaring coal fire was really rather pleasant.

Each morning before I left for work Mum would get up early, turn the cooker on to generate a bit of heat and fill the sink with hot water. Getting up when it was cold was never a pleasant experience, and going to a toilet outside when it was freezing was an utter nightmare.

Mum stayed positive throughout, though: we were managing, she said, and had a roof over our heads. It may have been a roof that was crumbling, had holes in it and was falling to bits, but it was a roof all the same.

Major building work had been going on for years now, most of the properties around us had been knocked down, and there were new-builds all around us. Nancy, Alan and the children had already been rehoused. Their house was lovely and we were constantly invited around for tea, and sometimes when Mum was at work in the evenings, I would go over to have a natter and a cuppa with Nancy.

Mum and I would talk for hours about what it would be like to live in a new house, so it was with great excitement that we tore open the letter from the council. It informed us that our flat had been declared uninhabitable and we were to be re-housed.

'Where is it, Mum?' I shouted excitedly. We looked at the address.

'Never heard of it,' she said, 'but it can't be far away.'

We grabbed our coats and went in search of this new-build. We went all around the estate where the new flats were but couldn't find the street anywhere. 'It's got to be here somewhere,' said Mum. 'We've got our confirmation letter, and it must be built or at least nearly finished, because we have an address.'

'You looking for somewhere?' said a voice.

Mum showed the lady the letter. 'It's over there,' said the lady. 'On the next estate, where the houses are.'

We thanked her quickly, unable to believe what she had just said.

'Surely not,' said Mum. 'A *house*? Can't be. Surely not.'

'Come on, Mum, it's just over there. Let's go and look.'

Our hearts were thumping. I may have been a teenager, but I grabbed Mum's hand and we walked slowly over to the next estate, neither one of us actually believing that we could have been offered a house. Brinkburn Street – we were here. We walked along the street looking at the numbers, and there we were standing outside our beautiful new home. We peered through every window, trying to see what it looked like. We should have been jumping up and down with excitement, but we were struggling to believe our luck, so we just stood there looking at each other, then at the house, then at each other again, until Mum said, 'We must look utterly ridiculous standing here like this. Let's go and find out for sure.' We linked arms and walked to the housing office and were told that, because our flat had been recently declared uninhabitable, we were to be moved with immediate effect and could collect the keys to our new two-bedroom-and-a-box-room house in two weeks, when it would be completed. But what on earth was a box room?

I think if Mum could have skipped back home, she would have done, such was the excitement that day. We went straight to the telephone box at the end of the street to ring her friends and her sisters.

We had a full flat that night. Mum's brother Uncle Benny had brought my Aunty Margaret and cousins Pat and Jacky over, and Aunty Tilly had sent Uncle Bill to see what help we needed. Mum's younger sister, Aunty Mary, was arriving from Cumbria at the weekend. Nancy, Dawn and Lisa were there too. We all trooped round to look at what was to be our house again, everyone peering through the windows trying to see as much as they could, then it was back to the flat for tea, sandwiches and cake. What a wonderful evening that was. Surrounded by family, all chatting and drinking tea, all excited about the future and our dream house.

We did move in two weeks later. We felt as though we'd moved into Buckingham Palace. It was the most beautiful house in the world. It didn't matter a jot that we had no carpets. Me and Mum, our very own beautiful and grand two-bedroom council house – not forgetting the box room and, most importantly, a bathroom and an indoor toilet. Life just didn't get any more perfect than this. Happy days.

Fame at Last

It was Mum who saw the advert in the paper. An operatic society was being put together and auditions were taking place the following week for anyone wanting to join. I couldn't wait to get there: this was it at last! I would sing and dance, they would give me the leading role in their next production and I would be famous. Job done. Almost, anyway. When I arrived, the room was packed with people, and they all seemed to know each other. People had come along from all different musical societies and had worked together on different productions over many years. Some of them were semi-professionals. Honestly, if I'd been at the Oscars I couldn't have been more star-struck. The sopranos were singing in the corridors, the altos were adding to the harmony and the dancers had been asked if they would like to warm up. Oh, what an idiot I must have looked that day! I was sixteen years old, totally naïve, knew nobody there, and had given up dance classes with Newcastle Dance Centre some years earlier when studying for my exams and getting a job became more important.

I was beginning to think I should just quietly slip out the side door when the dancers were shepherded into the audition room. I was the only person in the room that didn't know anyone else, and I was furiously trying to think up any reason at all to get out of there as quickly as possible. Then, suddenly, there she was. Mavis, my teacher from years ago who was so kind to Mum and me when I first began to take lessons, walked into the room to introduce herself as the choreographer. Well, that was it. I began what was to become my whole life for the next fifteen years – dancing in musical shows.

I'll never forget the curtain being raised on my first opening night. I may have been in the chorus and only in a couple of dances, but I had arrived! Somehow, I would be recognized. I was on the way to stardom. But life never quite works out that way, does it?

God only knows how I lasted so long in musical theatre. Mind you, I never missed rehearsals, always turned up on time, was always eager and ready to go. Many years later I was told: 'Well, you were a constant source of amusement. We couldn't let you go – it wouldn't have been nearly as much fun. Not quite what I had been hoping to hear, thank you very much.

Orpheus in the Underworld was fun. During the cancan I managed to kick my shoe off and hit the conductor on the head. In *South Pacific*, the elastic holding up my grass skirt snapped and it fell off, much to the amusement of the audience. During another show I made a complete exhibition of myself (not in a good way, you understand) because we had to dance in high heels. I tripped, tried to steady myself and went careering across the stage before finally falling flat on my face – once again to a round of applause. When early on in life I practised taking a bow to thunderous applause, this wasn't exactly what I had in mind.

It was decided that for *Hello, Dolly!* they would build a platform in a semi-circle around the orchestra pit where the dancers would skip and cavort around with their partners. So there we were, singing 'Put on Your Sunday Clothes' and dancing the light fantastic around the semi-circular platform. My partner through sheer vanity had decided not to wear his glasses. Poised and elegant I span round, arms beautifully stretched out and – I have to say it wasn't totally my fault – smacked him in the face, knocking him into the orchestra pit, where he landed on the drums.

In *Camelot* I was a woodland creature. All the dancers had an animal head to wear. The curtains opened, there was gentle music playing and King Arthur was sitting centre stage in the magical forest. It was a very pretty scene and the woodland creatures were hiding behind the trees. Slowly, everyone came out from behind the trees and began to dance. Well, I say 'everyone'. My head had got stuck on the branches of the cardboard tree. I coughed to get the attention of the others. A girl called Maria glided past and said, 'What are you doing?'

'I'm stuck on the tree – get me out!' I said when she glided past the next time. So it was that each of the dancers, each time they danced past me, tried to knock or pull the head from the branch. The tree began to wobble and I really, honestly, seriously, envisioned myself walking off the stage with a tree attached to my head. Why me? I asked. Why is it always me? But I couldn't believe what actually happened. The dance ended and the woodland creatures waltzed off into the wings and left me standing there, still stuck to the tree.

Now, at this stage, while I could hear the hysterical laughter going on in the wings, along with shouts of 'For God's sake, don't move. You'll tip the tree over,' I should have been laughing myself – but I felt like crying when I realized that the scene did not change for another half an hour. King Arthur, bless him, at this point, turned round, put his hand to his mouth and whispered:

'Get off!'

'I can't get off.'

'Just get off now!'

'I can't get off, I'm stuck to the ****** tree.'

There were, of course, quite naturally, a few other words during this short conversation, which I will not pen here.

I know when to give up, so I removed the grips holding the headpiece together, took it off my head, left it swinging on the tree and walked off, to a round of applause from the audience. Oh well, at least I had been noticed.

The Christmas pantomime was another occasion to remember, but not necessarily for the right reasons. The lights were low and we were all in place. The setting was Aladdin's cave and I was dressed as a jewel, top to toe in silver – silver leotard, silver tights and a silver turban with a big diamond on the top. How very pretty. There were six of us, all as different coloured jewels, posed under the stage on trapdoors waiting for our slow ascent.

The curtains opened to 'ooh's and 'aah's from the audience. The backstage, design and lighting staff had gone all out to create a stunning set. The orchestra struck up and there was a hush in the auditorium. Ever so gently, the

My grandma Anne, who I never got to meet and who Mum was named after.

I saw this photograph of my adopted mum, Nancy, aged seventeen, for the first time in March 2013 – so beautiful and dignified, it brings a lump to my throat every time I look at it.

Everyone always asks if it's me in this photograph. My real mother, Molly, and I are so very alike, and I thank God every day that I got to meet her.

I can feel the wind in my hair and remember the screams of laughter as Dad stood me on the running board of the car and drove up and down the drive at Nazareth House.

A love story in itself, Tilly and Bill were married for forty-six years in a home filled with love, laughter and total acceptance. They were a joy to be with.

My first birthday. Every year Mum took me to Jerome's, a photographer in Newcastle, to have my picture taken.

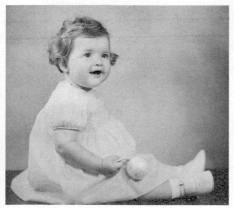

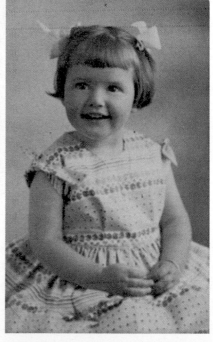

This photograph was displayed in Jerome's shop window, and Mum was so proud. She still talked about this many years later.

Mum, Christopher and I with one of the nuns from Nazareth House, in front of the chapel.

I love this photograph of Mum with some of the children as it shows the statue of Our Lady of Lourdes, which comforted Mum on her first visit to Nazareth House, in the background.

Christopher and I in the garden, holding hands as always. To the right of the photo are the branches of the magic whispering conker tree. Oh I do hope it's still there!

Christopher and I spent many hours at the park with Mum. They were such fun and happy times.

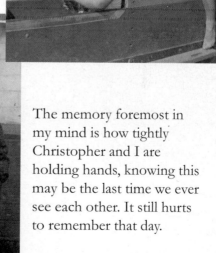

The memory foremost in my mind is how tightly Christopher and I are holding hands, knowing this may be the last time we ever see each other. It still hurts to remember that day.

All dressed up for a friend of Mum's wedding day, where I had the honour of being a bridesmaid.

Me with my doll, and the new cot Mum had bought for her. Behind me, there he is – the love of my life – Cliff Richard, plastered all over my wall.

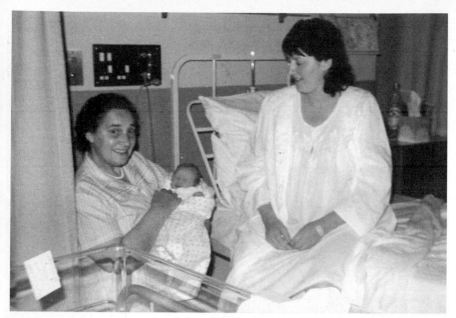

The day my beautiful daughter Gemah arrived. I just love the look on Mum's face – so very proud and happy. I never got a look in!

Mum, Gemah and I would spend all year looking at brochures and plan what was always a wonderful week at a holiday camp.

This was taken at my wedding to Harry.
Left to right are Christopher, who I never lost touch with;
his father, Danny; Harry; me; Julie (Christopher's wife)
with their son; and their daughter in front.

trapdoors opened and the platforms began to lift. I struck my diamond pose, arms stretched, toes pointing, head held high, perfectly still, and the jewels took their places in Aladdin's cave.

Clunk! Except me. The trapdoor got stuck, and all that got through was my head. Unfortunately, I could see the audience and they could see me and I could hear definite giggling coming from the auditorium, so I slowly bent my knees and crouched down. The people below were working furiously to bring the ramp back down but it was stuck fast.

'Climb up on to the stage,' someone shouted from below me.

'You've got to be joking – I'm a dancer, not a member of Billy Smart's circus! I can't swing myself up from here.'

A few very long minutes went by, and there was a lot of running about under the stage. Then suddenly there was a jolt, but it was upwards not down, and at this point I could be seen from the waist upwards so, professional to the last, I took my pose and held it. 'Brace yourself,' they said, and with another push the platform jerked up another few inches, sending me flying sideways. I had to grab on to the edges of the hole in the stage. And now the platform would go no further. Oh, the indignity of it all! Hands either side of the hole, I hauled myself up on to the stage and walked forward to take my place beside the treasure chest, adopted my pose and received once more a round of applause from my audience.

Don't you just know when it's time to give up?

Watching Handbags

I remember watching her walk up the aisle. She looked so pretty and so very happy. We had spent months looking at dresses and chatting about how she would look and feel on the day. My friend Elaine loved Alex very much and was really looking forward to the big day. It was all arranged and the wedding would be taking place on Saturday. Elaine had found her man in the black coat and the two of them had a flat to move into. I couldn't even imagine how exciting that must be, to be in love *and* have your very own place to live in together.

Elaine's dress was white and, with her auburn hair, she looked very beautiful. I was proud to be her friend. The only thing that spoilt the day for me was that I was not part of a couple, as everyone else around me seemed to be. There were a few friends from school who had all kept in touch with Elaine, all there with their boyfriends or husbands and, once again, I was on my own.

I think Elaine's wedding was the first time it really hit me that, when it came to the last dance, which was always a romantic slow song, I was the one watching the handbags. I was the friend, the one people said should be invited along because she was on her own and they felt sorry for her. The one everyone said was such fun to be around, was always good for a laugh, could be relied upon, would never let anyone down ... but, never, it would seem, was I girlfriend material. I never felt pretty and was always aware that my friends were more attractive than me. Fortunately, I still had my dreams, hopes and belief that one day my man in a black coat would simply appear out of nowhere. He was out there somewhere and I dreamed about him all the time. One day in the not too distant future, at the end of the evening when the slow music began, he would smile, take my hand, lead me on to the dance floor and someone would have to look after *my* handbag, because I would be busy tripping the light fantastic with the love of my life.

It was many years later that I realized this was never going to happen. I had been seeing someone, but he had tired of me and now wanted to be friends: I was a lovely person but he couldn't see it going any further. The truth was, he had fallen in love with my friend, but he knew it would be all right with me, because I was that sort of person and would understand. I cried, of course I did, but continued to be friends with both of them.

I was an aunty to all the children when they came along, and loved babysitting. I adored Elaine's boys and was very close to them. My great friend Pauline Walker had two girls, Jane and Claire, and I spent most weekends with them. I'll always look back on those days as absolutely wonderful and very happy. Pauline's house was always open to me, and she often laughs and says she invited me for tea one Friday night and I stayed for fourteen years – or at least that's how it seemed! Pauline, her friend Maureen, and Elaine were the ones who saw me through life's challenges and invited me along to all their family events. I always looked forward to these and enjoyed them, yet somehow, at the end of the evening, there I was either looking after the children or minding the handbags. This, it seemed, was my role in life and I decided that, if that was it, then so be it. I took my role as aunty seriously and devoted every moment I could to loving the children and spending time with them. They were the loves of my life and brought me hours of endless joy. I would always look forward to babysitting, and as soon as Pauline and her husband were out of the house Jane and Claire would jump out of bed and come thundering down the stairs and we would all settle down for a fun night in.

It was only in those odd moments that suddenly spring up out of nowhere that I began to realize I was missing out. Mum and I were walking through a shop in Newcastle one day when we found ourselves passing through the baby department and I caught myself looking at the prams and cots. To this day, I have no idea why at that moment, on that day, it should hit me so hard. That would never be me, I would never be a mum. I wanted to be the girl, about six months pregnant, who was standing looking at the cots, the man beside her holding a little girl's hand. I felt a lump in my throat and dragged Mum out of the department as quickly as possible, making some excuse or other. Why was it, I wondered, that some people had lots of boyfriends, or even married more than once, and no one anywhere gave me a second look?

Where on earth was the love of *my* life? I had lots to offer, I know I did. Mum's friends kept giving her stuff, saying that it was for my bottom drawer, that old-fashioned tradition of putting things aside for when you get married. Well, my load of treasures would have filled three wardrobes by the time I was twenty-two years old. I was on the shelf, and Mum needed the space back in the wardrobes. But I never lost hope entirely. He was out there somewhere, my man in a black coat. All I had to do was find him.

Skinny Again

We had talked about it, read about it, imagined it, and now we were ready. Elaine and I had decided that the fish finger and turnip sandwiches had to stop. It was time to regain our sylph-like figures and be skinny again. Elaine now had a young son called Steven who was three years old, and she was determined to lose her baby fat.

I didn't have that excuse. I think the fat fairy turned up one night, pierced a hole in me and blew me up. All I had to do was find the valve and let myself down again. That was my story. Actually, it was pies. Mince pies from the deli round the corner from the office where I worked. It was either a saveloy dip (a frankfurter sausage in a bun dipped in gravy) or two mince pies every day for lunch. I was only twenty then and fairly fit, so it took a while for my waistline to expand, but when it did, it didn't hold back.

Now, though, the decision had been made, and we were both very much looking forward to our first steps into the world of dieting. We told Alex, Elaine's husband, that to keep us focussed we needed to put a photograph of ourselves as we were now somewhere so it would constantly remind us of our goals. Alex took a photo of us both sitting on the sofa smiling, and said he would put it up for us.

The night of our first Weight Watchers meeting had

now arrived, and we were both a little late. New starters are supposed to turn up early. Unfortunately, it had taken longer than we anticipated to get through every last biscuit in the cupboard (and even then we didn't quite manage it), after a massive helping of sausages, beans, egg, chips and bread buns with butter and lashings of brown sauce. We were such classy girls.

We struggled to walk, let alone run, the last few yards to the meeting, but we made it and were weighed. Shock horror! It was worse than we thought, which made us all the more determined to succeed. At the end of the meeting we went through all the leaflets and got our beginners' talk and were feeling extremely positive about it all. We couldn't wait to get started.

'I have a few surprises over the next few weeks for you new starters, to help you get a flying start to the new you,' our consultant had announced. Great. We were looking forward to it.

It was wintertime and so already dark at 8 p.m. when the meeting finished. We walked the short distance to the bus stop and had our heads together looking over the leaflets we had been given when Elaine looked up and I heard her scream. There was a man standing just a couple of yards away from us, and he had opened his coat. There were things on display that should seriously have been kept behind lock and key, or a zip at least.

'Oh my God, he's got his –'

'Shut up and run!' screamed Elaine. I had never, and have never since, run so fast in all my life. We dropped the leaflets, Elaine grabbed my hand and we belted to the next bus stop. 'Keep running!' she said. 'Just in case.' After what felt like miles, we finally stopped running because we were totally out of breath and wheezing so much we couldn't even speak.

When we had calmed down and realized that we were probably completely safe, and now in a well-lit residential area near a main road, Elaine gasped, 'Well, that was a good start, wasn't it? We must have lost two pounds running away!'

My mind was racing, and I thought about our welcome speech earlier.

'I've had a thought,' I said. 'Maybe that was one of the consultant's surprises for her new starters. Hire a flasher to chase them home – now there's a flying start for you!'

We howled with laughter all the way home on the bus back to Elaine's house, with of course no leaflets to read.

When we got there we were still trying not to laugh, so as not to wake Steven up, but without success.

'Mam,' he said in a sleepy voice.

'Yes, son?' answered Elaine.

'Are you skinny yet?'

Our laughter at that woke up Alex, who was asleep on the sofa. After a few moments, though, he gave up trying to listen to what we were saying, as we were beyond hysterical by now. He simply shook his head and went back to the sofa with a sly smile on his face.

Eventually, we calmed down, Elaine put the kettle on and we both looked at the biscuit cupboard.

'Well, we don't actually start until tomorrow . . .'

'That's true. Today is still today and doesn't count.'

'It would be a shame to waste those chocolate biscuits and have to throw them out tomorrow, just in case I ate one . . .'

'It would, Elaine, it definitely would.'

'Let's have a biscuit and a cuppa then.'

We opened the cupboard door and there it was in all its glory, glued to the inside, the photo of the two of us (taken at a bad angle, I say) looking like a couple of frumps. Underneath it were written the words: 'Fat Boilers'.

The biscuit cupboard was closed and sealed and we sat down to enjoy a herbal tea.

Love in a Hot-water Bottle

For over fifty years Nancy continued to be a real mum to me, always there, giving, loving, caring, losing patience with my 'ridiculous notions', as she called them, always wanting to know where I was, how long I was going to be, still meeting me from the bus stop when I was thirty years old. Oh, how I miss that now! What wouldn't I give to see her just once more, standing at the bus stop in the freezing cold with a hot-water bottle under her coat for my walk home in the snow.

One year, my work Christmas party took place a coach ride away in Northumberland. It had snowed all night and the coach struggled on the return journey. It must have been about 3 a.m. when I reached our road, and ours was the only house in the street with every light blazing. I was halfway up the street when the door was flung open. There she was in her dressing gown and slippers, clutching a hot-water bottle and waving, shouting, 'Susan!' at the top of her voice and watching me walk the rest of the short journey home. I was utterly exhausted but, no, I couldn't go to bed, I had to have a cup of tea first, otherwise I would catch my death of cold. Only when she was quite sure I had not come to any harm – after all, I was only thirty years old – was I allowed to go up to my bedroom, where there were hot-water bottles on the pillow and at the bottom of the bed.

Never – *never* – would Mum go to bed before I got home after a night out. This was long before mobile phones, and she never stopped worrying about me if I was out of her sight.

Although I loved Mum with all my heart, some friends of mine had recently moved into their own flat and I began to feel as though this was something I would like to do. I wanted my independence, but how was I going to tell Mum? I felt nervous all day at work, knowing that I had finally decided to take the plunge and tell her that I had found a flat not too far away and was going to be leaving home. Aunty Elaine would be at work when I got home, so Mum and I would be alone. (When I was about five years old, Elaine had come to work in Nazareth House to help Mum look after the children. She was a wonderful woman with an incredible talent for making cakes, and she and Mum were such close friends she'd lived with us for a while in our first house in Byker. She was always Aunty Elaine to me; Mum thought it was disrespectful for children to call adults by their first name and I had never grown out of the habit.)

How well Mum knew me! I had planned to tell her straight away, but I was still struggling, and she said to me, 'Susan, if you have something on your mind I think it better you just tell me what it is.' So I did.

I was gobsmacked: she was fine about it and wanted to help, asking where it was, how many bedrooms, when I was moving in. I couldn't believe how well it was going and, although part of me was suspicious, I was also relieved.

My friends Maureen and Pauline came along and completely redecorated the flat for me, and it was completely and utterly the most beautiful home I had ever seen in my life – and it was mine. All mine.

Three weeks after telling Mum, I moved in, giving her a spare key. I couldn't believe that at last I had my freedom. I could do what I liked, when I liked. It was going to be so much fun. I had it all planned out. I would sit up late into the night watching TV in my lovely flat, have friends over and, most of all, have my independence.

I moved in on a Sunday and spent most of the day just walking round the flat, settling in. It was February and freezing cold, as the flat had no heating apart from a gas fire in the lounge. The dial on the washing machine looked extremely complicated and the windows in the bedroom had ice on the inside. Not quite what I would have wished for on my first day of freedom! I filled hot-water bottles, put on my PJs, a pair of socks, legwarmers and a thick dressing gown and snuggled down into bed. Pure bliss.

Who needed a warm house, hot running water and constant chatter? Not me. I had set my alarm for 5 a.m. to put the boiler on so there would be hot water for a bath before work. Of course the room was still cold, and I have never shivered so much in my life, but I was determined: this was my new life. All day at work I felt so grown-up. I wanted someone to ask me where I lived just so I could answer, 'Oh, I have my own flat, you know.'

All day I thought about what fun it would be going back to my own flat, making tea, watching TV – and, of course, phoning Mum to make sure she was all right and coping without me. I was a woman of the world, starting out on my own, venturing into the unknown world of paying bills and taking on responsibility for my own life. I didn't need anyone to look after me, I could cope perfectly well on my own, thank you very much. I remember that, just for a second as I took my key out of my bag when I got to the flat that evening after work, I felt a spark of loneliness, just a moment of fear. I shook it off, put the key in the door . . . and there she was. Mum.

Fire on, hot-water bottles in the bed, washing machine spinning, ironing done, and my tea cooked. 'I used my key,' she said.

I knew I would never have the heart to ask for it back. So much for independence! I knew the hours Mum worked and that I would have to accept that the nights she finished early I would find her in the flat pottering around and 'cleaning', as she put it. The lounge was dirty, she said, there was a tissue in the waste bin. 'God forbid,' I remember saying. 'That's shocking!' Big mistake. Mum was not impressed by this comment and decided there and then that my new independence had set me on the road to depravity and destruction.

I remember being so angry at the time, and yet, looking back now, I would give anything in the world to have her stand behind me just once more, looking after me and loving me. I'll always miss her just being there, a constant in my life. She was never one for emotional displays of love. Saying 'I love you' would have embarrassed the life out of her. But there was no need to say it because there, in every action, was love, support, care, dedication. If I did something wrong, she would be the first person to point it out and tell me where and how I had gone wrong and how to put it right – that was her way – but God help the person who criticized me or hurt me in any way. My mum, No-nonsense Nancy, would be ready for battle on my behalf every time.

I lived in that flat for only twelve months in the end, and most of that time Mum would be there when I came home from work, or I would go home and spend the night with her. In December 1986 I discovered I was pregnant. It wasn't going to work, living on my own in a third-floor flat with no heating, and I hadn't caught my breath before she had me back home, the furniture sold, our names down on the council housing list for a three-bedroom house and a smile on her face from one end to the other.

Mum never failed to amaze me. She wasn't even shocked when I told her. All she said was 'We will manage,' then, in the next breath, 'I am going to be a grandma.' I thought she would want all the details. I loved my child's father very much, and I wanted to tell her about him, but 'No thank you very much, I don't need all that stuff,' she said, and then that she needed to talk to Tilly.

She went straight to the phone and I could hear Aunty Tilly laughing on the other end and the pair of them chatting away excitedly. Aunty Tilly had many grandchildren of her own and was so thrilled about there being another little one on the way. It was music to my ears to keep hearing Mum say, 'I will be called Grandma!', then 'Must run now. Got to ring Elaine to organize a christening cake.'

I was only twelve weeks pregnant but I was so happy to see Mum happy. I was home once more and preparing to be a mum myself. This, I knew, was going to be the biggest challenge I had ever faced and yet, from the moment I was pregnant, I loved my baby and couldn't wait to meet her. 'I know what you need,' said Mum when she came off the phone. 'A cup of tea and a hot-water bottle.'

What an incredible woman and teacher Mum was. She instilled into so many of her children core values, mutual respect and good ethics, and taught us all that actions speak louder than words. Simply telling someone you care or that you love them is not enough; you must show them also, through your actions. So I look back today and remember once more those days, come sleet and snow, no matter how icy the roads, and Mum at a freezing-cold bus stop with a hot-water bottle under her coat waiting to walk home with me. The words 'I love you' were in every thought, word and deed.

My Man in a Black Coat

So where had *this* baby come from? Nancy did not want to hear the details, but I would have shouted them from the rooftops.

I'd always known exactly what he would look like and how he would make me feel. I'd dreamed about him for so long. He would make my feelings of loneliness go away, because to him I would always get it right, and even if I didn't he would never tell me so. He would take my face in his hands and tell me how much he loved me before kissing me. People laughed at me, saying that I didn't live in the real world and things like that only happened in books or in the movies. I felt so sorry for them. I couldn't imagine a life without dreams. After all, the people who wrote books and movies must at least base them partly on real life.

This man would tell me I was pretty. Mum always said that beauty is in the eye of the beholder. No matter how many times I looked in the mirror, I never felt pretty, but that was all right because he would think I was and would tell me so. All I had to do was wait for him.

I sighed. He would definitely be worth the wait. I would know him immediately — as soon as I saw him. My heart would skip a beat, he would wink at me, I would smile back, and that would be it. I would float up the aisle in an ivory wedding gown to gasps of admiration from family and friends, we would have lots of children and grandchildren and people would say to others, 'You need to take a leaf out of our Susan's book and wait for your Mr Right.'

And, of course, on our first Christmas Eve together we would go to Midnight Mass and, during the second verse of 'Silent Night', he would put his arm around me and I would know I had met my own man in the black coat. Life would be perfect.

And that's the way it happened. From the very first moment I saw him I was in love. Head over heels, cartwheeling, crazy and madly in love. No one else in the history of time had felt like this. Only me. This was different, special. Oh, how sorry I felt for other people. They could never possibly feel like I did.

My heart didn't just skip a beat, it almost stopped. There it was again: tall, dark and handsome. An old saying, but very fitting. He had an air about him; about the way he walked, so sure of himself. I stood in the middle of the office unable to move. Had my heart actually stopped? I thought it might have done. This was it. That was him. Oh, dear God in Heaven, it had happened. Today was the day.

'Hello,' said my workmate Julie. 'And what planet are we on today, may one ask?'

'Oh Julie, it's him! The one!'

'Oh, I see. Well, before you declare undying love for him and run off into the sunset to have a hundred babies, do you think you could finish typing the contract up? By the way, he is . . .'

'Perfect!' I cried. 'Absolutely perfect!'

'If you say so,' she said, with a sad look in her eye. Bless her – it was probably because she had never found her Mr Right.

I was on top of the world that day. He would fall in love with me, I just knew it. Not that he had actually noticed me, but I knew. A girl knew when she was on the way to being loved. It was just the way he looked at me every day. He had been part of the crowd when they had gone out to lunch last week, and they had laughed, talked and laughed some more. He had said I was something else. You had to be there to hear the way he said it to understand how special that made me feel.

I had read all about it. When you met your soulmate, it was simply a knowing, not anything that could be explained. I had read about past lives and people meeting and recognizing each other at soul level, and I was convinced I would know him in this way when I met him. The magazines were right, it was true: he was mine, I knew it. So much for all those people telling me to live in the real world – how smug could I be now? I imagined the shocked look on their faces when I introduced him. My hands may have been poised over the keyboard, but no typing of any contract or anything else was actually taking place. I was somewhere else entirely . . . in my house, with family and friends – everyone was there.

Oh, by the way, I would casually say while holding out a photograph of the gorgeous man himself, this is Harry, established mechanical engineer and looking to start up his own business. He is in love with me and the wedding is in July (I had always dreamed of a summer wedding). Congratulations in order, I think. They would all raise their glasses and then the rest of the night everyone would be fighting for my attention, asking all manner of questions and saying how lucky I was. Suddenly I felt a poke in my back, which brought me straight back to reality.

'Any possibility of the fingers connecting to the keyboard?'

'No imagination,' I whispered under my breath.

I was only the smallest step away from skipping down the high street on my way home. I was, however, swinging my bags and striding along with my head held high. Harry, Harry, Harry. I said his name over and over again in my head. It was a perfect name for a perfect man. It would be Harry and Susan Lambert – or Suzanne, as he called me. There were already two Susans in the office, so Suzanne it was. It sounded so cool when he said it, and the name stuck.

No one could burst this bubble, I thought. No one could take this joy away from me. After all, love made everything perfect, didn't it? What could possibly go wrong?

Harry was married. He already had a family. And I had been brought up to know right from wrong. I would put all thoughts of him aside. In my stronger moments, I managed it, but in weaker ones I would dream about what it would feel like to have his arms around me, to go shopping together, to be cuddled up on the sofa watching TV. Not life-shattering events to other people maybe, but everything to me. And dreaming was harmless. Nobody would get hurt because it wasn't real. Dreaming about being with him became my guilty pleasure.

He had said I was pretty, and when I sat and looked in the mirror that night there *was* something different in the reflection that looked back at me. I wasn't pretty, but there was a certain confidence there, a slight flush and a definite sparkle in my eyes. Tomorrow I would be just like the other people in the office, all sophisticated and smart. I laid out my clothes ready: black skirt, white blouse and high heels. Tomorrow I'd face the adult world, no playing the class clown, time to be brave and confident and see just what I was made of. I had to face up to it. Harry was wonderful, but we would have to be just friends, and he would admire me for who I was. That was enough, it would have to be. He had a family.

I tried so hard not to love him, but the thought of never being with him was simply unbearable: he was, after all, my man in the black coat. I just knew it. But I knew better too: I was Nancy's child and had been taught right from wrong. Never in all of my dreams had I considered it could turn out like this. Loving him hurt so very much.

In my stronger moments these fanciful feelings would be put to one side; in my weaker ones I still continued to dream. I'd have a stupid smile on my face every time I thought of him, but then the reality of the situation would hit and wipe it right off.

Reality, however, can be extremely tedious, so I continued to dream. That was harmless, surely. I would never actually take it any further; of course I wouldn't. I couldn't. It wouldn't be right . . .

Well, maybe just once – but only the once. Of course, it didn't turn out like that . . .

Mother Earth

And, yeah, it is written that from the moment we conceive and are with child our bodies are infused with all the necessary hormones that ensure we are able to carry out all the appropriate and natural talents that turn each and every one of us into Mother Earth. This includes knitting. In my defence, I must have slept through this early lesson in sex education at school – unless that's when they were rambling on about one over, one under (it's a knitting stitch, for those who are not Mother Earth) so, when I sat shocked to the core in the doctor's surgery, having been told I was indeed three months pregnant, my first words were not 'Dear God, I must have some three-ply immediately.' More like:

'Mum, this is 1987, you've got to be joking.'

No-nonsense Nancy did not joke. 'Everyone around is knitting for you. Your aunties have already started.'

'So I need to knit why?'

Apparently, for the thrill of making it myself.

'I can think of better ways to be thrilled.'

'Yes,' said Mum, her nose in the air and looking at my by now six months bump, 'so it seems.'

The subject was not dropped. Knitting machines were the new thing now for those shameless people who could not knit. Great idea – why buy some beautiful little baby cardigans for a few pounds from the local shops on Shields Road when I could spend hundreds of pounds on a knitting machine and spend months making them?

But it seems I was being ridiculous, so the next day found me in Fenwick's, blundering my way around the haberdashery department. Why is it that when you have no idea what you need you're always served by the know-it-all who is thoroughly conversant in her subject and looks across the top of her glasses and treats you like a silly little schoolgirl?

'Can one help, Madam?'

Who was this woman with the 'can one'? I was in Fenwick's, not Harrods. Definitely ideas above her station, this one.

'I'm looking for wool.'

'Wool, Madam?'

'Yes, wool. You know, the stuff you knit with.'

Sarcasm never works well on the haughty upper-class sales assistant, and this one was already beginning to look down her nose and purse her lips. I wanted to tell her that if she was going to do that properly she would need a few lessons off Mum, but decided to keep my mouth shut.

Sarcasm ignored. 'Does Madam know what ply?'

'Madam doesn't know what ply is.'

'Thickness. I would suggest four.'

'Then I shall have thickness four, thank you very much.'

She patted the bun on the top of her head, adjusted her glasses and glanced over at the security guard. Oh, surely not, I can't be thrown out of Fenwick's department store when I'm six months pregnant for not speaking posh and having no knowledge of ply. Obviously, being pregnant and Mother Earth, not having this know-how was a punishable offence.

'Does Madam have a pattern?'

'Madam does.'

I didn't.

'Then it will tell Madam how many balls of wool Madam requires.'

Yes, she has me now and she knows it. Smug expression is plain for all to see. No idea what ply is, no knitting pattern and, of all the challenges ahead – motherhood, pain, sickness – good God, this was turning out to be more difficult than I imagined labour to be. And I imagined that would be pretty tough. She was winning, and she knew it. I squared up to her.

'Twenty, I will take twenty balls of the cream.'

She looked down at my bump, up at my face, down at the bump, back up.

'How many babies is Madam expecting?'

'Six' I replied. 'It was a good night.'

Step backwards, shocked through. One to me, I thought.

So there I was on the way home on the bus with a carrier bag full of cream four-ply, knitting needles and no pattern.

Mum was right, of course, so I persevered, and it *was* a thrill and gave me a wonderful sense of achievement to knit a baby cardigan myself. Back and front sewn together, two sleeves completed, bought the buttons. Job done. Unfortunately, Gemah is now twenty-five years old.

Bubble and Squeak

It was Sunday, and Nancy never missed Mass, which meant I didn't either. I wasn't sure today, though, whether I was going to make it. Every bone in my body ached and the pain in my back was becoming worse by the minute. I thought back to Easter Sunday. It had been boiling hot and I was nearly six months pregnant and not looking forward to a Mass that would be a long-drawn-out affair with tea and biscuits afterwards in the hall. Could I be excused, do you think? I remember asking. After all, it was a fifteen-minute uphill walk, my ankles were swollen and I had been up all night with heartburn. No chance, it was Easter Sunday, and pregnancy was no excuse. Today had to be different, though. In two days' time, on Tuesday 28 July, my baby was due, although everyone said that babies never came on time and certainly not on their due date. I turned over and, once again, the pain made me feel slightly sick. No way was I going to get out of bed and walk to church today. 'Sorry, Mum,' I said. 'It's just not going to happen.'

'Very well,' she said. 'I will pray for both of us.'

Nancy was worried and excited at the same time. A grandchild! A girl, of course, she just knew it. And any day now. She had loved

every moment of Susan needing her. She was aware of how her daughter followed her round the house these days, seeming to need her now more than ever, even one day asking her to sit outside the bathroom door when she took a bath because she felt a bit strange. Tilly was excited for her, too; they had talked about grandchildren often.

'Imagine, Tilly, a daughter and a granddaughter – so much more than I had hoped for.' Nancy loved this grandchild with all her heart, and she wasn't even here yet.

'Nancy,' people had said, 'it could be a boy.'

'Well, of course it could,' she said. 'I'm not a fool, thank you very much.' Secretly smiling, she said to herself, 'Could be, but it's not. It's a girl, without any shadow of a doubt. It's a girl.' They had looked at the name Scott William, after Susan's father, if it was a boy, and Gemah Louise for a girl. As soon as she heard the name and looked at the meaning – 'little gem' – Nancy had known. Yes, it's a girl! Thank you, God. The pink cardigans and baby-gros were hidden, though; no need to put any pressure on Susan, who, after all, didn't know she was having a daughter, bless her. That day at Mass, Nancy prayed for her granddaughter's safe arrival, knowing it would be any time soon.

The next day, I could hardly move and the pains in my back were worse than ever. 'Know what you need,' said Mum. 'A cup of tea and some bubble and squeak.' For those unfortunate people who have never experienced this delight, bubble and squeak is all of the Sunday-dinner leftovers thrown into a frying pan and made into a kind of pancake of vegetables and potato. You eat it with lashings of brown sauce, and it is totally and utterly wonderful. It was all I could think of that Monday morning. Bathed and dressed, I sat in the comfy armchair smelling the aroma from the kitchen and constantly turning my head to check if it was ready yet.

'Mum, will it be ready soon?'

'Not long now, love.'

'Will I get the trays ready, Mum?'

'No, be patient. Only a few more minutes.'

I heaved myself out of the armchair, grabbed a plate and stood like Oliver with my plate held out.

'Here we go then, love,' called Mum, and she was just spooning the long-awaited bubble and squeak on to my plate when my waters broke.

'God hates me!'

It's a Girl!

I was in hospital within the hour. Oh, the indignities! I wanted Mum, but no, she was at home, apparently having the house painted for my return. Why, oh why? I asked myself. The new baby was not going to notice, as far as I was aware.

Nancy sat on the stool beside the telephone. The painter had left for the day and she had cleaning to do. Just for now, though, she allowed herself to wonder. All these years she had loved Susan, cared for her, fought to keep her, and today she knew in her heart that Susan always had been and always would be her precious child, and, no matter what happened, they would face life together. Susan being in pain was not something Nancy could think about. It had been a very hot day, and Nancy had no idea how long she had sat watching the phone. It was beginning to get dark now and there was a moment when she wondered, Is something wrong? She jumped when the phone rang, but it was Tilly. 'Go to bed, Nancy,' Tilly told her. 'You and I both know from my experiences that it can take a while. Tilly knew, of course, that there was never any chance of Nancy going to bed. 'Let me know when it happens,' she said. Nancy sat there hour after hour waiting, drinking endless cups of tea.

She opened the bags she had kept hidden under the bed. Every-thing was pink: bonnets, gloves, dresses, bibs, all with little ducks and teddies on them. The pram was ready in the corner of the room and Nancy changed the cream cover for a pink one with little pink and cream bows. That's better, she said to herself. All ready now. A granddaughter, Gemah Louise! 'Grandma' she kept saying over and over to herself, hardly able to believe it. She had been a mother for thirty-two years, and she had done her best, she thought. Susan was a good girl, and they were still close. Nancy hadn't asked about the situation with Harry – it was all too embarrassing; best put all that to one side. Yes, Susan was a good girl and she would be a good mother to this child.

Fenwick's toy department once more, she thought. Only this time Nancy would have money in her purse. Her granddaughter wouldn't be spoilt, of course, that would be wrong; and yet Nancy dreamed about looking at all the dolls and prams and seeing the delight on Gemah's face. In five months' time it would be Christ-mas, and it was going to be the best ever. Nancy was not sure how many Christmas Days they would all have together. After all, at some point, Harry and Susan would get together maybe. But Nancy couldn't think about that today. I will take a leaf out of Susan's book today and dream, she thought. She smiled to herself and continued on a sweltering-hot night in July to plan Christmas Day 1987.

She was asleep, propped upright on the telephone stool, when the phone rang at 5.15 a.m. Her precious granddaughter, Gemah Louise, had made her way into the world at 4.55 a.m. on Tuesday 28 July, the day she was due, Susan was fine and the baby was perfect in every way.

Tears running down her face, Nancy replaced the phone on its hook.

She looked round the room at all things pink.

A boy, indeed! She smirked, turned off the light and went to bed.

Celebrations

In July 1987 I gave birth to my beautiful daughter, Gemah Louise. It wasn't until the moment I held her in my arms that the understanding of the full story hit me. I was tired and exhausted after a long labour, and when my daughter looked at me and her tiny hand held my finger I was totally overwhelmed. This then was what it was all about . . . love. Two grandmothers, two women, destined never to meet yet bound together by the child that was me. One to spend her whole life crying and grieving for the child who had been so cruelly taken away, and the other who had the child and grieved for the moment she might be taken away. How sad for both of them. I closed my eyes, thanked God for my precious child and promised always to respect and honour the bravery of both my birth mother and my mum.

I couldn't believe how quickly the time passed. I was so very happy, and Mum and I seemed to spend much of our time laughing. I loved every single moment of motherhood. Harry was involved as much as he could be, but much of his time was spent working away, and spending time with both families was important to him. And to tell the truth, I loved my family unit of Mum, Gemah and I, with Harry visiting as often as he could. I hadn't realized how much Gemah's arrival would complete me: she was my everything, and every day with her and Mum was a day to be treasured and enjoyed.

Mum had promised, of course, that she would never interfere: Gemah was my child and she respected that. Yeah right. The first night home I went to sleep with my hand in Gemah's Moses basket, holding on to her hand. I woke up in the early hours of the morning with my hand dangling down the side of my bed to find an empty space. Where was Gemah? I crept into Mum's room and there they were, Mum sitting up in bed cradling her grandchild. 'Put the kettle on love,' she whispered.

Two and a half years sped by. Then, it was a late morning on a Sunday in February 1990, and Gemah and I had been out with Harry enjoying a couple of hours in the nearby park and were hurrying home for one of Mum's full English breakfasts. We were full of chatter as we burst into the house, both shouting for Mum, telling her we were home. There was a silence throughout the house and the breakfast was on the kitchen floor. I raced around the house and finally found Mum. She had collapsed on the landing upstairs.

My wonderful mother had suffered a debilitating stroke and was to spend the next two months in hospital.

I remember well the day the doctor told me to prepare for the worst: even if Mum did recover, the chances were she would not walk again. But no way was that going to happen – this was me and Mum against the world again – so I walked up to Mum, took her hands in mine and said, 'OK, have you finished with your attention-seeking now?' Mum didn't speak, but she did give a little laugh.

Progress was slow and, one day, without my knowledge, Mum was transferred to the rehabilitation unit. I will never forget that day. I walked into the room and there she was, still sitting at the tea table. Tea was long gone, and there she was facing a blank wall. Fortunately, I wasn't actually arrested that day for grabbing the wheelchair and trying to leave the hospital with her there and then. Thank God for Harry, who was a great support to me during this time and spent many hours running me back and forth from the hospital.

I did the next best thing: I fought back, as she had done so many times for me. Gemah was the apple of Mum's eye and followed her everywhere. I have never to this day seen a smile so full of love as my Mum's the day Gemah was born. All I could think of after my horrendous labour was seeing Mum and showing her the beautiful, incredible granddaughter I had given her. I knew she would walk in and hug me, loving me for making her a grandmother.

Not exactly. It seems she turned up a whole hour before visiting time, paced the corridor and then marched in, smiled at me and, as I put my arms out, said, 'Hello, love,' walked straight past me and picked up her granddaughter, her eyes full of tears. Charming.

I knew what I had to do now.

'Listen,' I said. 'You are going to get better. You will get up and walk, or they will not let you come home, and how am I supposed to cope without you? I'm only thirty-five – far too young to cope!' I knew this would make her giggle. 'And Gemah is wandering all over the house looking for you. How is she supposed to cope without her grandma?

Tomorrow morning I will be back and we are going to show the physiotherapist just what you are made of, OK?'

I knew how it felt to be needed and I trusted whole-heartedly in the power of belief. If Mum believed we could not cope without her, she would do all she could to get better. Eight weeks later, after many hours of physio-therapy, Mum came home, in time for Easter. No-nonsense Nancy had fought and won yet another battle.

The New Gloves

Nancy had to keep it together today. People like her didn't make scenes; they kept their feelings to themselves. She was keeping her mind focussed on ridiculous things, but it helped. She was wearing her best clothes, new shoes and brand-new gloves. Her old ones had seen better days, and she explained to Susan how necessary it was to have new gloves on this particular day, black to match the handbag that came out only on the most special occasions. 'Leather gloves,' she had said to Susan. 'I need black leather gloves for tomorrow.' Susan had just smiled and said, 'OK, Mum, that's fine. We'll get you some new gloves, I promise.' They had met after work and gone to Fenwick's, and now Nancy's outfit was complete.

She checked her handbag one more time. She knew it was there but, still, one more check. Yes, she had it, and she snapped the clasp shut and made her way out the door to the waiting taxi. Today was definitely special enough for a taxi. There was to be no nonsense today, she had been warned. They had laughed — well, Tilly had — when they had talked about it: 'A proper knees-up it should be,' Tilly had said, and Nancy had been shocked. 'Nancy Harmer!' Tilly had said. 'Still that no-nonsense attitude after all these years. You know it doesn't wash with me. Anyway, it's my knees-up, so there!'

They had never spoken of love. There had never been any hugs or demonstrations of affection, yet it was all there. For nearly fifty years they had been the best of friends, had never fallen out, had always supported each other through tough times, watched each other's children grow up and celebrated as each new grandchild came along. They knew each other's thoughts, and words were not necessary. When the time came for help, somehow they were there, beside each other.

Was it only last week? thought Nancy now. She counted the days: nine. How can a life suddenly change and be completely different in only nine days? It had been a Sunday. Tilly had been poorly after her last heart attack but had been feeling much better, on the mend she said, so Bill was bringing her for tea. Well, it was going to be a good one, and all the stops were pulled out. Anne, Tilly's daughter, was also coming, with her daughter, Lorey, the youngest grandchild, only eight months old, just six months younger than Gemah. Nancy loved it when they all got together. She had dragged Susan around the supermarket the day before, to buy scones, best butter, salad and ham – all Tilly's favourites. 'How long is Aunty Tilly coming for?' Susan had asked. 'Only we've bought enough food for a week here, Mum!'

Susan had laughed at her when she said, 'Better safe than sorry. I would hate to run out of food.'

'God forbid!' she had replied, and Nancy had had to tell her off.

It was a big day, though; she hadn't seen Tilly for at least three weeks, and that was unheard of. It was, of course, in the hands of the gods that Tilly and Nancy should spend this special day together.

The table was set for a party of at least twenty people, and the usual chaos ensued, with two young babies, Bill trying to watch the football and Tilly and Nancy talking non-stop. Whenever Tilly was in a room, it lit up. She was the centre of her family's universe, the one that held everything together. The family would all laugh and make fun of her. They always said, for example, that if she went into town with a hundred pounds in her purse she would spend the lot and have to borrow her bus fare home. Tilly was a born carer, always looking out for people to look after, any stranger in need. Life and soul of the party, was what people said about her, salt of the earth, down to earth and with kindness in every part of her soul. In the early days when there wasn't a lot of money Bill came home one day to find that Tilly had fed all the workmen in the street with bacon butties and cup after cup of tea. Poor things, she said, it was cold, they needed feeding up. Tilly, like Nancy, firmly believed that an endless supply of tea and a bacon butty could solve anything.

Once more that Sunday the house was filled with laughter. After tea everyone sat around relaxing. The babies had just woken up and Nancy had gone to make another pot of tea — after all, it must have been a good ten minutes since the last one — and Tilly said, 'Come on now, give me those babies,' and there she sat with a child on each knee. Bouncing Gemah and Lorey up and down, she looked at her friend and said, 'Isn't this just perfect, Nancy?'

'Yes, Tilly, it is,' replied Nancy.

Today, Nancy was once more concentrating on her gloves, counting the stitches. It was something to look at and think about.

Tilly was late. Tilly was always late. Nancy smiled. Fitting that she should be late today.

Then Susan put her hand on her shoulder and Nancy knew Tilly had arrived. She would have to stand up now, of course she would — 'No nonsense, remember, Nancy' — but just for one second she thought her knees might fail her. She was hardly aware of Susan's arm around her back, helping her up. Head held high, both hands on the bench in front of her, Nancy looked straight ahead. She didn't look sideways as Tilly passed. She couldn't. There was total silence until Tilly arrived at the front of the church, and it was then that the music began.

It wasn't until Bill glanced sideways and Nancy caught his eye that her knees did her the injustice of letting her down and she had to sit back on the hard bench. She thought about the bench at the coast where they spent most Sundays if it was sunny, about meeting at the bus stop, Tilly and Bill with the sandwiches and Nancy with the flask of tea and the biscuits for an afternoon in the flower gardens at the coast. There they would sit, tea towels spread across the bench, putting the world to rights, chatting about everything under the sun. If it was especially warm they would have an ice cream and a walk along the promenade.

Four weeks ago, Nancy and Tilly had been looking at the photographs Susan had taken with her new camera of herself and Tilly laughing and squinting at the sun, happy and carefree, with a scone and a cup of tea, and the coast in the background. They had laughed so much at the sight of themselves that Tilly had spilt her tea all over the photo. Nancy didn't think she would bother any more. No more tea and biscuits at the coast. She looked around the packed church; she hadn't been listening to the priest. She could almost hear Tilly whispering in her ear, 'Nancy Harmer, I do believe you're not listening in church. Shame on you!', and then laughing.

That last Sunday really had been a wonderful day. Everyone had left and Nancy had only just finished clearing up and was reading Gemah a bedtime story when the phone rang. It was Susan who took the call, from Bill, and Susan who sat beside her for the rest of the night while she adjusted to the thought of a life without Tilly.

A celebration of life, that's what they called it now. Ridiculous. It's a funeral, that's what it is, always had been and always would be. What was there to celebrate?

Nancy closed her eyes and whispered, 'Goodbye, Tilly. God bless.' She wanted to say that it had been fun, but that seemed too flippant to say in church. She returned the tea-stained photo she had of them on the bench at the beach to her bag and shut the clasp. Then, nonsense or not, Nancy cried.

It was much later that evening, and the priest was tired. It had been a long day. He had been fond of Tilly; she and Bill were good people. He knelt at the altar and said one last prayer for her. He did his usual rounds, then began to switch all the lights off as he made his way out. One last look.

The last set of lights was switched off and the church was in darkness except for the altar lights. That was why he didn't see them.

They were still there, on the bench, the new black leather gloves. Nancy didn't want them any more.

Christopher and Julie

It had been so many years since I had seen him, yet there was still a place in my heart that would only ever belong to him. From the moment I had set eyes on him as a child there had been that spark, something wonderful that the separation of years could not destroy. I was not alone in my pain in those early years when he returned to Ghana. Mum had suffered too. We both loved him, and although he was with us for only a few years, in that time we had spent every possible moment together. The separation, when it came, had been an almost physical pain.

Mum said in later years that it was never any good anyone telling you that it was pointless to love someone. Love just arrived unannounced sometimes and it was wrong to close your heart to it. There had been so many children, each of them special in their own way, and it was impossible sometimes not to feel pain when they left Nazareth House. Nancy always wondered, for years and years afterwards, where they were, whether they'd coped and adjusted, whether they were happy. Christopher had been different. The pain of him leaving had been raw for many years, even though Danny always made sure we received photographs and letters letting us know how they were. I could not have loved him more if he had been my biological brother.

Years went by and the letters between us as we grew older became fewer, although we never forgot each other. I was forty years old now, Gemah eight and Mum seventy-five when this particular letter arrived. Mum was so excited she was at the front door waving it in the air when I came home from work. Gemah was very excited too: her grandma had been telling her stories about Christopher since she had been collected from school. 'Mum, Grandma's read the letter hundreds of times,' she said.

'Not quite,' Mum replied, but the sparkle was there in her eyes. 'Read it, Susan. Go on, read it now.'

Christopher. I hadn't thought about him for some time now, and I sat down, Gemah and Mum watching me, both of them already knowing the words in the letter by heart.

Christopher gave us all his news. He was very happy, and married to Julie, and they had a daughter who was four years old. Christopher's father lived near them and they were having a wonderful life. Christopher's letters had always been full of kindness, words of love for his sister, Susan, and mum, Nancy. He had never forgotten us and throughout his life he had remembered that kind gift of a case of toys and photographs for his long journey by sea to Ghana. His family was now living in Manchester, only a three-hour car journey away, and they were coming to Newcastle in a few weeks' time and wanted to drop in and see us. We were so happy that day, the three of us, jumping up and down and planning our day together with Christopher and his family.

It was a long three weeks, and Mum, as usual when anyone was coming to visit, was spring-cleaning the house.

Why any visitor would feel the need to get on to their hands and knees and look round the back of the toilet or stand on tiptoe to look in the back of the cupboards to check for dust was beyond me, but I had long since given up trying to understand Mum's passion for 'sorting and cleaning the cupboards out'.

We watched out of the window for at least an hour before they were due. It is almost impossible for me to describe how it felt the moment I saw him again. God had answered my many pleas to bring him back to us. He walked towards us, waving and smiling, and I will never forget that first hug. I hadn't seen him for so many years, and here he was in front of me. Julie was lovely, and they were such a caring and compassionate couple, part of a large church community, and quite simply the kind of people who it is marvellous to be around and an honour to know.

What an incredible day that was. We laughed, we cried, we laughed some more. Mum got the photograph album out and we talked without stopping to draw breath.

'Please come back tomorrow for breakfast before you go back to Manchester,' Mum pleaded, and they did. After breakfast, Christopher, laughing, said Mum had filled them all with so much food he'd had enough to eat for a week. With sadness but also feeling great joy at having seen Christopher and meeting his family, we said good-bye, but with promises of telephone calls and to keep in touch.

The next time I was to see them, something very wonderful and exciting would happen.

Family Days

Harry moved in with Mum, Gemah and myself in 1995. It was a time of adjustment for all of us. I loved Harry very much and it was great to spend time, all of us together as a family. Mum was always making Harry laugh – we were used to her naivety and her funny ways of saying things –. and sometimes she would laugh along too, with no understanding of why something was funny, just joining in the fun.

Mum's arthritis was beginning to get much worse and the stairs and daily chores were becoming more and more difficult for her. I began to worry about leaving her in the house alone in case she fell, which she had done on a few occasions now. My Aunty Mary, who lived in Workington in Cumbria, was quite simply a Godsend. She would often come and stay for a few days to give me a break. I really don't know what I would have done without her. At the drop of a hat, she'd be there looking after Mum, doing things around the house and, when she came through, the three sisters and their brother Benny would all get together. Their older brother lived in London, so they didn't see him very often. The joy in my life was to be with all my cousins and their children. By the end of the day my whole body would be aching with laughter. There would be all the stories about when they were young and what they got up to. It was a happy home filled with laughter, and Mum was at the centre of it all. Mum and I hadn't had any access to a car when Gemah was younger and Uncle Benny took us everywhere and often came on holiday with us. This was my family, and I was their niece and cousin, and now Gemah, Harry and I were together. I was very happy indeed. There was always an anniversary, wedding or some other family event to go to, and the grandchildren – Gemah, Michael, Jamie, Daniel and Adam – always had birthday parties which were fun, messy and absolute bliss.

Every third Sunday Mum and I would bake all afternoon, and at 7 p.m. on the dot my Uncle Benny would arrive to see us all and we would have supper together. He was a good, kind man and we were all very close. On the Saturday, Mum would be up early and at the shops, saying, 'Come on then, time for the meat counter,' and buy meat for more sandwiches than anyone could possibly eat on one Sunday evening. It was always for 'Our Benny', who would enjoy it and who, living on his own, couldn't possibly be eating properly.

It was one of the grandchildren's birthdays and, naturally, the whole family got together, with what seemed like enough food for the whole street. The children were playing and you had to shout to be heard above the chatter and laughter. I remember Mum saying how lucky they all were and how good life had been to them. 'Well, we've been able to laugh, Nancy,' said Mary. 'Just as well!' said Margaret, and off everyone started again on their stories and memories.

These people had suffered the loss of their mother, when Mary was only eighteen months old, and the loss of their father in 1970; Benny had spent his early life in and out of hospital; they had lost a sister, been through a world war, been evacuated, split up as children, lived in houses that people today would condemn, and here they were, laughing, happy and thankful for their lives. They had learned the importance of family, of sticking together through adversity, through love. I'd spent many days with all these people. I had no blood tie to them and yet they were my family through and through. To my Aunty Tilly and Uncle Bill, my mum's sisters and brothers and extended families, I was simply 'our Susan', their niece or cousin. And all from being Nancy's child. I admire them all greatly and thank them for the honour of being part of their family.

The Lop-sided Cake

It was a household the same as most others today. The presents had all been unwrapped hours ago and the television blaring since 7 a.m. There was an amazing smell coming from the kitchen and the table was set for Christmas dinner. We had a red-and-gold-themed table this year and had spent Christmas Eve making it just perfect. Mum had even bought little presents for everyone to put on the table. The usual decorations hung from the ceiling and garlands stretched across every room. We had coloured lights on the tree and around the windows. It was our traditional fairy grotto, in fact, with lights draped around the many pictures on the wall. Every time Gemah brought anything home from school, from the very first scribble when she was three years old to her now beautifully drawn pictures, they were put on the wall with sticky tape or Blu-tack, where they could be seen every day, and now covered most of the walls in the dining room, kitchen and hallway. So very many years ago, yet even now when I close my eyes I can see my perfect home, filled with love, laughter, memories and those treasured pictures and poems.

Children were outside already, failing miserably to ride their new bikes through the snow, Gemah was playing on her new computer game and we could hear the CD of

Christmas carols that had been bought for Mum playing in the kitchen. It was a very noisy house, just as it should be on Christmas morning – that is until Harry, unable to cope any longer, asked if there was any chance of turning the noise levels down to megablast. The TV was switched off, and Mum and I got on with the job of cooking Christmas lunch, to the strains of 'Silent Night', Mum's favourite.

Mum was unable to stand for long periods of time now, so she was sitting at the kitchen table preparing the vegetables. As well as ourselves, we were expecting Uncle Benny and Aunty Elaine, the friend of Mum's who made the most delicious cakes. She was so good at decorating them that now, every birthday she had, Gemah's excitement was more about what her cake from Aunty Elaine would be like than her presents. There had been a fairy castle, Red Riding Hood's cottage, a mermaids' lagoon . . . each one more incredible than the last. I was so glad she was coming for dinner today.

Mum, as always, loved to tell us Christmas stories, and this year was to be no different. 'What's the story this year, Grandma?' asked Gemah.

'One moment,' said Harry. 'Before we start, I'll get the sherry out.'

Every year, Mum had a glass of sherry at Christmas. 'Yes, please, Harry,' she said now, as though she was really looking forward to it. Truth is, she absolutely hated the stuff, but it was Christmas and you had to have a glass of sherry to be sociable, she said, so a thimbleful was poured into the glass for her, and it lasted her until at least four in the afternoon. Every year it was the same. So, sherry in hand, we all sat around the kitchen table while the meat sizzled in the oven.

Many years ago, she began, there had been great excitement in the orphanage not only among the children but among all the staff and nuns. The Lady Mayor was to visit on Christmas morning. This was a very big occasion for Nazareth House, and the children were going to be brought into the nuns' parlour to greet her at 11 a.m. All the children with long hair were to be sat down on Christmas Eve to have rags put into it to create the perfect ringlets, the very best clothes were to be got out, and 'I,' said Mum, 'decided it was time to get out my red lipstick. I only used it on very special occasions. In fact, it had been at least two years since I had worn it. This was a very special treat for me too and I was very excited at the thought of actually meeting the Lady Mayor. It was all anyone was talking about, from the cloak and chains she wore to what on earth you would say if she actually spoke to you.'

Discussions were taking place as to what to give the Lady Mayor as a gift. Mother Superior asked Cook if she could spare some of her ingredients to make another Christmas cake, and everyone agreed that would be a wonderful idea. Cook always made the Christmas cake, and Aunty Elaine decorated it. Mother Superior asked for it to be a traditional cake with holly and red ribbon, and the day before, the ingredients having been prepared days earlier, the cake was placed into the oven and Cook turned her thoughts to the million other things she had to do that day. Aunty Elaine was upstairs in the nursery with all her bits and pieces ready to decorate it for the Lady Mayor. She had taken over the table in the television room for the purpose, and now all she had to do was wait. Time passed. By four in the afternoon she was thinking to herself, I really should have had that cake by now. I need to take my time with it.

Unknown to her, downstairs, in a very hot and busy kitchen, Cook was having hysterics. The cake had been taken out of the oven and, to everyone's absolute horror, it had sunk on one side and was lop-sided. Cook was screaming, the young girls who were helping in the kitchen were running round being totally useless and not knowing what to do. The noise from the kitchen brought Sister Mary Joseph running to find out what on earth was going on. She entered to find a kitchen in complete chaos.

'Would someone like to explain this?' she asked quietly.

Young Norma spoke up. 'Well, you see, Sister, it's the cake. It, erm, well, it's lop-sided.'

Cook groaned and had to sit down. Sister Mary Joseph gently asked everyone to move away from the table so she could take a look. There was silence as she moved forward to do so. She smiled, turned to Cook and kindly said, 'Cook, I'm sure we can think of something else for the Lady Mayor and . . .'

'Damn the Lady Mayor!' shouted Cook. 'It's my reputation I'm worried about! A lop-sided cake – I'll never live it down!' Sister Mary Joseph gasped in shock, Cook fainted and, once more, chaos ensued.

It was then that Aunty Elaine walked into the kitchen to find out what had happened to her cake. Everyone was talking at once, waving tea towels in Cook's face, dabbing her brow with a wet cloth. Elaine simply ignored them and walked forward and stood there, staring at the cake. Cook came round. 'Thank you,' said Aunty Elaine, and she picked up the cake and walked out of the kitchen, never once taking her eyes off it. She asked to be left alone, closed the door and shut herself away to deal with the lop-sided cake.

At just after nine o'clock that evening, Elaine asked for Mother Superior. Everyone was huddled outside the television-room door when she arrived. They crowded in behind her when the door was opened, and there it was in all its glory. A Christmas cake made in the shape of a snowy ski slope with little people skiing down it. There was a moment's hush while everyone took it in, then everyone began to talk at once: 'How did you do it?' 'Oh my, it has to be the most wonderful cake I have ever seen!' 'What are the people made out of?' 'Wait until the Lady Mayor sees this!' . . . and so it went on. Elaine had saved the day and Mother Superior was very happy and thanked her over and over again.

The next morning, there was much hustle and bustle, the best china was sitting on the table in the parlour and the children and members of staff were ready to greet the Lady Mayor. It was all very official and, after she had arrived, the Lady Mayor walked around the parlour, talking to the children. They were on their best behaviour, the girls remembered to curtsey and lots of ringlets shimmered and shook. Then the time came for the cake to be presented from the children and staff of Nazareth House to the Lady Mayor.

There was a hush, apart from a few gasps of wonder, as two of the children ever so gently and slowly walked forward to present the Lady Mayor with the most wonderful lop-sided cake ever.

To say she was delighted would be an understatement. She had never seen the like, she said. She thanked Cook and said it was the most incredible thing she had ever seen.

Cook had the grace to blush.

There was a hush in our kitchen that day, too. The CD had stopped playing. We had all been enthralled by the story of the lop-sided cake.

Until, that is, the smoke alarm went off and four people jumped up to deal with their own Christmas kitchen disaster!

The Proposal

It was December 1998 and preparations were one again in full swing for Christmas. That means I was running around the shops like everything was going out of stock and stressing about food, presents, cards and whether it would all be done in time. The usual Christmas, in fact. A couple of months earlier I had started up a car-hire business with my friend Caryl, and we were still in the early days of getting it up and running, although we did have a few very busy weeks ahead of us due to the party season.

This particular morning I got up early, had a quick shower and began scanning my 'to do' list for the day, thinking there might not be enough hours to get through it all. Caryl had the car business in hand and was meeting someone from the media later that day to be interviewed while driving the car – a big white stretch limousine twenty-eight feet long. Brave girl. I had the ultimate joy of food shopping today, had to pick up a last few presents, meet Caryl later that evening and fit all the other daily chores in between. Harry and I had been so busy we had hardly seen each other the last few days, so I left him a little poem on the kitchen bench saying how much I loved him. Gemah was spending the day at Gillian's house – she was my best friend and lived round the corner – so I was all set, ready for the day. Half an hour later, while I was standing freezing cold at the bus stop, it started to snow. Great, I love snow – but not today, thank you very much.

Four very long hours later I arrived home. I trudged up the street with what felt like a hundred carrier bags. I'm sure my arms were a couple of inches longer than when I set out. Next year I promised myself I would go food shopping wearing a suit of armour. On one single aisle I had been pushed, battered twice in the back with a trolley, had my foot stood on, been kicked in the ankle by a screaming child (I knew how he felt, I could quite easily have had a tantrum myself) and hit on the side of the head by someone carrying a large box – and all for the sake of squirty cream. Why do normal, upstanding citizens become demons the moment the shops open the last weekend before Christmas? And, more to the point, why are we running around like headless chickens buying enough food to feed the whole street when the shops are open again two days after Christmas? Such were my thoughts as I slipped and slid along, the snow having now turned to sleet. You know those beautiful cards in the shops with their wondrous scenes of pretty snow-laden cottages and children playing happily in the snow? Well, real life just isn't like that. Why not have a picture of a soaking-wet woman, hair flat to her head and arms laden with Morrison's carrier bags, skidding along in the slush doing more twists and turns than Torvill and Dean?

Naturally, of course, just to finish the day off, my keys were nowhere to be found. There is a place in my hand-bag where there is a secret, magic hole. When I need to retrieve my keys, transferring all my other bags into one hand and tipping over sideways with them, balancing my handbag on my knee, using my teeth to hold the straps up and my free hand to look for the keys, they are nowhere to be found. Gone. Hidden in the secret, magic compartment and never to be seen again. Time to give up and boot the door with my foot.

Harry answered the door with a questioning look on his face as if to say, Why are you booting the door down? 'Do Not Ask,' I said in my most exasperated voice. So he just took the bags and I collapsed into the nearest chair. At that moment I caught sight of myself in the mirror, and it wasn't pretty.

Harry was in the kitchen putting all the food away when I called through to him:

'I'm going to have a cuppa then make dinner. What would you like?'

He came through from the kitchen and smiled at me.

'I think I would like to get married.'

And there I sat. His bride-to-be. The new 'not-waterproof' mascara was smudged across my face, my hair was plastered to my head, water was dripping off my nose . . .

'*Yes!*' I screamed, and jumped up to hug him, then turned and ran out of the front door, slid up to Gillian's door, burst into the room where they were all quietly sitting watching a Christmas movie and yelled, '*I'm getting married!*' We were all jumping around excitedly, Gemah and I hugging each other, and in the next half an hour we had it all sorted. Gemah and Gillian's daughters, Laura and Rebecca, and her niece, Natalia, would be brides-maids, and Gillian, my wonderful, funny, supportive and caring best friend, would have the greatest honour. 'Oooh, what's that then?' she said, visions of being the maid of honour springing into her mind.

'You're organizing it,' I said with a smile on my face. 'And I'm thinking February.'

'February.'

'Yes.'

'This next February?'

'Yes.'

'The February that's in ten weeks' time?'

'That's the one.'

'Insane, that's what you are,' she said, 'but let's do it!'

We gave each other another hug, then I returned home to start planning things with Harry. 'Oh, by the way, Gillian,' I said before leaving, 'we'll have a look round the department stores next week. No bridal stuff, I just want an evening-gown-type dress, something I can wear again maybe, something sophisticated. Nothing too fancy, OK?'

'Yeah, right,' said Gillian, and after I'd left she rang the bridal shop to make an appointment for the next day.

I was getting married, and I hurried home to make myself look half decent and celebrate with the man I loved.

It's always good to finish a day with laughter, and later that evening I popped round to see Caryl and ask how the interview had gone.

Now my friend Caryl is wonderful at this sort of thing and, as always, had turned up perfectly groomed, not a hair out of place, in a designer skirt and jacket with matching shoes and bag (everything always matched with Caryl). They had brought along a film crew and the clip was to be shown on the north-east news later that week. They first interviewed her sitting in the interior of the car with all the party lights and music playing, then asked her to drive the car round the block so they could film it in motion. The interview team got out of the car and the film crew were waiting as Caryl emerged from the driver's seat, sophisticated as always, swinging her legs to the side. She walked to the front of the car, got in and shut the door. Click. Only one problem. The keys were on the back seat. Caryl closed her eyes in horror.

'Is there a problem?' asked one of the crew.

'Just the one: the keys are on the back seat.'

'Oh, is that a problem then? What do we have to do?'

'*We*,' said Caryl, 'will have to crawl through the privacy glass and retrieve them. Now I need your assurance that you do not have your cameras switched on and you will not be taking photographs.'

They all had a bit of a laugh and a chatter about it then turned away as my lovely, sophisticated friend got on all fours and crawled on her stomach through the privacy glass. She landed face first on the shiny polished leather seats in the body of the limousine. I have to say I do wish it *had* been filmed. I would have paid good money to see it.

Anyway, I wasn't too worried. I'm sure she would have been wearing matching designer knickers.

The Perfect Angle

Gillian did absolutely everything. She totally ignored the evening-dress idea and dragged me to a bridal shop, where I was shown an ivory satin and lace dress with little bows on the train. Well, that was it. I was whisked away to try it on, and from the moment the dress was over my head I felt like a princess. I walked out of the cubicle with a smile on my face that said it all. 'Told you,' she said. 'I knew I was right.' Yes, Gill, you were so right.

While Caryl and I, along with her husband and my Harry's help, carried on getting our business off the ground, Gillian arranged the wedding almost single-handedly. Venue, flowers, wedding lists, invitations – anyone with any questions would call Gillian. Aunty Mary was coming through to look after Mum; it had been arranged that Uncle Benny would take them to the wedding.

Gillian also arranged a brilliant hen night. A coach came to collect us all from her house and take us to Whitley Bay's finest bars, then back to her house for a buffet and more partying. Not one ever to allow anyone to be on their own, when Harry arrived home she was straight over to drag him to the party. It was a fantastic night with lots of laughter, dancing and singing into hairbrushes.

I was to be married from Gill's house and, to put it mildly, I was highly stressed the night before, so, with

Gillian threatening to slap me if I didn't go, she sent me to bed with a pillow sprinkled in lavender essential oil.

I lay there, thinking back to just a few months before, at the end of November, when Christopher had called to say that they would all be coming through to Newcastle for the weekend for a friend's wedding and could they pop in and see us. Sunday lunch was arranged, and it was a double surprise when Danny, Christopher's father, came with them. Mum was ecstatic to see him and it was fantastic to see them talking about the old days. Danny told Harry all about Mum and how knowing how much she had loved and cared for his son had made life bearable for him. He had tears in his eyes talking about her, and it was a very emotional day for all of us. Later in the afternoon Julie took me quietly to one side and asked me a question.

'Why have you and Harry never got married? He is divorced now, isn't he?'

'Yes, about four years ago, but Julie, he hasn't asked me.'

'You would like to?'

'More than anything.'

'Well,' she said, 'Christopher and I will pray for you when we get home.'

'That is so kind,' I replied, 'but may I suggest double knee pads? You may be down there for a while.'

I smiled now, remembering that it was only two weeks later when Harry proposed. Julie was one of the first people I called, telling her that she and her family were definitely guests of honour at the wedding.

And now, tomorrow was the day. Finally, my secret dream was about to come true. I thought I would never sleep with all the excitement. When Gillian came upstairs to check on me and saw that I was still awake even after she had sprinkled lavender in my bath water and on my pillow, she walked over to her bedside drawer, said, 'What the hell!' and poured the whole bottle over the bedclothes. I slept.

It was a crazy household the next morning, with all four bridesmaids and the bride having their hair done. Joanne, my hairdresser for the past fifteen years, was doing our hair as a wedding present, bless her. I was stressing because I thought my fingers were swollen and the ring might not fit. 'No problem,' shouted Gill across the noise. 'I will bring my little jar of Vaseline just in case. Now, will you stop worrying?'

People were in and out all morning, and by eleven o'clock we were all stressed and hungry. So there we were with rollers in our hair, sticking on our false nails, eating microwave chips with brown sauce (classy chicks). The button holes and the flowers had arrived the night before, and Gillian had been sneezing all morning, so pretty much the normal wedding-morning chaos. 'I don't know how many times you're going to try that hat on,' I said to Gillian at one point. Now, if you're not the sort of person that wears hats it's quite a strange feeling when you wear a hat with a wide brim. Gillian's outfit was a beautiful pale blue, with the hat the same colour, and she would look great whatever angle she wore it.

Eventually, the limousine pulled up outside. Might I say

that this was not my limousine, the one I actually owned with Caryl and hired out for weddings. I remembered thinking to myself that at least I'd have no problems hiring a car for the wedding. But no, the lovely Caryl had taken a booking two weeks before for the car to be used in a promotional event on the morning of my wedding. Guess who was in the car. Mr Blobby. Caryl, calm as always, said she would sort something out, and hired me another white stretch limousine, which I had to pay for, but hey ho! Mr Blobby's needs come first! Our own limousine was being brought to the church after the service, so all was well. The night before, Caryl and Gill had put beautiful ribbon bows at the end of each pew in the church, so the aisle looked very pretty. Sharon, another great friend, had made orders of service and had put them on all the pews. I truly was blessed with wonderful friends. It was all set. We were ready.

I left the house with my bridesmaids and Gillian. The driver, in full chauffeur's uniform, was standing by the car, the door open. All eyes were on me and I was loving it. I glided across to the car, smiling at everyone, Gillian carrying my train. The sun was shining and it was a clear, crisp February day. Everything was perfect. We got into the car looking all serene and sophisticated, then, when the car was halfway down the street, Gillian screamed, 'Oh my God, we forgot the Vaseline!' The poor driver nearly crashed the car. As it was a limousine and there was no room to turn around, he had to reverse all the way back up the street. Gillian ran into the house, then back out, and jumped into the limousine holding on to her hat.

When the neighbours began to come out into the street, she shouted, 'Please don't ask!' and we were away once again.

We all burst out laughing, and asked the driver to put on my CD to play on the way. There we were, all six of us swaying from side to side, singing along to Jason Donavan's 'Any Dream Will Do'. It was very probably not the most dignified wedding party the driver had ever seen, and Gillian was still stressing about the angle of her hat.

When we arrived, everyone was there on the steps of the registry office waiting for us. There was Mum, looking so proud, my family and friends, all the people I loved here in one place. Photographs were taken, then I walked up the steps to be greeted by my husband-to-be. Once all the forms had been checked and signed, everyone took their places.

Gemah took my hand and was by my side as I prepared to marry her father. Laura, Rebecca and Natalia were behind me. Gill looked at me, and tears began to form in her eyes.

'No tears, Gill.'

'No tears, Sue.'

'Love you.'

'Love you too.'

Now, if this was a scene in a movie, Gillian would then float off to take her place before I glided down the aisle.

However, the double doors were not yet fully open ready for my entrance when, head held high, proud as Punch, Gillian turned, walked through the door – and got her hat stuck. My screams of laughter could be heard inside the room (not a usual occurrence before the bride makes her entrance). 'I like that angle best, Gill,' I shouted, as she hastily adjusted her hat just before the doors were opened wide and Michael Ball burst into song, singing 'Love Changes Everything'.

It was a fun and beautiful ceremony, and when it was over we got back into the limousine to head for the church, where we were having a blessing. This time, I walked down the aisle with Dad to the traditional bridal march, my bridesmaids behind me. The priest carried out the blessing of the rings and, as my wedding band was taken off to be blessed and returned to me, Gillian sat there once again as she had at the registry office, with her fingers hovering over the clasp of her handbag ready to retrieve the Vaseline if necessary.

The Jarvis family were all there. I had known them since Mum and I moved to our very first home. We had all attended this church for many years now. Their daughter Lucy had the most beautiful singing voice, and I used to love listening to her on a Sunday. She sang the love theme from *Titanic* and it was the icing on the cake. Everyone loved it.

Then the organ began to play and Harry and I turned to make our way into the world as husband and wife. There behind me was our daughter, who I treasured with all my heart and soul, my mum, who I could not have loved more, Harry's son, who was a brilliant best man, and my family and friends.

And there they were, Gillian and Caryl, one of them walking up the aisle, so dignified with her hat at a perfect angle, giving waves the Queen would be proud of, the other whipping all the bows from the edges of the pews as she waltzed up. 'Well, we can use them on the limousine for other weddings,' she said.

Crazy but perfect friends.

We had a buffet reception in the afternoon so that we could all mingle and chat with each other, and then my father stood up to make his speech. He said all the usual things about how proud he was of me but then made my heart stand still when he turned to look at Mum. 'However, before we toast the bride,' he said, 'I want you all to raise your glasses to Nancy, to whom I owe a debt of gratitude I can never repay. The woman that Susan has turned out to be is down to Nancy. Many children have passed through her hands, and none have been luckier than my daughter. Thank you, Nancy.' At that moment I loved my father more than I had ever done before.

The toasts continued and Harry made everyone laugh with sarcastic comments about my cooking (well, we can't all be Fanny Cradock). Nothing had gone wrong and everything in the world was wonderful that day. In the evening my friend Susan brought over all her friends to put on a country-dancing session and later we had a disco. Lucy sang for us again, and I looked around the room feeling so special and lucky to have all my friends and family there.

The Last Dance

She was sitting quietly now, a smile on her face, because she knew what was to come. That perfect moment that would make everything all right from this moment on. A secret she had never shared and kept close to her heart, just in case one day . . . When you have prayed and hoped and dreamed, always wondering, imagining, how you might feel, it's a momentous feeling when it becomes real. She closed her eyes, hardly able to believe it.

It was the signal that everything was going to be different now: there would always be that strength by her side, someone to fight her battles, protect her from criticism, make her feel special. When those thoughts surfaced, as they often did, telling her she was nobody special, that she would never amount to anything much, that she had the worst pair of legs ever, that she was a plain child, he would fight the demons and she would stand tall because he was there.

She closed her eyes and thought of Gemah, and how much she loved her. Do all mothers feel this way, she wondered, or is it just me? It's not only that I love her, it's so much more. Gemah was dancing around her grandma, and her heart beat just a little faster, as it always did when she watched her. She had been a good mother, she hoped. No matter what else, she knew in her heart that she had tried her best.

Inside, her heart was beating so fast and she was unable to believe that this dreamed-of moment was now fast approaching. Amazing, she thought to herself, that someone can feel this amount of emotion, trepidation, and no one can see it. She had dreamed about this day, as most young girls did, dancing round the room with net curtains on her head, picking flowers in the wood and practising her walk. How many weddings had she sat there by herself, hoping, yet never quite believing anyone would ever want to marry her? How many times had she smiled, congratulated, celebrated the weddings of others with a heaviness in her heart that no one could see?

At this point in the day, she supposed most brides might be thinking to themselves, Well, that's it, all done and dusted – but not her. For her this was the beginning.

It was time. The lights were low, the tables were littered with debris, there were streamers everywhere and balloons were floating across the dance floor. The evening was over, except for one thing.

No one in that room, not even her husband, could possibly know what this moment meant to her. She looked up, and he was walking towards her. She closed her eyes, her heart thumping. Oh dear God, it's real! It really is happening!

He took her hand, and the man in the black coat led his wife on to the dance floor for the last dance.

Somebody else watched the handbags.

Titanic Trauma

Nancy had never had a boyfriend. There was no need for all that nonsense apparently, and anyway, didn't she have enough children to look after without that kind of thing?

Now that's perfectly reasonable if that's how you feel, but please tell me how you are going to do the birds and the bees thing for your growing daughter when the time arrives?

At the age of ten, I can't remember ever thinking about boys, and my memories at that time are ones of school, homework and days out with Mum, and reading every magazine I could lay my hand on for all the gossip about famous actors and actresses.

I remember one day I arrived home one evening from school and after tea Mum asked if we could have a little chat in our room. These words came with embarrassed little glances and sideways looks and nods. I was worried. This looked and sounded serious. Had I done something bad, said something wrong? The time arrived and there she was, wringing her hands, banging the cushions about, handing out biscuits, stirring the tea over and over, straightening ornaments, clearing her throat . . . What was going on? This was so unusual. Mum was always so composed.

She sat down beside me and, looking straight ahead,

eyes averted as far away from me as possible, said, 'You don't kiss boys.' Stunned silence from me. I had no intention of kissing any boys, thank you very much. I didn't even particularly like them. 'You know when girls get' (vigorous nodding of the head and a cough) 'when they get . . . involved.' Excuse me, are we doing some strange kind of sign language or code signals here? What on God's earth was she talking about? Of course, there was no way that Mum was ever going to say the word 'pregnant', and she would have had to wash her mouth out with soap and water for a week if she'd said 'sex'. It took a lot more embarrassing mumbling before I was allowed to leave the room, thinking that I had better be more careful the next time I behaved with wild abandon and kissed the Cliff Richard poster above my bed.

That was the entirety of my sex education from Mum. Possibly, it wasn't a problem, though, as my summer exam results from school were in my bag and I had finally reached the A+ status. Twice, in fact. Religious education and music. Well, that's my career sorted, I thought: I will be a singing nun.

In my whole life I never heard Mum say either 'pregnant' or 'sex'. You'll remember how excited and proud she was at being told that she was to be a grandma when I was 'with child', and she began the round of visiting and phoning friends to give them the good news?

Well, I thought, time had moved on now, I was grown-up, and it would all be different. Or that's what you would think. But no, absolutely not. The 'Wonderful news, Susan is —' was followed by eyebrows raised up to the hairline, pursed lips and head tipped to one side. Oh well, at least the vigorous nodding had stopped.

This all explains why anything to do with (dare I say it?) sex was never discussed in front of Mum. It would have embarrassed us more than her, I think, and we were always extremely vigilant when watching TV. I thanked God for remote controls so we could quickly switch channels if a programme became embarrassing instead of making a rugby-tackle dive to switch over.

One particular Christmas will always stick in my mind. It never fails to make my family laugh, no matter how many times we relive it. I wasn't yet married, but Harry was living with us, and that year Christmas was made even more special as we were having family for dinner. It was a fun-filled day and Gemah was helping to prepare all the festivities. The house was decorated, as always, like a fairy grotto, with hundreds of fairy lights, lanterns and garlands hanging from the ceiling. We always kept the most special treasure until everything else was done, and then out of the box came the fairy made out of a toilet roll and cotton wool that Gemah had brought home when she was in reception class. It brings tears to my eyes to remember those wonderful moments: myself, Mum and Gemah placing the fairy on top of the Christmas tree, then turning all the lights on.

They were such happy days, and Mum was enjoying life. She had fought back from a horrendous stroke and we were happier than ever. Gemah, of course, got away with all the things I never did. She was the apple of her grandma's eye, and they simply adored each other. I sometimes think it must have been so hard for Harry – we were such a tight-knit group – but he was always lovely with Mum and shared many a laugh and good time.

This Christmas we had gone totally over the top with the decorations; it was simply wonderful. Harry came home from work that night, walked in the door, looked around him, shook his head and said, 'You've obviously run out of decorations. You need some more?' Very funny.

That day it was very busy in the kitchen, as it was Mum, Gemah, Harry and my uncle for lunch, then my aunty and cousins for tea.

We had a fantastic dinner, then the rest of the family arrived. After more chatter the sherry was brought out and we all collapsed in a heap ready to settle down for the film on TV. *Titanic*. I have only myself to blame for what happened next, as I had already seen the film.

I was only half watching it and snoozing when I felt my cousin dig me in the ribs. There they were, Jack and Rose on the *Titanic*, about to have sex in a car on the boat deck. The music began to play – but the beauty of Jack and Rose becoming one was forgotten in our house. It all happened at once. My uncle quickly picked up the newspaper and started rustling it about, pretending to look for something in it, everyone started talking at once, I suddenly decided it was time for a cuppa, and Mum had escaped to the kitchen to look for biscuits. The film carried on as we all pretended not to notice, and the louder the music got, the more Mum was clashing and banging the cupboards in the kitchen to cover it. The iceberg couldn't come quick enough after that!

Gemah was upstairs in absolute hysterics and would have been heard laughing downstairs if it hadn't been for all the clanging and crashing going on in the kitchen. Yes, I know Gemah was only eleven at that time but, fortunately, she had been given a little more sex education than I had. Well, to be fair, anyone had!

Unfortunately, the rest of the film went unwatched. Mum decided it was time to prepare for Christmas tea – and this about two hours after we had eaten enough food for a week.

It was a fabulous day and we all thoroughly enjoyed ourselves. When our guests left, we settled down, exhausted, in front of the TV. It was all over for another year.

'Enjoy the film, Nancy?' said Harry with a cheeky wink.

'Disgusting,' she said through pursed lips and, nose in the air, sailed forth to the kitchen to wash up.

The Letter

Bill had been thinking about Nancy today. She had been a good friend, the best, and a wonderful auntie to the children. He was a quiet man with a dignified air about him, a mop of wavy grey hair and a twinkle in his eyes. The soft Irish lilt in his voice was still very apparent, even though he had left Ireland over sixty years ago. That was back at the beginning, where it had all begun; his whole life had been mapped out in front of him then. The priesthood was definitely his chosen path. He felt happiest in prayer, and his religion was of the utmost importance to him. Like many others, though, he hadn't reckoned on the war and the changes it would bring about. He was so determined on his life's path he would still have fought to become a priest, but then one day it all changed. Tilly. He fell in love with her the moment he set eyes on her.

Falling in love had not been on his agenda. And he and Tilly were so different. He was the sensible one and Tilly – well, Tilly didn't have a sensible bone in her body. Life was to be enjoyed; it should be fun. Why be sad when you can laugh? She had captured his heart in their first moments of meeting. They had married, had four girls and a house filled with laughter. They had celebrated anniversaries with their children, grandchildren and great-grandchildren. His Tilly could answer the door to visitors, disappear into the kitchen and twenty minutes later emerge with a trayful of scones and cakes that would make Mr Kipling look like a novice. And in all the years they had been married, he couldn't remember ever seeing a recipe book in the house. She would just throw the ingredients into a bowl, and that was it. Perfection. They had disagreed, of course, over many things, because they were so different, yet they had done it without falling out. It was impossible to fall out with Tilly — she would just laugh at you and do her own thing anyway. He had loved her very much. She had been his Tilly and he didn't regret a thing.

His breath was short now, and he didn't always feel that he was functioning as he should do, but he turned his attention back to the letter he was writing. It was almost finished, but not quite. There was still the final explanation to be written. He would never know if they had understood. He thought they would: they were good people, his girls. Bill and Tilly had been good parents; their relation-ship had had the perfect balance, Tilly with her sense of fun, the girls happy in the knowledge that they were loved, Bill ensuring that they were all taught core values and respect. There was that word again: 'respect'. His shame would be in the hands of his maker when they read this, and he would be back with his Tilly. Life was just too quiet without her. Nancy, he knew, would understand.

It was getting dark outside and his eyes were tired. And, in truth, it wasn't only his eyes, he himself was tired. Drained. The letter was finished now. It had taken him weeks to write it, to find the right words to explain it properly. He loved his girls, all four of them. He was proud of them. They had been lucky, himself and Tilly, the girls had grown up to be wonderful daughters. They were all married now, and they deserved to know. Bill smiled, thinking about his great-grandchildren. They were coming into a very different world to the one he had been born into, and he was glad of that. They would not be made to feel the shame. Would they feel as though they had missed out by not knowing their ances-tors? He very much hoped not. It was Anne who had asked the most questions, but they all wanted to know. He was bitterly ashamed. It had been a heavy burden to carry all these years. He had always managed to laugh it off when the girls asked who their grandfather was. His name was Thomas, he told them, and they would make up stories about where he might be and who he might be, and they would laugh, and Bill would go along with it, then change the subject. Respect and dignity were important to him, and he had kept his shame a secret to maintain it.

It wouldn't be long now, he thought, he knew there were days when he couldn't remember what he had done, whether or not he had eaten. Not that it mattered. There wasn't a day went by that one of his family wasn't knocking on the door making sure he was all right and filling him with food. The times when he was alone he spent remembering the old days. Families should stay together, they should stand together and stick by each other no matter what. Money had nothing to do with it. There was too much talk about money these days, about how it could improve life. It was one of the things he disagreed with strongly.

Tilly and Bill had got it right. There had been times in the early years when lack of money had been a daily worry – for him, anyway; Tilly would always say that something would turn up, and she had been right. And then there was Nancy, always there, caring for and loving the girls. He smiled, remembering one year when there had been so little for Christmas and Nancy turned up late on Christmas Eve with presents the nuns had said she could take for Tilly's little ones. Not wanting to wait until Christmas Day, she had rushed out after work and turned up laden with presents from Santa for the children then hurried away for the last trolley bus home. Nancy had been much more than a friend: she was family. The Smalley family had stood together and fought for each other, as *it should be. Their daughters had been fantastic and their grand-children were kind, thoughtful, good people too. Yes, he thought, smiling to himself. The Smalley family had got it just right.*

If only there wasn't the shame – but that was his, not theirs. He wondered how many times he had heard as a child that you had to pay for your sins. Pay-back time. Penance, they called it. He had sat in the confessional many times over the years, asking for forgiveness. Well, he would be meeting the big man soon now. Let's see what He has to say about it all.

Bill Smalley was an honest, truthful, kind, caring, respectful and dignified man, a man any child would be proud to call their father, a man anyone would be honoured to call their friend. The penance was not his to pay.

It was time to go home now. He just knew it. He could almost hear Tilly whispering to him, 'What took you so long?', and then laughing.

The letter. He had read and re-read it. It was addressed to his girls, his precious daughters, Maureen, Anne, Kathleen and Marga-ret, and in that order, as was only right and proper, Maureen being the eldest. They needed to know the truth, though, and now was the time. It had to be written down so he could be forgiven and his girls would finally know the truth. The shame. His Tilly had understood, and how many times had she told him that it did not matter; he was all they needed. His girls would understand too.

After eighty-six years, it had been written down, and the question had been answered. Thomas was a made-up name, and he had never known his father. That was the shame Bill Smalley had carried with him all those years.

'I am so sorry,' he wrote. 'Please forgive me.'

He wrote his daughters' names on the envelope, saying each one out loud as he did so, and left the letter where they would find it.

Alongside the heartbreak and deep sadness they felt at the loss of their father, they also felt anger. Anger that he should have felt even the smallest amount of shame for something that was no fault of his own. Whispers of injustice and prejudice had played their part and once again taken their toll.

If any one of us experiences even half the joy, love, integrity and honour the Smalley family had, thanks in no small way to their parents, Tilly and Bill Smalley, then we should consider ourselves very lucky indeed.

His daughters did understand and, if possible, loved him even more for it. There was absolutely nothing to forgive.

Full Circle

Mum's recovery from her stroke had been much better than anyone expected, so it was with great sadness a few years later that we came to realize that she was now suffering from dementia. I continued to love and look after her until such time as I was no longer able to. Then Mum needed nursing care.

When I got married in 1999, thankfully Mum was well enough to attend the wedding and finally got the long-overdue credit due to her when my father as part of his speech asked everyone to raise their glasses to her. I have said it before and I will say it again: I have never loved my father more than at that moment.

It was shortly after my wedding that it became apparent that Mum was suffering from dementia. I was still Nancy's child, and we had loved and looked after each other for decades, but now it was out of our hands. We could no longer be responsible for each other's welfare. There was no sense of freedom or relief knowing that from now on Mum was going to be taken care of by someone else, just a heavy feeling of loss and loneliness. She was my mum, my responsibility, no matter what the carers said, and I knew what I wanted for her and what I had to do next.

The day Mum was transferred to the temporary respite care home was particularly hard. It was a lovely place, and she was welcomed by the staff, who all chatted and got to know her, and of course Gemah and I were there too. We didn't leave her side all day. It must have been nearing tea time when we were politely asked to leave so Mum could adjust to her new surroundings. This, I thought, was like leaving my daughter at nursery school for the first time, knowing that, no matter how wonderful the staff were, nobody could ever love and look after her the way we could.

I took Mum's hand in mine and explained that we would still see each other all the time. Gemah and I would come every week, and on games nights, and we would have fun together. I knew she was watching us as we walked out of the door, and it wasn't until I got outside that I broke down and cried for the inspirational mother I had left behind. My daughter, as always a tower of strength to me, held my hand, her own tears also falling for the grandma she loved so dearly. It was made no easier when I was told later, having called to check, that she had settled in but kept asking for me.

'Yes, well,' I could hear her saying, 'you just have to make do and get on with it.' The roles were reversed now, and it was my time to fight for her – and believe me, I was going to rise to the challenge. During the next few weeks our determination to find Mum's future home kept us going as we knocked on doors and made numerous phone calls, never taking no for an answer. Eventually, I think to get rid of us, we were given an appointment with the person who could make the decision of whether or not Mum could have a place in the nursing home of our choice. We pleaded our case and won.

Mum's new home was in a beautiful building, and my daughter and I spent many hours settling her in, putting all her photographs up and making sure she had all her treasures around her.

Every morning, after she had been washed and dressed, Mum was taken to sit in the conservatory before breakfast, from where she could look out upon the grounds of Nazareth House and have a clear view of the church, whose bells had rung at six o'clock every morning. Mum had come full circle, back to the beginning.

Bingo!

It was games evening that night – bingo and a sing-along – and Gemah and I were going along to join in and help Mum have a fun evening.

Mum's short-term memory had been a problem for some time now, but lately she also seemed to be losing her long-term memory. This was especially sad, as she loved to reminisce about the old days. Gemah and I spent as much time as possible with her, always afraid that, one day, she wouldn't recognize us.

The game activities were fantastic, as they helped keep Mum's mind active, and although sometimes she didn't really understand what was going on, she did enjoy all the involvement.

We stood at the doorway and watched her, still so very dignified, regardless of all the indignities she now had to bear. There she was in her wheelchair, sitting at the games table waiting for us, a chair on either side of her.

The staff said she was a joy to look after, always happy to agree to anything they asked her to do and always quiet and polite with a smile on her face.

What had happened to No-nonsense Nancy? The thought brought a lump to my throat. She had been a force to be reckoned with and, even as an adult, one look from her would be enough and I would back down (sometimes with a bit of a giggle, though).

Gemah squeezed my hand then walked forward, arms outstretched, and called, 'Hi, Grandma!' The Blackpool illuminations were nothing compared to the light in Mum's eyes when she saw her granddaughter. Her whole face lit up. She looked round the room. 'This is my granddaughter, Gemah, and my daughter, Susan.' This was always what she said, never just our names but 'granddaughter' and 'daughter'. She was so very proud of us. I leaned forward and kissed her and we began to set out the bingo board and markers. I was chattering away, explaining the game, and then Gemah nudged me. There it was . . . the look!!

Mum tapped me on the knee. 'Thank you,' she said. 'I'm not completely stupid.'

I had been wrong: No-nonsense Nancy was still with us. Gemah burst out laughing, gave her grandma a hug, and the game began. Mum was concentrating hard, but we had been told to let her do it herself, it was good for her, so we sat back and watched.

'Two and one, twenty-one.'

Mum put the marker on twenty-one and smiled.

'Brilliant, Grandma,' said Gemah.

'One and six, sixteen.'

At which point she picked the marker up off twenty-one and placed it on sixteen.

It was just too much. Gemah and I burst out laughing. We just couldn't control ourselves. Mum joined in too, not knowing why she was laughing, but there we sat, the three of us, laughing so much we ended up wheeling Mum out and into her room so we didn't disturb the others. That was a great evening. It took so little to make Mum happy. All she ever wanted was our time.

Once we had composed ourselves, we took Mum back to the lounge and everyone settled down for a sing-song. There was some discussion as to what CD to listen to. Last time it had been Bing Crosby, and the week before Al Jolson.

'Ooh, I love Dean Martin,' said Jenny, one of the other women there.

'Me too.'

'Very well, Dean Martin it is.'

While the CD was playing, Linda, Mum's main carer, came on duty. 'Come on then, Nancy,' she said. 'Spill the beans – who was the love of your life?'

Mum turned her head to look at me with those beautiful pale-blue eyes of hers, and smiled.

'You were,' she said 'You.'

No words!

Molly

I don't know why I looked at the death notices in the local paper that day. I'd asked Dad more and more questions over the years, and he had told me as much as he knew, so I now had not only Molly's name but the names of some of her family too. But there it was in black and white. I had read the words over and over again. I remember saying to myself, It must be her. Maybe if I said it out loud it would become even more real. So I said it: 'It must be her.' Frozen inside, unable to think straight, I read the words one more time. The names were right. Molly and her husband's full names were there, and the name of my older sister, Sarah, plus other siblings whose names I hadn't known. How can you have brothers and sisters and never know them? I remember thinking. It was so wrong. Not to have those years of growing up together, finding common interests, fighting, yet always sticking up for each other.

Her name was Molly. Molly, the lady who had given her baby away not because she didn't care or because it was an inconvenience, and certainly not because the child wasn't wanted. The growing child inside her had been loved from day one, and Molly had never forgotten her. Molly had been brave and given a woman she would never know the gift not only of a child but a life filled with love, treasured memories and the only chance she would ever have to be a mother.

Once more I was crying, not silently, but out loud now. The tears were streaming down my face as I read the words again and again, just wishing and praying they were not true. Of course, I knew they were. How much pain had poor Molly had to suffer, and how frustrating for me to stand by and not be able to help, to put my arms around her and say, 'Mum, I love you, and I am so sorry.' Molly had lost a child forty-eight years ago through no choice of her own, and now she had lost her son. Since Christopher, I had known that the most wonderful thing in the world was to be able to take someone's hand and simply hold it. Words were not always necessary, but holding hands was special; it could say so much. I wanted desperately to hold Molly's hand.

The time that evening seemed to be dragging. It had been lovely so far, everyone out, lights dimmed, candles lit, a glass of wine and a good book – until I picked up the newspaper.

It had been some time since I had thought of Molly. Life was busy these days and my vivid imagination and dreams of fame and fortune seemed a lifetime away, replaced by a sense of responsibility and reality. Since the day Gemah was born I had at last felt the most incredible sense of belonging. The missing pieces no longer mattered: I was filled totally with my love for my child. Gemah was sensitive, fun, creative, imaginative and a delight in every way. She could do no wrong, she was perfect, and I loved her completely.

It was true then. Molly had lost her son, and I had lost a brother who I never even got to meet. And for the first time in my entire life I knew where my birth mother and the family I had never known were going to be. I knew where they were going to be next Tuesday at 11 a.m.

What should I do? My heart ached for Molly, and I was the one person who couldn't help. It was not somewhere I should be, I thought, but then maybe this was the only opportunity I would get to ever see my mother. 'I just need to see her,' I told Gemah and Harry. They were wonderfully supportive and said they would come with me.

'It's OK,' said Harry. 'We'll sit at the back then leave as soon as it's over. Do you think you'll be all right with that?'

'I will. I promise I'll be fine. I just want to see her.'

It was so much worse than I could ever have imagined. The moment she stepped out of the car, Harry and Gemah grabbed my hands. There are simply no words to explain what it feels like to see your birth mother for the first time. And this was no lovely park or beach, where I'd always imagined we'd run to each other, our arms held out, and finally, at long, long last, speak words of love and forgiveness, and hold hands. No, this was a cold crematorium filled with sombre faces and tears, and there she was, head down, one arm linked through her husband's, one hand on a walking stick, surrounded by her family as she entered the chapel to say farewell to her son.

I sat crying that day as much for my loss as for hers. I simply could not take my eyes off her. She was so beautiful to me, so dignified. But she also looked as if she was in total shock. I watched her and told her over and over in my mind how much I loved her. My brother and sisters were also there, and I watched them too and prayed for their loss.

I took one last look at my birth mother as everyone began to file out. We managed to slip out without going up to her. That would have been wrong. This was Molly's family, and I did not belong there with them today. Harry put his arm around my shoulder and Gemah took my hand, but before I got into the car I turned and took one last look, as Gemah whispered, 'Love you, Grandma.'

'Let's go,' I said. 'I got to see her, which is more than I could ever hope for, and when I close my eyes I will always be able to see her. That's enough for now.' And we went home.

I didn't cry at all that afternoon, I just wandered around the house feeling sad, trying to recall Molly's face every time I closed my eyes.

'You still trying to see her, Mum?' said Gemah.

'It just feels so unfinished,' I said. 'Like having a bar of chocolate and someone saying, "Ooh, that's lovely, but you can't eat it. You just have to look at it."'

Gemah burst out laughing. 'Mum, you're so funny sometimes – but listen, I've had an idea, and it's a good one.'

We went out and bought a beautiful bunch of flowers and a card. We wrote a message to my brother and Gemah's uncle, told him how much we would have loved to meet him and promised to say prayers for him.

It was early evening and had just begun to drizzle when, for the second time that day, we made our way to the chapel. We found a lovely tree in the garden and placed the flowers under it. We chatted away and told my brother all about us, sent our love to him and promised we would always keep him in our thoughts.

'Better,' said Gemah. 'Much better.'

I said that it was lovely to say goodbye and that I did get to spend a few moments with my family – some people didn't even get that much.

'Dad said he's going to do everything he can to find her, Mum. It's easier now with the Internet. Don't worry, Mum, we'll find her.'

I went to visit Mum in the care home that evening. What an emotional rollercoaster the day had been! But now that I was feeling stronger and calmer about the day, guilt was setting in. I had spent the whole day thinking about Molly and my family, and there was Mum, who had probably sat looking at the door all day wondering where I was and when I was coming.

As always, there she was, in front of the TV. She turned her head the moment I walked into the room and smiled. Mum didn't say much these days, and I chatted away to her, talking about Gemah and what she had eaten for tea – all small talk. It was all here, I already had it all: a wonderful mum, mother, parent. What on earth had I been thinking earlier today? Now, I just wanted to put it all behind me and pull myself together.

'Hello,' said one of the carers. 'She's been looking for you all afternoon. I hear you were at a funeral?'

'Oh, well, yes, I was.' I turned away, not wanting to explain any further.

'Are you all right? Was it someone close?'

'No,' I told her, God forgive me, then I took Mum's hand and we continued with the small talk.

Hugs

It was only two days later that Harry came and sat beside me and said that he had something for me. He handed me a piece of paper with Molly's home address on it. It had been quite easy, he said. There were lots of sites on the Internet where you could search for names and addresses. Finally, after all these years, I knew where my birth mother was, and it was, at most, a fifteen-minute car ride away from where I was living.

That night I sat down and wrote to my mother for the first time. I explained how sorry I was to learn of the loss of her son and that I did not want to intrude on her grief. I talked about myself, and my family, and said I hoped that one day when she was feeling up to it we would be able to meet. I told her that I loved her and was grateful for the sacrifice she had made. I told her that what I wanted most in the world was to give her a hug and hold her hand.

The most difficult thing to do was to hold on to the letter for four more weeks. I thought it appropriate to leave it that long after the funeral. Then Harry posted it through her letterbox. We were too afraid it might get lost in the post.

That was a long weekend. I checked my phone constantly, just in case she had called, but by Sunday evening I had given up hope. Harry said that there had definitely been someone in when he posted the letter, because he could hear a dog barking. Goodness only knows what the family was still going through, I thought. I knew I would have to be patient, and that I had to accept that I might never hear from my birth mother.

Molly was watching TV, watching without hearing or taking any notice of what was being said. On her right was her little candle corner with pictures of her son and anything she could find that would remind her of him. She had loved him so much, as she did all her children. It was simply wrong to lose your child, she thought, and unfair. No one understood. No one could. Life went on, and she had a husband, other children and grandchildren, a whole family who loved and cared for her. Molly loved being a grandmother, and it was a busy house at Christmas when everyone came around, as they often did. Molly was proud of every single one of her children, but today it was only her son she could think of. It had begun to get dark, but Molly didn't put the lights on. The candles were so pretty and the reflections were dancing on the photographs. Molly jumped when the letterbox rattled and the dog started to bark. What rubbish is being put through the letterbox now? she thought.

Within seconds, on seeing the name Susan, Molly knew exactly who the letter was from. For four weeks, Molly had felt very little. She was frozen inside, numb, nothing mattered; she could not cry, had not cried even at the funeral. Oh, how she wanted the release of tears! And what sort of mother was she that did not cry for her son? Molly read the letter once, then went back to the very beginning – 'Hello, Mum' – and a spark of warmth began to spread through her. At last they came, tears of joy, despair, sadness, anger and, again, joy. My son gone and my daughter given back to me, she thought. It helped, it really did. Her husband had always known about the child Molly had given away, but the children had yet to be told.

Sunday dinner eaten, we were snoozing on the sofa when Gemah shouted out, 'Mum, your phone is ringing.' I was still half asleep when I answered.

'Hello?' There was a pause, then:

'Hello, darling, I'm your mum.'

'Mum, oh Mum . . . are you all right?'

'Much better, darling. You helped me to cry. It has been so hard and I have been numb. Your letter brought warmth. I needed so much to cry, and I am holding on hard to anything I can to help me feel better, and I truly believe that your brother sent you to me. The children are being told by their father tonight, and next week we will all get together. I never ever forgot you, darling, and of course I want to see you and I want to hug you too.'

There was so much to be said, so much they both wanted to know. It had been forty-nine years since Molly had cried herself to sleep, missing her child every single second of every day and wondering how she was supposed to carry on and put this behind her, as everyone said she would. You do not put it behind you, she thought. You just learn

*to get on with it the best you can. Now, next week, she would once
more hold her child in her arms and give her daughter Susan the hug
she had waited for all these years.*

Girls' Night In

It had been threatening to snow all day. Gemah was working and wouldn't finish until 2 a.m. and the first flakes were beginning to fall. But cold or not, the party season was in full swing and parking would be difficult, so I had decided to take Gemah into work and to collect her afterwards. We loved these late nights together and always had a good laugh and a natter on the way home as she told me all about her night. I couldn't help but have a giggle, watching the girls fall out of the club, half dressed and freezing cold, carrying their shoes and walking in the snow in their bare feet. One poor girl was lying on the ground and the paramedics were wrapping her up in tinfoil. Then the car door was yanked open and Gemah jumped in and kissed me.

'Hiya, Mum. I've had a great night.'

'Look at that poor girl over there, Gemah.'

'Bless her. Oh well, you know you've had a good night when you go home dressed like a Greggs pasty!'

Even at 2 a.m. my lovely girl was always fun to be with, and we were chatting and laughing as usual as we made our way home through the sleet.

We had no idea that today would be so different, that our world was soon to be rocked and that from that moment on everything would change. My mobile phone was ringing. We knew, of course, that a call at that time of the morning was not going to be good news. Gemah answered, and I waited. 'We'll be there in five minutes,' she said. 'I'm with Mum. I've just finished work.' I was already turning the car around. In the past few months, Mum had been in hospital quite a few times with various ailments, each one seeming to make her a little weaker.

We got to the hospital, parked the car, forgetting all about the parking fee, and hand in hand through the now heavy falling snow we ran to the emergency department.

She was frightened. No-nonsense Nancy was no longer there, just a lonely figure sitting in a wheelchair with tears in her eyes. We ran straight over to her. Gemah threw her arms around her and I knelt in front of her and took her hands. 'Susan,' was all she said. Sometimes it is impossible to find any words, and sometimes they are totally unnecessary anyway. I wish I had known at that moment that it was the last time I would hear her say my name. I would have closed my eyes and listened with my whole heart. Mum didn't take her eyes off me, and the tears fell from her eyes and down on to her cheek.

I had to find out what had happened, why she was here. The carer who was with Mum told us that she had been feeling poorly, not eating and had been a little unresponsive, so they had decided to have her taken into hospital and to call me. It was one of the most wonderful decisions ever made, as it brought Mum, Gemah and me to one place on what was to be our last day together.

The rest of the day was spent with Gemah and I sitting either side of Mum, Gemah holding one of her hands and me the other, each of us telling her everything that was happening and chatting to her endlessly about anything at all. Of course she was going to get better, just like all the other times; all it would take would be more medication to put right whatever was wrong, we were certain of that, my daughter and I. Those beautiful blue eyes just stared into ours. Mum was quite content as long as we were there. Gemah took her hand away just to get a tissue and Mum's hand hovered in the air towards her granddaughter until Gemah took it again and Mum smiled.

So she knew who we were, and it comforted her and us to know she felt safe. Gemah and I tried not to look at each other, both of us slowly beginning to understand in our hearts that this time *was* different.

By late afternoon we were all totally exhausted, and Mum was asleep. We had been up all night, and the nurse told us to go home and get some rest. After ensuring that the nurses had our mobile numbers, we finally went home.

We called on John, who had been Gemah's boyfriend since she was fourteen years old, and they sat together, John as always a tower of strength to her.

'Come on,' said Harry. 'I'll take you out for a couple of hours. There's nothing you can do and, if they ring, I will take you there immediately, I promise.' We had only been out for half an hour when the call came, and we all rushed to the hospital.

I must have been totally numb, because the word 'unresponsive' didn't register with me at all. Gemah and I stood closely together, asking stupid questions like 'When will she be awake?' Does she need medication or something?'

It was left to Harry to place his hands on my shoulder and say, 'Suzie, it means she isn't going to make it. I am so sorry.' I froze, then looked over to where she was lying.

'We have made her as comfortable as possible,' the nurse said. 'Would you like to stay with her? She's not in any pain at all.'

I shouldn't have left her before, we should have stayed, but we were assured that during the short time we were away she had been asleep and unresponsive.

Harry gave us both a cuddle. 'Is there anything I can do?' he asked. I thanked him and said Gemah and I would be all right now and we would like to be on our own with Mum.

We sat again either side of her, held her hands and settled down for our last girls' night in together.

We reminisced and laughed about all our times together, all the crazy things we had done, and willed Mum to laugh along with us. 'It's nearly Christmas,' we said, 'and we're going to buy you a new outfit for Christmas Day, not to mention new slippers.' We decided on a new skirt, blouse and cardigan, and Gemah said she had the most lovely hand cream for her.

'You'll love it, Grandma, it smells absolutely gorgeous and will make your skin feel fantastic. On Christmas Eve you can have a lovely bath and put it on all ready for Christmas morning.'

I wish I could have helped Gemah more. There had been a bond between her and Mum that it was special to be a part of. Mum absolutely adored Gemah and she could do no wrong, yet she always insisted on Gemah understanding the core values of life. It was the perfect balance. Yet here she was, my daughter, being the strong one, asking me if I was all right and speaking to the nurses for me, making sure everything that could be done was being done.

We had been awake for hours now and were beginning to feel both emotionally drained and physically exhausted, yet still we chatted and laughed, not knowing how much time we had left.

There was something I needed to tell her, something I wanted her to understand. 'Mum,' I said, 'I've found Molly. I met her for the first time a few months ago. Mum, she is absolutely lovely and she wanted me and missed me all these years. I told her all about you, what you did for me, how much you loved and cherished me, and said I considered myself a very lucky girl. Oh, Mum, she was so pleased and was so happy that I had been so well looked after.

'I need you to know, Mum, that I love you with all my heart. No mother could have done more for her child than you have done for me, and as for that chat when I was young about you not being my real mum, take it from me, you are my real mum in every single way. I will look back knowing that I was loved every single day of my life, that even when things went hideously wrong you would either comfort me or do your chin-in-the-air thing and tell me, "Yes, well, that's the way it is." It always brought me down to earth. Looking back, I can now see how you must have suffered, how frightened you must have been when I was young, and I will remember you always for your strength, your compassion and simply for the inspirational person you are.'

There was a tiny movement.

'Gemah!' I said. 'Did you see that? Do you think she heard?'

'Very possibly, and, knowing Grandma, her reply would be, "No need for dramatics and all that nonsense."'

Of course, we both burst out laughing.

The nurses brought us more comfortable chairs and some pillows, and there we sat, all three of us, holding hands. Somewhere, very faintly, 'Silent Night' was playing on the radio. We knew it was Mum's time, but maybe it was worth one last try.

'Grandma, please, if you can, stay for Christmas. You know we need you. Nothing will ever be the same without you. Grandma, please. We need you here with us.'

Her breathing was beginning to grow shallow, and we had said all there was to say. We had been blessed to share our journey with her.

We kissed her and put our heads on her shoulder, all three of us bonded together for one last time, and No-nonsense Nancy went home.

The Special Clothes

The next few days were a blur. My Aunty Margaret, Aunty Mary and my cousins all came over and were wonderful. My cousin Pat helped organize all the arrangements and took much of the stress from me. I was absolutely useless; I was wandering around in a daze. I had never thought about how I would feel when the time came, and at that moment I felt completely numb, totally at a loss. When I went to bed that first night, I remember I sat up and looked out of the window at the stars. Where are you? I was thinking, and immediately in my mind I could hear her voice: 'Well, I'm not swinging on a star, that's for sure.' I smiled. Mum was always so down to earth.

Our local newspaper wrote a beautiful article about her and her dedication to children, which I know she would have thought was making a fuss, but I thought it was lovely and hoped it would reach people from the past who might like to attend her funeral.

Harry made the necessary arrangements, because Gemah and I had a very special assignment. Every year we would buy Mum a new outfit for Christmas. 'And this year is going to be no different,' said Gemah. We chose a lovely red pleated skirt, a cream blouse and red cardigan and, of course, matching red slippers. We talked about Mum all the time as if she was still with us or could at least hear us. It was our way of coping. We were mighty pleased with our purchases and the next day we were taking the special clothes to the funeral home, where they were going to dress her. These wonderful people were even going to put the cream on her hands which Gemah had bought her for Christmas.

The next day found Gemah and I running around all over the place tying up loose ends, so Harry offered to drop the special clothes off for us. We had already discussed what we wanted with the funeral home, so that was a great help. Nothing could go wrong.

But, honestly, you couldn't make it up! The clothes were in a Morrison's carrier bag. Harry, who was rushing around working and trying to help us with the arrangements in between jobs, threw the bag in the back of his van, and off he went. Lo and behold, also in the back of the van were his work clothes . . . Yes, you've guessed it: also in a Morrison's carrier bag.

The bag was handed over. I can only imagine the look on the funeral administrator's face on being told that these were the special clothes that the family would like Nancy Harmer to wear. Luckily, the angels must have been looking after us that day, because Harry came home early for a cuppa, bag in hand.

'Why didn't you drop Mum's clothes off?' I asked.

'I did.'

'You didn't.'

We both looked at the carrier bag.

We dived into the car, not speaking, just totally focussed on getting to the funeral parlour before it closed. Typically, their line was engaged and we couldn't get through on the phone. When we got there, we literally burst through the doors and explained the mistake. It was all right: the bag was still there. I sank down on to the nearest chair in total relief.

We left with sombre faces, as befitting the occasion, got outside and roared with laughter all the way home.

If my mother – my beautiful, dignified and serene mother – had gone beyond the veil and met God Almighty dressed in a navy-blue boiler suit, polo-neck jumper and a woolly bobble hat, the thunderbolts would have rocked the earth!

It was a beautiful service, and Mum was honoured, as she deserved to be. We had Josh Groban's 'You Raise Me Up' playing as she was brought in. Gemah was so strong for me that day, and so brave. She didn't let go of my hand until it was time for her to stand up and read out her poem. I didn't take my eyes off her, and the words, as always when Gemah writes, were inspirational, beautiful and so very meaningful. Mum would have been so proud of her. How fitting, I thought, that Mum had gone home at Christmastime. So many of our memories and the stories we had to tell had taken place at Christmas. Mum had loved Midnight Mass and the carol services during December, so for the service we had decided to have Christmas carols instead of hymns: 'Away in a Manger' and 'Silent Night'.

I never knew until the day arrived whether I would be able to stand up and read out the words I had written. All I can remember is sitting on a hard bench and Gemah's hand in mine. I was thinking that it felt so small, so cold, but the time had come, and Gemah smiled at me and squeezed my hand.

'You can do it, Mum,' she said.

After all Mum had been through for me, of course I could. I walked forward, stood in front of everyone and said the following words:

> 'I'll try not to be selfish
> And wish you were still here,
> For the place that you have gone to
> Sits in my heart so dear.

> 'For now you sit with angels,
> With them you talk and pray,
> And this year you will spend your time
> With God on Christmas Day.

> 'The angels gathered all around,
> The gates were opened wide,
> And trumpets blared as you walked in
> With angels at your side.

> 'No more pain or sorrow,
> No more loss or fears,
> Just love and pure contentment,
> No need for human tears.

> 'Happy Christmas and God bless,
> Once more complete and whole,

For a moment in my heart, Mum,
But forever in my soul.'

I remember so little of afterwards. I know that people
came up to me saying they had known her years ago, but
I was so numb it is all a blur. We had a get-together in the
time-honoured tradition, but I was glad when it was all
over and I, too, could go home.

Home

They were right, of course: there was much rejoicing that day. She was a character, and had certainly been missed around the place. The choirs of angels were rejoicing and could be heard throughout the heavenly realms. The angels had made her the most beautiful wings you could imagine, out of the purest of soft, white feathers.

Peter opened the gates with a smile on his face.

'Peter.'

'Nancy.'

'These gates could do with a bit of a polish.'

He smiled. She had been a miss. Nancy smiled back and sighed. It was good to be home, but she still felt the love of the people she had left behind.

Suddenly, silence fell, and she could hear the whispers being carried on the gentle breeze, reminding her of the love here. Time stood still and a hundred thousand angels caressed her soul.

He was there, she knew it. Nancy closed her eyes and felt the beautiful energy that surrounded her.

She was remembering.

So many young souls here that had returned home early. She looked after them, loved them, greeted them, helped them to send messages of love to earth. Her beautiful, heavenly children. She would hear them talk about their earth mums, about their devotion and unconditional love, about how it felt to be held in their parents' arms, and about their families and friends. Nancy would listen and wonder.

'I would like to be a mum,' she said. 'Without the nonsense, of course.'

He laughed. 'I could do that for you, but it may be a challenging journey.'

'I'll cope.'

'I will surround you with children to help you feel at home.'

'Could I . . . please could I . . .' She was faltering.

He loved her so much. 'What is it, my child?'

'Could I have Tilly?'

He promised. And God never breaks a promise.

'Oh, and if you have a spare moment knocking about, I wouldn't mind a granddaughter.' Nancy opened her eyes. Susan, Gemah and I will have a good laugh about our journey when they come home, she thought to herself. Until then I will hold them in my heart.

'The children are waiting for you,' He said, and was gone.

The heavenly choirs were singing once more, and the angels surrounded her.

'What is it with the wings? It's very kind, but you know I don't like fuss . . . Heavenly choirs . . . very nice and thank you so much, but you know it was a hard journey, that one, and to be honest all I really want is some peace and quiet, a nice cup of tea and a mince pie if there's one going.'

They all smiled. It really was good to have her back.

Suddenly, there was a low rumble, which grew louder by the second. Nancy looked up and waited.

At that moment thunder rocked the earthly skies as Heaven's gate burst open and thousands of children ran to greet her with open arms, once more tugging at her skirt, wanting stories, so happy to have her home.

Nancy smiled. 'First things first, my darlings,' she said, as she turned her head and called out: 'Can someone please tell me where in God's name is Tilly?'

Reflections

Hindsight

Hindsight, thought Billy, is a great thing, so they say. If only I had known. No one ever knew what Susan thought as a child; she kept so much to herself. He had never truly understood how much his little girl loved him, never known how many times she had stood on the bathroom bench holding on to the bars on the windows facing the long driveway, her eyes closed, praying that when she had said her three 'Hail Mary's and two 'Our Father's and opened her eyes she would see the car with the running board, with her daddy driving it and waving. Many hours she would stand there, until Mum got annoyed and told her not to be ridiculous. She would sneak back, though, as soon as she could, when she was supposed to be in the playroom, to try again.

Nancy had lived in fear, Susan had told him, of Billy walking in one day and taking Susan back, as was the original agreement. I didn't know that. Why on earth didn't I see that that's what she was thinking? I assumed that even Nancy would know that I would never have taken Susan away from her when I got married — how many times did I call her 'Susan's mother'? Wasn't that enough? Apparently not. I could have saved her years of worry, thought Billy now, and he finally understood why Nancy always seemed to be cool and sometimes even unfriendly to him. Hindsight, he thought again.

Had he been a good father? he wondered. Had he done enough? He had loved his little girl — he had tried his best, hadn't he? They had spent wonderful days together, and it was those days he was thinking about now. They had been looking at old photograph albums today. Susan was writing a book and wanted to know if he had photographs of them together. He watched her laughing when he put them in front of her, album upon album, hundreds of photographs showing her growing up, taken at every stage of her life. She was surprised to find so many of Christopher, herself and Dad together. He'd had to remind her: 'Well, you wouldn't go anywhere without him.' There were photos of holidays with Mum and the Smalley family where he and Eileen had driven up to spend the day with them all. Billy could never have known how Susan's heart had warmed that day. Every photograph she looked at, her daddy was smiling at his child with an expression of love on every inch of his face. When she was a young child she had played hairdressers with Eileen and written her a note telling her what to do when she went to bed to ensure her hair was perfect in the morning. Eileen had kept it all these years in the back of that album.

Well, he thought, they still got together, Susan still came to see him, he was part of her life. She had been laughing on her last visit, saying how impressed she was by his computer skills. It was how he kept in touch with everyone, and he loved how himself and Gemah emailed each other often. Today he had taken a photograph of them all – 'Dynasty', he called it, laughing. There was himself and Eileen, his children, Jane and Susan, his grandchildren, Miranda Kay and Gemah, and Gemah's son, his great-grandchild, Séamus.

Billy had been brave and stood up to them, and had every right to be very proud of himself. Now aged eighty-five, he had watched the world change, and he too had fought against the authorities many times. On more than one occasion he had been called to Nazareth House and asked to sign papers, for the good of the child, naturally. There was a doctor, they said, who was interested in adopting Susan, and Billy should forget his own feelings and think of the child. Billy had looked them straight in the eye and said, 'This means handing over any right to my child, does it?'

'Of course,' they explained. 'It's for the best, Mr Robinson.'

Billy had smiled at them, taken the pen and watched the smug look on their faces disappear when he put a line through the paper, turned on his heel and walked out. They never asked him again. He knew without any doubt that Susan was perfectly well looked after by Nancy. To be honest, he didn't know what he would have done without her. Had he told her that? Not then, maybe, but at Susan's wedding he had taken his chance. He had been shocked to see Nancy and how much she had changed. Still so proud, though, and she had every right to be so.

Billy was back in the past again. Men simply didn't look after children – well, not by themselves anyway, not back then. Nancy had been looking after Susan since she had been brought to Nazareth House and he was perfectly well aware that Susan called her Mum. Nancy had more than earned that right, and his daughter was a very happy young child. There had never been any chance that Nancy would tolerate any injustice or bullying because Susan had been born out of wedlock and of course she herself would have been totally unaware of any prejudice. Susan would know none of this: she was too well looked after and loved by them all. It was only now, at eighty-five, that he had found out that this, in fact, was not true. I could have made sure, he thought. Hindsight.

The fault did not lie with Billy; he hadn't known anything about it. In truth, there had been days when his young daughter had wondered, Does my daddy love me? Will Daddy come back again?, because the whispers in the child's ears that she was unworthy, unloved and should be grateful for having been given a roof over her *head even though she was a disgrace were screaming in her head. Yet deep down there was a peaceful knowledge that touched her heart every time Mum took her hand or cuddled her, every time Daddy turned up and threw her up into the air, took her out for the day, got to the top of the drive then grabbed his well-turned-out daughter and stood her on the running board, pulled the tidy bow from her hair and drove along, the wind running through her hair, listening to her squealing with delight. Susan had indeed loved her daddy very much, and days like these were simply perfect, all the whispers forgotten.*

Could he have done more? That's a question most of us will ask ourselves at some point in our lives. Again, hindsight.

Billy had not given his daughter away; he loved his child and had brought fun into her life. He knew his child was with a mother who would undoubtedly protect and guide her through life, teach her good values and, most of all, love her. He would retract the original agreement; it would simply be too cruel to take Susan away from Nancy. He was still her father, however, and he would be part of her life always. Still, he thought, were there things he could have done differently?

Hindsight, he thought once more, is a great thing.

Photographic Proof

I was watching him today, as I always have done, with a smile on my face. Dad never failed to make me laugh. Today, though, I felt very much like crying, but I couldn't tell him that. Never once that I can remember have I thrown my arms around him and said simply, 'Dad, I love you.' Yet I could have done quite easily; there was a closeness with my father that came perfectly naturally. So why didn't I ever say it? I thought. The simple answer was fear. Those whispers, deeply buried, yet still able to surface at a moment's notice. What if somehow it embarrassed him? What if he didn't say it back? Safer, always, to say nothing.

Then, today, it was there in front of me for all to see: a father and a daughter. There was no mistaking that expression on his face: he was watching me, smiling at me, laughing with me and loving me. I had waited fifty-seven years to understand this. Always doubting, hurting, wondering. Today I was going to let all that go and simply believe it.

I was shocked to discover just how many photographs Dad had taken when I was young. There were hundreds of them. Had I simply forgotten how much time we spent together and remembered only the times I had waited for him, hoping to see his car coming down the drive? Time can be confusing to a young child. As an adult, I thought there had been weeks when I hadn't seen him; I had always thought he must be too busy. Even now, when I close my eyes sometimes, I can see those bars and feel the pain of thinking that maybe the whispers were true. After all, if you were told something often enough, it felt like it must be true. God forgive them, I think.

Dad had said today, 'Do you remember, Susan, when I came to see you every Sunday?' But no matter how tightly I squeezed my eyes shut and tried to remember, I couldn't. I could, however, remember him on those incredible days when he did come to see me, when we sang crazy songs, when he'd throw me up into the air and take me on days out, letting me run wild. And Eileen had always made sure that I was tidy and clean before taking me home.

Even now, Dad was still so much fun. I was remembering one particular summer when I came to stay with him, Eileen and Jane, as I often did. We were all going to Mass that particular Sunday morning, I recalled, except for Eileen, who was at work until lunchtime and had left strict instructions to put the chicken in the oven before leaving for church. Dad, said Jane, was now well into parish life, and they always went to Mass on a Sunday. He was also one of the readers. I loved those times: me, Dad and Jane sitting in church, just like every other family. Nobody could possibly have known how that felt; it was everything I had dreamed of.

I remember stealing a look at Dad, who was nodding and leaning forward as though he was taking in every single word of the gospel. I looked at Jane and we stifled a giggle. 'You're lucky you weren't here last Sunday,' she said. 'He stood up in the pulpit, lifted his arms and shouted, "And it came to pass," like he was doing a Frankie Howerd impression. A drama to be played out at every chance possible!' She laughed. Who, I thought, does that remind me of?

Dad turned to us both then, smiling, then whispered, 'Do you have a pen?'

Jane said, 'He must be inspired by something the priest has said,' and Dad sat there with a serious and serene expression on his face as we scrabbled in our bags for a pen and some paper.

'Here, Dad,' I whispered. Dad continued to look at the priest and began to write on the back of an old envelope. Jane and I were intrigued. Then, still looking straight ahead, eyes on the priest, he passed us the piece of paper:

'I forgot to put the chicken in the oven.'

I will never know how Jane and I didn't get thrown out of church that day, but we did leave early, as soon as communion was over, and continued to howl with laughter all the way home.

I was remembering all the good times now. When I was about twenty-five, Dad and Eileen took Jane and me to Devon on holiday. The excitement was unbelievable. This was my first family holiday with Dad, and it couldn't come quickly enough.

We were just like any other family going on holiday: a car full of suitcases, a mum, Dad, two daughters and a dog. About ten minutes into the journey, the sandwiches were out and we were merrily on our way. 'Might just be a slight problem with the car,' Dad said, 'but nothing major.'

Ten hours later, in a car that had started to overheat half an hour into the journey, a dog that was being sick, and having made what seemed like a hundred stops and starts, we eventually arrived at our holiday cottage. We collapsed, exhausted, into our beds that night, all wanting to get up early next day.

It was so hot the next morning we all made our way to the beach and, once there, Dad, Jane and I decided to hire canoes. Eileen was happy to sit on her towel on the beach and watch us through her binoculars. 'Are you sure you'll be OK, Dad?' I asked, uncertain.

Dad stood tall and began: 'I've sailed the oceans, been on boats rocking from side to side that would terrify you two. I could snap my fingers and dive into the sea and save you both in a split second and . . .'

'Got the picture, Dad,' I screamed, laughing, and Jane and I ran ahead to grab our own canoes and paddles.

'Don't go out too far,' Dad was shouting. 'It's not safe,' but of course his words fell on deaf ears. We had heard quite enough.

The sea was calm and I was ecstatic. My sister and I were side by side, paddling backwards and forwards, enjoying a wonderful day in the sun.

Then: 'Where's Dad, Jane?' I asked.

We scanned the horizon.

'Oh, look, Susan, he's over there!'

'Bit far out, isn't it?'

'Nah, he'll be fine. He's swum the oceans, remember?'
More gentle canoeing in the sun.

'Ah, bless him! Look, Jane, he's gone in for a swim.'

'Aaaah.'

Ten minutes more paddling back and forth across the gentle waves.

'He's waving at us, look. Give him a wave, Susan.'

We waved. More sisterly relaxation and boating in the sun.

'Jane – where's Dad?'

Suddenly: '*Help!*' she was screaming at some nearby swimmers as I paddled my canoe furiously to Dad, who had gone too far out, fallen into the water and was now holding on to his upturned canoe with his arms and wrists, his fingers having gone numb. His paddle was too far away for him to retrieve.

'Grab my paddle!' I screamed at him, 'I'll pull you in.' Unfortunately, as I threw my paddle towards him, the wind caught it and I hit him on the back of the head.

I was about to jump in but, just at this point, Jane arrived with two men, and they grabbed Dad.

The poor man was so embarrassed. 'I'm fine, honestly – apart from my daughter smacking me on the back of the head with a paddle and trying to drown me.'

'You OK, Dad?' shouted Jane.

'OK? Am I OK? I've been waving SOS signals for twenty ****** minutes, and you two just sat there bobbing about and waving back like demented idiots!'

It's times like this, when you realize how near you have come to tragedy, that your heart beats so fast you feel sick . . . so why were Jane and I trying hard not to look at each other, knowing we would laugh if we did?

The two men took one of Dad's arms each and began to swim in with him. As soon as he found his feet on the ocean bed, Dad shook them off, thanking them, but saying he was perfectly all right, thank you. He turned round to say, 'Goodness knows what –' to us, but we never found out what because, just as he turned his head, his canoe, which had drifted in behind him, was carried forward on a big wave, hit him on the back of the head and he fell face first into the sea.

Of course now we were absolutely helpless with laughter. Dad got up, fell over again, got up again, and wobbled over to Eileen, who, not daring to laugh, handed him a towel.

Naturally, for the rest of the day we were subjected to countless stories of how he saw his life flash before his eyes and how the angels had hovered waiting for him.

Later that evening, Eileen said, 'All right, Billy, that's enough. Let's just enjoy our evening.'

'Hmm,' he said, as Jane and I linked arms with him, looked at each other and burst into song: 'A life on the ocean waves . . .'

Billy smacked us both gently on the back of the head and chased us down the street.

Billy – my crazy father, who cleans the windows listening to Ravel's 'Bolero', thinks it's funny to dance to the music in the supermarket, has endless quotes to match every situation and makes me laugh so much every time I see him – you did not give me away, you did love me, and the memories I have of you will always make me smile.

God bless you, Dad. You did your best, you did what was right and I love you.

Mum

All over the world somewhere today there are families with grandparents, great-grandparents, mothers, fathers, children, grandchildren who gather together to celebrate family occasions. Yet the rooms they gather in may have been a little emptier had it not been for the brave souls who gave away their babies. As a result of their sacrifice, new families were formed and childless couples became parents and maybe grandparents. Women who cried every month because they were beginning to realize that their dream of becoming a mum was starting to look unlikely, impossible maybe, because they feared looking ahead into a future with no prospect of family life, or at least not the one they had hoped for all these years, were given the chance to have a family life.

There were no IVF babies until 1978. Before that the only hope for these women was to find an 'unwanted' child from a 'fallen' woman. But many of these children were not unwanted, they were adopted because the mother was forced into giving up her child, shamed into it by her own family and by society. And neither were these mothers fallen women. These were the women who gave us the children of our future. Every child born into this world is a gift from God, so whoever you are, or were, you deserve our thanks for contributing to our future. May

God forgive those who did not treat you with the greatest respect for your sacrifice.

Thank goodness for the way we live today, where no matter what relationship a child is born into, all that matters is that the child will be loved, nurtured and taught true values: empathy, the importance of accepting others, respect and, most importantly, love. I believe with all my heart that a child raised surrounded by love will survive, because that is what the soul of a child cries out for most. Love.

I am, always have been and always will be Nancy's child. I am honoured to have shared my journey with her. If Mum ever looked back and reflected, I hope she knew without any doubt that she could have done no more and that there was never a moment when I didn't know how much she loved me. At some point in each day she is there in my thoughts, and I miss her as much today, so many years later, as I did the day she left us to go home. Her favourite colour was blue, and her pale-blue cardigan still hangs in my wardrobe as a daily reminder of her – as if I needed one!

I cried the day Séamus was born not only because I had become a grandmother – another of my dreams realized – but because Mum was not there at our sides pushing her way in, wanting to be in the middle of it all and taking over. When I close my eyes I see her there as I remember her best. Brown wavy hair, bright-blue eyes and a smile that could melt my heart. Her little brown bag with the lipstick and compact, which she had for the last twenty years of her life. I laugh when I think of her no-nonsense attitude, and those looks that told me I had gone too far. She had perfected them over many years, and then Gemah came along and got away with everything by climbing up on to her knee and saying, 'Love you, Grommy.' No-nonsense Nancy would give in, smile at her and say, 'All right then, love, just this once.' Amazing. Her eyes followed Gemah everywhere, and she was safe in the knowledge that her granddaughter, daughter, sisters, friends and many other children making their way in the world today loved her. No-nonsense Nancy had got it just right.

She touched so many people's lives and changed them for the better, leaving her kind words and thoughts in their hearts. Children grew up knowing love, understanding true values and living with respect for others. Mum trusted you first and let you know how much she valued your respect for her, and she got it every single time. The children who were called unruly were calmed; the young, frightened, angry, screaming child received the look and was allowed to continue to scream. Mum would simply stand there, watching the child and looking at her watch until she would finally announce, 'Finished now, pet, because the tea is ready, and the sandwiches look really rather good tonight,' and put out her hand to lead them to the TV room, chatting all the time about how everything was going to be all right. It took no effort; it all came completely naturally to her. When Aunty Nancy said it was going to be all right, it was going to be all right. Fact.

She had known fear and loss. Not a single day went by that she didn't miss Tilly, Bill and her brothers, Benny and Michael. That first weekend without Uncle Benny we had gone shopping as usual and she made her way straight to the meat counter to get different types of meat for sandwiches for Benny. Then suddenly she turned to me and said, 'Oh, it doesn't matter any more now, does it?', her eyes full of tears. Every third Sunday for many months after he had gone she would say, 'Our Benny would be here tonight.'

Well, I know that Mum is up there somewhere, both her and Tilly no doubt causing trouble and drinking endless cups of tea in Heaven's café, forcing sandwiches and cake on Benny, Michael and Bill and, without a shadow of a doubt, rushing to our sides to comfort and help us when we need them.

Aunty Tilly and Uncle Bill had nine grandchildren and sixteen great-grandchildren, the youngest of whom is called Tilly, and now two great-great-grandchildren. They would be so proud of them all. I arranged a get-together at our house at Christmas of 2009, and it was noisy, fun and absolutely wonderful.

They say that life is a continuous circle and that we come here many times to learn and to challenge ourselves. They also say that we choose our parents, as they are the ones who will teach us many of life's lessons. If that is the case, I chose well, and pray to God that He will once again let us be together. It was an amazing journey.

Any regrets? Only the one. I should have told Mum over and over again that I loved her. I should not have cared whether it would embarrass her or not, I should have said it out loud and shouted it from the rooftops – and yet wasn't she the one who taught me that love should be shown in every action, not just spoken in words? My actions always said, 'I love you, Mum,' but oh how I wish I had said it too. I say it now every day in the hope that she hears me. Love you, Mum.

Life's Lessons

Today as I look back on my life and reflect, I realize that I have been fortunate enough to encounter many kindnesses, great friendships and a great deal of love. I have laughed often and am grateful to the people in my life, who I will always remember for their inspirational words and their thoughtfulness.

Our parish priest, Father Featherstone, told his congregation once: "There is no one quite like you. There is no other person like you in the whole world. You are unique. You are special.' I have always remembered that Sunday morning in church and how wonderful those words made me feel.

When I was fifty-six and working in an office, there I was laughing and joking with my colleagues – in between working, naturally! – and I don't know to this day why, but my boss, Steve Foster, gave me an opportunity to do something I had no qualifications for yet had always wanted to do. That was to stand up in front of people and do presentations. I was never happier. The knowledge that someone believed in me enough to give me an opportunity of this kind was overwhelming. Steve was probably the person most suited to tell me how to do it, where I had gone wrong and where I could have improved, but there was none of that. Just help, gentle guidance, support and encouragement. It was food for my soul, and I will never forget how he made me feel. He made me feel accepted and worthy.

I remember now that first presentation, a room full of people, all of whom I knew, many of them friends more than colleagues. Karen Franklin, my buddy, who I made sit at the front so I would have someone nearby I knew was rooting for me, and Frank McChrystal, technical genius, ensuring that I didn't make a complete idiot of myself by crashing the system (which I had done twice during the practice run). The night before, I had stood up tall in my bedroom and delivered my presentation to all my teddy bears sitting in a row in front of me. They were a great audience: they smiled, encouraged me and clapped loudly when I was finished.

After half a dozen trips to the toilet, and having checked and re-checked my notes a hundred times, the lights were dimmed, PowerPoint at the ready. I walked to the centre of the room to greet my colleagues.

If only they'd had the foresight to dress as teddy bears, I would have been fine. They did, however, clap at the end of my presentation. I had succeeded because someone had believed in me and given me the opportunity to shine. Thank you so very much, Steve.

These people and many more have taught me invaluable life lessons. I realize that I have, of course, got it wrong sometimes. To those of you I hurt in any way, may God forgive me. I am so very sorry.

I am stronger now than I have ever been. Faced with

unfair prejudice or injustice, I will stand tall, chin in the air, turn on my heels and walk away with my head held high. I am, after all, Nancy's child.

And on a Final Note

So what happened to Nancy's child, the drama queen, to her dreams of being a princess who was always going to be rescued by a prince, of being a mermaid, a famous dramatic actress who could incite so much emotion the cinema would have to hand out tissues at half-time, a comedy actress making people laugh until they cried, maybe even a famous ballet dancer whose dancing touched people's souls?

Well, it didn't quite turn out that way. I never managed to be a mermaid, caressing moonbeams and swimming the oceans. However, I did get a badge for retrieving a brick from the bottom of the swimming pool, so that's something. And I did manage to make people laugh and receive applause – but not quite the way I intended.

Ballet was never for me but, thanks to Mavis Whiteside, I did win a Latin American dancing competition when I was eleven years old, was the *Sunday Sun* Latin American Champion and had my picture in the newspaper. That makes me practically famous, I reckon.

I certainly felt like a princess the day I got married, so one to me there.

And as for dreams coming true, I got to hug my birth mother and meet my brother and sisters, and I will never forget that moment. They were good and kind to me and I will always be grateful to them for that.

So what happened to the drama queen's dreams of fame? Well, who needs fame anyway? I have a lovely, supportive husband, an incredible daughter, son-in-law and grandson, an inspirational mum, amazing friends and a lifetime of wonderful memories.

Strangely enough, the only thing I never dreamed of doing . . . was writing a book!

To Maureen, Anne, Kathleen and Margaret

I only took the smallest step,
It took no time at all.
Just a single moment,
When I received the call.

Surrounded by such gentleness,
My heart and soul were eased.
No more doubt or wondering,
My worries were appeased.

So close was I, my darlings,
Although you never knew.
I hadn't gone that far,
I was standing next to you.

We faced our trials together,
Stood closely by until,
The challenges would show themselves
And we drew closer still.

I know life can get hard sometimes,
And yet somehow I knew,
I must have got it right somehow,
There was no penance due.

They ask me many questions here,
'Was it what you thought?'
All those joys and challenges,
Lessons to be taught.

I closed my eyes and saw you,
All four of you right there.
I sent you love to let you know
That both of us still care.

My children, how I love you,
It was worth it all, it's true.
And yes I'd do it all again
To share my life with you.

    –Dad

To Mum

Today again I thought of you,
There was no reason why,
But there you were, my mother,
As I slowly closed my eyes.

It just crept up upon me
With my grandson on my knee,
Shared precious time together,
My family and me.

'We'll meet again one day,' you said,
So where were you right now?
Up in Heaven in the sky,
When will it be and how?

Why did I still feel empty?
It wasn't what I'd planned.
To feel the pain, still missing you,
The need to hold your hand.

Why weren't you here around us,
Hands there on your hips.
In our lives amongst us,
With your helpful handy tips?

TO MUM

We never doubted ever
How much we meant to you,
Yet did you know, dear Mum,
How very much we loved you too?

'Where are you, Mum?' I whispered.
'Where's this place they talk about?
Why can't you come and visit us?
Sometimes I have such doubt.'

'Typical,' said Nancy.
'There they go again,
Question after question,
Who? What? Why? Where? When?'

Nancy sighed and turned to Tilly.
'It's typical once more,
The kettle nearly boiling.
Hold the cuppa now, don't pour.'

'More questions,' shouted Tilly.
'I'll leave the tea to stew.
We love it when they call us.
Hold on, I'll come with you.'

In a single breath, no time at all,
My soul no longer cried,
For there you were, my mother,
Standing by my side.

I knew that you could hear me.
It took my breath away.
'Listen close,' you whispered.
'There's things I have to say.

'Heaven isn't in the sky.
We do not spend our days,
Swinging on the moonbeams,
Soaking up the rays.

'It's where we are, right next to you.
And every thought and word,
We take and hold within our hearts
And every prayer is heard.

'Your hand is never empty.
Just close your eyes and know
My fingers close around yours.
I never did let go.

'Of course I knew you loved me,
I know you love me still.
You were my child, you cared so much.
I know you always will.'

'Do you miss us, Mum,' I whispered.
'Of course not,' she replied.
'Why would we miss you, darling,
When we're right there by your side?'

  –Your daughter, Susan

To My Grandma

Wings are for heroes,
I won't be needing those.
Just teach me love I'll honour,
Through highs and through lows.

You brought up a child,
Loved and nurtured her each day.
Heaven sent you your baby,
She just found you a different way.

You were shunned in the street,
For having children of many colours.
Little did the ignorant know,
You played the part of many mothers.

You made our world a better place.
Now your spirit's free to roam.
The world did shed a tear,
The day God took you home.

If inspiration can open hearts,
Even reach out to a few,
I pray you can live on through others,
And they can help change the world too.

Yes, wings are for heroes,
No flash or fancy clothes.
You taught us love we'll always honour.
Go fly, my dear Grandma, you were so very one of those.

–Your granddaughter, Gemah Louise

Acknowledgements

To Daniel Bunyard, my publisher, who gave me the opportunity of a lifetime, and Punteha, Senior Features Writer for *Take a Break*, who started me off on this journey. Bless you both for your constant guidance and your belief in me, without which this book would never have been written. Thanks also to *Take a Break* magazine for organizing the competition which led me to start writing this book, and to Sarah Day for all her patience and the wonderful job she did in editing it.

It is a beautiful and rare soul that walks alongside you during life's challenges, smiles, takes your hand and encourages you to try again. I have had the honour and privilege during times in my life to have those people at my side.

Krystynne Gabriel (Teacher of Light and a Channel for Goddess Light and the Starlight Energies; www.elestial-star.co.uk). Out of sheer curiosity I went to one of her angel workshops and my life changed from that day on – thank you not only from myself but from all those, and there are many, to whom you have given a part of yourself. Forever looking to others' needs, not only listening but hearing with such a caring heart even during your own life challenges. Always there at the end of a telephone or email, with a permanently open door to those of us who are struggling to cope.

I love Krystynne's home. From the minute you set foot in the door, you feel calm. Hundreds of crystals and angels are all around you, and a friend is immediately by your side, listening and hearing one hundred per cent, never for one moment judging, just caring and letting you cry – seriously, Krystynne should have shares in Kleenex – and, most importantly, giving you chocolate! There is always a big tin of chocolates in her house. Chocolate helps ground us, apparently. Well, that's a good enough excuse for me, thank you very much. Bring on the chocolate bars!

My precious friend Cassy. From the moment we met I knew it would be an honour to be part of your life. Always there for me, even through those times when your bravery shone through the challenges you were facing. May angels constantly be at your side.

Richard Alnwick, one of the most gifted, creative and kind people I have ever known. It has been an honour to be part of your journey in life, and of Pauline's, your mother, who simply accepts me wholeheartedly for who I was, have been and will be. Five minutes in your company and my heart is eased and life is well again. God bless you both.

Frank McChrystal, for his technical wizardry. I was not blessed with any degree of technical understanding whatsoever. You are however not only a technical wonder but a genuinely kind and caring person. Thank you for your patience.

To Catherine, who was so looking forward to reading

the book but unfortunately went home early. Our thoughts turn to you many times, Catherine, you were such fun and a genuinely lovely person. I have asked Mum to break with tradition and get out the wine and give you a hug from Margaret and the girls. May God bless you always.

To my many friends, old and new: I have been so lucky to have you all in my life. Some of you I have known for over forty years and together we created some of my greatest memories. You are all friends in the truest sense of the word, always there when times were fun, and there twice as much to love and support me through the hard times.

Pauline Walker, who made me part of her family and whose girls are now both parents themselves. For all those wonderful weekends when your house was mine and you all made me feel so special, so loved and so needed, may God bless you for that.

My lovely friends at ADT, where I worked, who were the first people to read my story and encourage me to keep writing, who would read my ramblings during their lunch hour and constantly support me.

My crazy and wonderful friends Gillian, Sharon and Caryl. We have laughed and cried together, and here we still are, caring about each other. Lives move on, and we may not see each other as often as we used to, yet we live still safe in the knowledge that at the drop of a hat we will be at each other's side if needed.

Elaine: to have a friend spanning forty-six years of my life is incredible. When we get together, all we ever do is reminisce and laugh. You were the first person to accept me totally for who I was, and you were and still are one of the kindest, sweetest people I know. We do not talk of love but, as Mum would say, it is there all the same in the way we care about each other. Thank you, Elaine. Your friendship is priceless.

Nicola Baines and Sarah Whibley, now with children of their own, who have accepted me into their lives without knowing how much it means to me to see their children and my grandchild all together celebrating birthdays, or simply days, together. Family days, you see, mean so much to me. Thank you, my darlings.

To Eileen Cockburn, whose friendship I value more than you could know. To be invited by yourself and Colin to your family table is something I am most grateful for.

The Smalleys and Nancy's family for welcoming me all those years ago and forever treating me as one of your own.

My cousin Pat, for all her research and keeping me right with times and dates. You are one of those rare people in this world who truly has a heart of gold. Through all the many challenges she has been thrown in this life, she has faced each one with courage, grace and dignity. I admire you greatly, Pat, and am proud to be your cousin.

To Andrea Bocelli, RyanDan and Josh Groban. Every word in this book has been written while listening to you sing. You inspired me with your music, which brings to the world all that is most beautiful. Thank you.

My husband, Harry, for his constant support, encouragement and, most of all, his patience during the writing of this book and his kindness to Mum.

My son-in-law, John, who I love so very much, and my grandson, Séamus, who brings smiles, laughter, acceptance and a heart full of love.

Finally, my daughter, Gemah Louise, a beautiful, caring and compassionate soul. You make my life one of pure joy and constant laughter. I am so very proud of you and love you beyond words. I see in front of me every day in a beautiful Egyptian frame the words written in Egyptian script by your own hand: 'Mum, for a moment in my heart, for ever in my soul.' Gemah, I smile when I think of you; I close my eyes and I see you. No matter what challenges I have faced, I would do it all again just to share one moment of my journey with you.

He just wanted a decent book to read ...

Not too much to ask, is it? It was in 1935 when Allen Lane, Managing Director of Bodley Head Publishers, stood on a platform at Exeter railway station looking for something good to read on his journey back to London. His choice was limited to popular magazines and poor-quality paperbacks – the same choice faced every day by the vast majority of readers, few of whom could afford hardbacks. Lane's disappointment and subsequent anger at the range of books generally available led him to found a company – and change the world.

'We believed in the existence in this country of a vast reading public for intelligent books at a low price, and staked everything on it'
Sir Allen Lane, 1902–1970, founder of Penguin Books

The quality paperback had arrived – and not just in bookshops. Lane was adamant that his Penguins should appear in chain stores and tobacconists, and should cost no more than a packet of cigarettes.

Reading habits (and cigarette prices) have changed since 1935, but Penguin still believes in publishing the best books for everybody to enjoy. We still believe that good design costs no more than bad design, and we still believe that quality books published passionately and responsibly make the world a better place.

So wherever you see the little bird – whether it's on a piece of prize-winning literary fiction or a celebrity autobiography, political tour de force or historical masterpiece, a serial-killer thriller, reference book, world classic or a piece of pure escapism – you can bet that it represents the very best that the genre has to offer.

Whatever you like to read – trust Penguin.